# INTERNATIONAL PSYCHOL🌐GICAL SCIENCE

## PROGRESS, PROBLEMS, AND PROSPECTS

### Edited by Mark R. Rosenzweig

Published under the auspices of the
International Union of Psychological Science.

American Psychological Association
Washington, DC

Published by
American Psychological Association
750 First Street, NE
Washington, DC 20002

Copies may be ordered from
APA Order Department
P.O. Box 2710
Hyattsville, MD 20784

This book was typeset in Century Condensed by Harper Graphics, Inc.,
Hollywood, MD.

Printer: Edwards Brothers, Inc., Ann Arbor, MI
Cover designer: Hasten & Hunt, Inc.
Technical/Production Editor: Olin J. Nettles

**Library of Congress Cataloging-in-Publication Data**
International psychological science : progress, problems, and prospects / edited
by Mark R. Rosenzweig.
    p.  cm.
    Includes index.
    ISBN 1-55798-168-X  (acid-free paper)
    1. Psychology.  I. Rosenzweig, Mark R.
    [DNLM: 1. Psychology.  BF 121 I607]
    BF121.I56444    1992
    150'.9'049—dc20
    DNLM/DLC
    for Library of Congress                 92-6993
                                            CIP

*Printed in the United States of America*
*First edition*

# Contents

# Contributors

**Larry E. Beutler,** University of California at Santa Barbara

**Wayne H. Holtzman,** Hogg Foundation for Mental Health, University of Texas at Austin

**Qicheng Jing,** Institute of Psychology, Chinese Academy of Sciences, Beijing

**Çiğdem Kağıtçıbaşı,** Bogazici University, Istanbul, Turkey

**Paulo P. P. Machado,** University of California at Santa Barbara

**Lars-Göran Nilsson,** University of Umeå, Sweden

**Kurt Pawlik,** University of Hamburg, Germany

**Mark R. Rosenzweig,** University of California at Berkeley

# Preface

T his book presents an up-to-date portrait of psychological science from an international perspective. It was prepared to answer questions from many sources and countries: from psychology professors and practitioners who ask for current information about the scope and achievements of modern psychology on an international basis; from students who want to know how psychology differs among countries and regions of the world; from colleagues in various countries who want suggestions about improving the recognition and status of psychological science in their respective countries; from national psychological societies seeking suggestions about preparing data banks of their members and national resources; and from national and international organizations that want information about the recruitment of young scientists.

For all of these questioners, and others, this book attempts to survey the progress, problems, and prospects of psychological science. It reveals much new information about the resources for psychological research around the world—human resources, financial resources, and organizational resources—as well as the differing status of psychology in different regions of the world.

Two main methods were used to develop this portrait of psychological science: an international survey, and reviews of accomplishments in some of the main fields of psychological research.

The international survey was conducted in 1991 by the International Union of Psychological Science (IUPsyS) among its 48 national member organizations located around the world. From this survey, we obtained a profile of resources for psychological research, as well as information about the recognition and status of psychological science in the different countries and regions. Results of this survey are presented in Chapter 2, along with related information from other sources. In light of this information, Chapter 2 ends with several conclusions about the resources available for psychological research, the recognition and status accorded to this discipline, and important actions for psychologists and psychological organizations to take.

The survey was based on a questionnaire mailed in January of 1991 to all 48 national member organizations of the IUPsyS and to certain other major national psychological organizations. (The text of the questionnaire appears in the Appendix, pp. 289–296.) In the cases in which a response was not received by March, a follow-up letter was sent, and, if necessary, a further letter was sent in April. In some cases in which the national organization did not respond, the questionnaire was completed by knowledgeable individual psychologists from the country. A few responses were received as late as October, giving a final total of 38 questionnaires, an 80% rate of return. Table 1 in Chapter 2 shows all of the countries that had a national organization in the IUPsyS in 1991; those for which a questionnaire was returned are indicated with an asterisk.

All of those who returned questionnaires are cited in the Acknowledgments. Those who returned questionnaires by the end of May 1991 were sent drafts of Chapters 1 and 2 in June along with a request for comments, suggestions, and corrections, and several of those individuals returned helpful responses. Further drafts were given to the members of the Executive Committee of the IUPsyS at their meeting in August, and some of these individuals offered further helpful suggestions. The help and cooperation of all of these psychologists has made this the most complete and informative international survey of psychological science yet made.

The portrait this book affords is of psychology as of spring 1991. Germany was already unified; the Society of Psychology of the German Democratic Republic had dissolved, and many of its former members had joined one of the two constituent organizations of the Federation of German Psychological Societies. The U.S.S.R. had not yet been replaced by a commonwealth and some independent countries.

Following Chapter 2, experts in seven different major areas of psychological research review the current status of their respective areas, drawing upon research done around the world. These reviews, which make up Chapters 3 to 9, represent only a sampling of the main areas of psychological research, but they give a good idea of the variety of research methods and findings of modern psychology. To present reviews of all of the main areas would require tripling the size of this book.

A truly international treatment is guaranteed by the facts that the authors come from six different countries, including developing as well as industrialized countries, and that each of them has done research abroad, has engaged in cross-cultural research, or both. All of the contributors have donated their efforts to this project, and the royalties from the book go entirely to the IUPsyS to further the development of psychological science around the world.

I regret any errors and important omissions that may appear in the book and ask readers to inform me of them as well as to send me information to update facts, figures, and conclusions presented here.

Mark R. Rosenzweig

# Acknowledgments

H elpful suggestions on formulating the 1991 IUPsyS questionnaire were made by Pamela Ebert Flattau, Wayne H. Holtzman, and Kurt Pawlik. Information on the following countries was supplied by the following individuals in response to the IUPsyS questionnaire. We thank them for their help with this survey.

Argentina: E. Nicenboim. Australia: K. M. McConkey. Belgium: A. Vandierendonck. Brazil: A. M. B. Biaggio. Bulgaria: S. Ganovsky. Canada: P. L.-J. Ritchie, D. Bélanger, T. Hogan, M. Sabourin, L. Forget. China: Lin Zhongxian. Colombia: R. Ardila. Czechoslovakia: P. R. Rican. Denmark: P. Foltved. Egypt: F. A. L. H. Abou-Hatab. Finland: H. Hamalainen. France: G. Tiberghien. Germany: G. Dahme. Hong Kong: D. J. Lam. Hungary: K. Szilagyi. India: J. B. P. Sinha, D. Sinha, A. K. Dalal, B. N. Puhan, A. Prakash. Indonesia: B. N. Setiadi. Israel: Y. Amir. Japan: M. Tomita. Mexico: J. J. Sanchez Sosa, V. Colotla, G. Rodriguez Ortega, J. Urbina. Netherlands: C. J. de Wolff, G. Wolters. Nigeria: I. S. Obot. Pakistan: S. A. A. Shah. Panama: M. E. de Aleman. Philippines: F. Punongbayan. South Africa: K. F. Mauer, R. J. Prinsloo. Spain: J. M. Prieto. Sweden: B. Göransson. Switzerland: F. Gaillard. Turkey: N. H. Sahin. U.S.S.R.: E. S. Romanova. United Kingdom: V. Bruce. United States: American Psychological Association: L. Lipsitt, A. Solarz, W. Camara, J. Kohout, J. Buchanan, G. VandenBos; American Psychological Society: L. Herring, A. G. Kraut, S. Brookhart, G. M. Pion. Uruguay: E. J. Tuana. Venezuela: L. M. Sanchez. Yugoslavia: S. Radovic. Zimbabwe: K. Myambo.

Thanks are also extended to all of those who offered comments on the successive drafts of Chapters 1 and 2.

The authors appreciate the efficiency and skill of APA Books, which has permitted this survey to be published rapidly and accurately. We also thank staff members of APA Books for helpful suggestions on the presentation of several chapters.

# CHAPTER 1

# What Is Psychological Science?

Mark R. Rosenzweig

T his brief introductory chapter is meant especially for readers who are not already well acquainted with the scope, methods, and fields of psychological science.

Psychological science is now part of the life and culture of every industrialized nation as well as of many developing countries. Many concepts, terms, and applications that are familiar to most of us were coined, or were given their current usage, by psychologists. Many of these were unknown a century ago or, in some cases, even a few decades ago, such as *intelligence quotient, mental age, psychotherapy, biofeedback, children's educational television programs, learning to learn, mental measurement, behaviorism, Gestalt psychology, personality assessment, personality test, projective test, psychodynamics, short-term memory, memory span, memory trace, teaching machine,* and *behavior modification.*

All of these terms and ideas come from research about behavior and experience, research that started a little more than a century ago when researchers began to use scientific methods to study these areas. The first laboratory dedicated to the study of human experience was founded at the University of Leipzig in 1879. The first scientific study of memory was published in 1885; it was a book by the German psychologist Hermann Ebbinghaus. The oldest still-continuing journal devoted to research on behavior and experience was started in 1887: the *American Journal of Psychology.* The first International Congress of Psychology took place in Paris in 1889; the series of international congresses continues productively, under the auspices of the International Union of Psychological

Science since 1954, with the XXV International Congress of Psychology in Brussels in 1992 and the XXVI Congress in Montreal in 1996. The first national psychological organization was founded in 1892: the American Psychological Association. Although modern psychology started over a century ago in Europe and North America, recognition of its scientific status took time to develop even in those parts of the world. In many developing nations, modern psychology started only after the Second World War, and in some of these countries it is still struggling to become established as a scientific enterprise.

The pioneers of psychological research believed that knowledge and understanding of human behavior could be achieved by following the canons of scientific investigation, and this remains the key tenet of psychological science. Experiments and controlled observation are used to study behavior and experience. Hypotheses are formed and subjected to empirical tests; on the basis of these test results, the hypotheses may be abandoned, revised, or maintained. When possible, laws of behavior and experience are formulated. Many of the pioneer psychological investigators were interested only in gaining knowledge and understanding, without any thought of application, but others sought from the start to apply psychological findings in such settings as the school and the workplace.

As psychologists have concentrated their investigations on different aspects of behavior and experience, many special areas of psychology have come into being. Separate associations, or divisions of larger associations, and specialized journals are devoted to scores of special areas of research. Special fields have also developed at the interfaces between psychology and other disciplines, for example, engineering psychology, health psychology, sports psychology, educational psychology, psychopharmacology, the psychology of music, and even psychoneuroimmunology. Figure 1 presents a diagram of some of the subfields of psychology and their related disciplines.

Many aspects of psychological research contribute to human development. The United Nations Development Programme (1990, 1991) has recently begun to measure human development around the world using, at the start, three components: health, knowledge, and standard of living. Health is a major focus of psychological research, and Chapter 7 of this book is devoted to health psychology. The acquisition and use of knowledge is another focus of psychological research; Chapter 3 on the cognitive psychology of learning and memory treats some aspects of this work. The standard of living is related to psychological research in such fields as industrial/organizational psychology and consumer psychology.

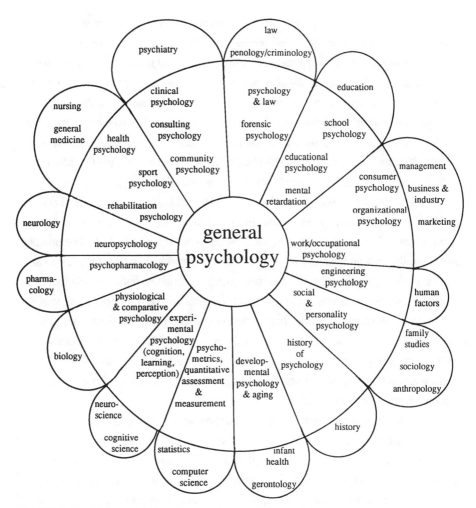

**FIGURE 1**   The main fields of psychology and their relations to other disciplines.

## What Is the Domain of Psychological Science?

### The Main Fields of Psychological Research

One way of classifying the main fields of psychological research is shown in the Appendix to this chapter. This list of fields has been used in national and international surveys, and it appears at several points in this book. It should be noted that other classifications also exist and that all such classifications are somewhat arbitrary because there is much overlap between neighboring fields and because many psychologists are active in more than one field of psychology. Although such a classification is useful in many ways, it may have the disadvantage of making the discipline appear to be fragmented. The classification of the main, traditional fields also omits many important growing fields such as health psychology, ecological psychology, psychology and the law, and human–machine interactions; such new fields are helping to redefine some of the traditional fields. In spite of these qualifications, the classification in the Appendix to this chapter has been widely used, and the data related to it are useful, especially when one bears in mind its limitations.

The questionnaire sent in 1991 by the International Union of Psychological Science (IUPsyS) to its national member organizations, and to certain other major psychological associations, asked for information about these fields in each country.[1] The first question asked whether research activity in each of these fields was high, moderate, or low. The responses showed a similar ranking in most countries, including both industrialized and developing nations, indicating similar research interests around the world. There was a tendency for developing countries to put more emphasis on research in the "health ser-vice provider" fields (clinical, counseling, and school psychology) and for the industrial-ized countries to put more emphasis on research in the academic/research fields. (The relative amounts of research efforts in the different fields will be taken up in detail in Chapter 2; see Table 3 of that chapter.)

Another item in the questionnaire asked if there were fields of psychological research that were characteristic of the country and that tended to differentiate it from other coun-tries. Most countries did not name a special field that their psychology emphasized, but some did. Thus, although most psychologists are working on the same main areas of psy-chology around the world, some psychologists in certain countries are investigating topics of special local or regional interest. Some of the later chapters (3, 7, 8) bring out differences in research topics and/or methods among different countries and regions of the world.

**What Psychological Science Is Not**
Many members of the public confuse psychology with other disciplines such as psychia-try, neurology, and psychoanalysis. They may also confuse psychology with pseudo-sciences such as astrology or dianetics.

---

[1] *The full IUPsyS questionnaire is given in the Appendix to this book.*

Consider first the distinction between psychology and psychiatry. Psychiatry is a medical specialty practiced only by people who hold medical degrees and who have taken a special program of study in psychiatry and have passed examinations in this field. Some medical doctors also have degrees in psychology, but this does not make them psychiatrists or clinical psychologists. Such physician–psychologists may work in any of a variety of fields, including developmental psychology, studies of drugs and behavior, and brain mechanisms of memory. In North America, psychologists who practice clinical or counseling psychology must have a doctoral degree (PhD) from an accredited university and must be licensed or certified for professional service in the state or province in which they work. Most doctoral programs in clinical or counseling psychology in the United States and Canada require five or more years of graduate study after earning a university degree (B.A. or B.S.). These doctoral programs include courses in such areas as statistics, learning, biological or physiological psychology, social psychology, developmental psychology, and abnormal psychology, in addition to specialized courses in clinical or counseling psychology. Doctoral programs leading to the PhD also require extensive research experience and the creation of an original dissertation, neither of which is required for a doctorate in psychiatry. In addition, doctoral programs in clinical or counseling psychology include a series of supervised experiences (practica) in clinical or counseling psychology and a one-year internship. The doctorate in psychiatry requires a residency in psychiatry. Although the interests and activities of psychologists and psychiatrists may overlap, the distinctions between them in terms of training and licensing are clear.

Psychology is sometimes confused with psychoanalysis, the system of psychology and method of psychotherapy devised by Sigmund Freud. Even within the area of psychotherapy, psychoanalysis is only one of a large number of methods. Chapter 8, "Research on Psychotherapy," mentions the explosive growth in the number of kinds of psychotherapy and discusses experimental research to measure the effectiveness of different kinds of psychotherapy for different kinds of patients.

During the development of psychology, it took time to separate scientific approaches from other approaches to human behavior and capacities. For example, at the first international congress of psychology in 1889 (the International Congress of Psychology), the president declared in his inaugural address that the primary intention of the congress was to make psychology a pure science that would base its progress on observation and experimentation; nevertheless, there was a good deal of interest at the congress in "spiritism," and mediums gave demonstrations of purported communication with

---

the dead. Interests such as spiritism were largely abandoned in further congresses, but such topics were not completely eradicated. For example, in Germany in 1929, the German Association for Experimental Psychology dropped the word "Experimental" from its name and opened the gates to nonscientific, literary approaches and to graphology, psychoanalysis, and holistic psychology (Lüer, 1990). This was, however, an exception to the overall course of development.

The struggle to define an area of science and to prune away dubious content has taken place in sciences in general. The long efforts of chemistry to outgrow and shed alchemy are well known. Throughout the sciences, errors and even occasional cases of fraud are hard to prevent, but the self-correcting methods that are a part of science overcome these mistakes sooner or later. A well-known example of fraud that took 40 years to expose was the contrived skull of "Piltdown Man," a combination of a human skull and an orangutan's jaw. More recent cases of error in physical science include polywater, a supposed form of water in which the molecules are linked in polymer chains, and cold fusion.

Because of the desire to increase human performance in many areas of activity, and because of insufficient knowledge of a field, many people tend to be gullible about claims for unconventional programs, especially if they are backed by testimonials. In 1985, the National Research Council of the United States appointed a committee, consisting mainly of psychologists, to study the claims of a number of programs said to enhance human performance by unconventional means. Two reports have been published so far (Druckman & Bjork, 1991; Druckman & Swets, 1988). Part of the committee's work was the investigation of a number of programs or techniques marketed commercially to improve learning or performance (e.g., Suggestive Accelerative Learning and Teaching, also called Superlearning; the mental practice of muscular movements; Hemispheric Synchronization; and subliminal self-help audiotapes). In each case, the committee found inadequate evidence that the program was of value. In some cases, the assumptions on which the program was based lacked scientific credibility. In other cases, the program contained several factors, and studies to date were inadequate to determine which factors may produce positive results. The 1988 report included a 12-page chapter on principles and techniques of evaluation to help people in business and in the military understand how to evaluate programs critically and systematically. Such efforts are needed to help eliminate or at least reduce erroneous or fraudulent programs said to be based on psychological research or, more broadly, on research in the behavioral, neural, and social sciences.

Gullibility and deception are common aspects of behavior. Thus, it should not be surprising that gullibility and deception have themselves been topics of psychological investigation for a century (e.g., Binet, 1896; Hyman, 1989; Jastrow, 1900).

## How Should Psychology Be Classified Among the Sciences?

With its wide scope and different histories in different countries, psychology has been classified in many different ways among the fields of science. Some aspects of psychology suggest that it be classified with the biological sciences, whereas other aspects suggest that it belongs to the social sciences. The statutes of the IUPsyS state that it works to promote "the development of psychological science, whether biological or social, normal or abnormal, pure or applied" (Rosenzweig & Holtzman, 1985, p. 765). Responses to the 1991 IUPsyS questionnaire (Item 7) show that in different places, psychology is classified as a natural science, a biological or life science, a medical science, a behavioral science, a social science, an educational science, a humanity, or in a class of its own. In two thirds of the national responses to the IUPsyS survey, psychology was classified differently at different universities within the country, and even within the same university there may be psychology departments in different categories. In three quarters of the national responses, psychology was classified as a social science, but only in one quarter of the countries was this its sole classification. However, this differed between the industrialized and the developing countries: Only one respondent from an industrialized country classified psychology solely as a social science, whereas 39% of those from developing countries classified it only as a social science. Half of the respondents from industrialized countries classified psychology as a biological or life science, and so did 33% of those from developing counties. On the other hand, half of the respondents from industrialized countries (but neither Canada nor the United States) reported that at least some of their universities classified psychology as a humanity, but only 24% from developing countries did so.

Psychology is given a class of its own in 45% of the industrialized countries, at least in some universities, but this is true in only two (11%) of the developing countries in our sample. In the United States, publications of the National Science Board and the National Science Foundation put psychology in its own class; its neighbors are, on one side, the life sciences (including agricultural sciences and medical sciences) and, on the other side, the social sciences (including economics, sociology/anthropology, and political science). Psychology was also given its own class in a major international study of funding of research organized by the U.K. Advisory Board for the Research Councils and the U.S.

National Science Foundation (Irvine, Martin, & Isard, 1990); here again it was placed between the life sciences and the social sciences.

The variety of classifications of psychology in different countries and different universities, and particularly that of psychology as a humanity in almost half of the European countries in our sample, may both reflect and help to perpetuate confusion or doubt about the nature of psychological science. In view of the research programs of modern psychology, such as those described in this book, it would be more accurate either to acknowledge that the domain of psychology overlaps those of the biological, behavioral, and social sciences or, as many organizations already do, to give psychological science a class of its own.

### Does the Scientific Status of Psychology Depend On Its Ability to Predict Behavior?

The difficulty of predicting behavior has been used to raise doubts about the scientific status of psychology. In fact, accurate predictions are hard to make about any system or event that is even moderately complex. Many museums of science and technology have a rather simple demonstration of this: A few rods are linked together at joints that allow the rods to swing either clockwise or counterclockwise, making a complex pendulum. One sets the rods in vigorous motion and then watches what happens. The rods farthest out in the system soon begin to behave in ways that appear to be unpredictable. They may stop briefly, then begin to turn in the opposite direction, and then reverse again. If one sets the system in motion again, trying to do so in the same way as before, the motions of the rods are different from the previous time. Thus, even a moderately complex system may exhibit what is called "chaotic" behavior and be hard to predict. Weather systems are notoriously hard to predict, even though they are physical in nature. It is said that some weather systems are so delicately poised between different possible outcomes that a gull flapping its wings can change the outcome. A recent book (Casti, 1991) is devoted to the difficulties of finding certainty in fields ranging from mathematics, the weather, and biological development (how does a complex organism develop from a single fertilized egg?), to fields involving human behavior: the stock market and the outbreak of war.

In many cases in which large collections of units are involved, however, the behavior of the mass is predictable, whether the units are molecules of air or people. For example, you can risk your life on the fact that people in England drive on the left side of the road, whereas people across the Channel in France drive on the right. Within defined circumstances, some aspects of the behavior of individuals and groups can be predicted on the basis of detailed observations, creative hypotheses, and carefully controlled tests of alternative hypotheses. Many examples of psychological research demonstrate such progress, as Chapters 3 to 9 will show. This permits useful applications of psychological science, but the scientific status of a discipline does not rest upon the accuracy of its predictions but upon the objective and systematic methods used to reach its findings and laws.

## Developing a Portrait of Psychological Science

To draw a portrait of current psychological science from an international point of view, we will discuss in Chapter 2 a survey on the themes and resources of psychological research. This survey of psychological science is part of a large-scale movement to survey particular sciences and the overall scientific enterprise. A few examples of this movement are as follows: (a) To get information on the funding of research, in order to make policy recommendations, agencies of the United Kingdom and the United States gained the cooperation of France, Germany, Japan, and the Netherlands for a major study: *Investing in the Future: An International Comparison of Government Funding of Academic and Related Research* (Irvine et al., 1990). (b) The U.S. National Science Foundation published in 1988 a special report titled *Profiles—Psychology: Human Resources and Funding*, as well as similar reports on biological sciences, chemical engineering, and computer sciences. (c) UNESCO published a book of status reports on teaching and research in psychology in 13 countries in Asia and the Pacific (Shouksmith & Shouksmith, 1990). These attempts to gather and disseminate information on the potential, support, and needs of the sciences should help to realize the contributions that the sciences are capable of making. From these reports, we can also see some of the ways in which psychology shares the potentials and characteristics of other sciences, as well as ways in which it differs; I will point out some of the similarities and differences in Chapter 2. The main questions considered in Chapter 2 are as follows.

*What are the main topics and problems that psychologists are investigating? To what extent do these vary in different countries and regions of the world?* Chapter 2 discusses the main topics that psychologists are investigating. I will draw upon the international survey undertaken for this book, along with other sources, to present a picture of the scope, objectives, and emphases of current psychological research. Some examples of current research—methods and findings—will be presented in detail in Chapters 3 to 9, and specific research topics will be named later, but first let us note some of the questions about human resources and other resources for psychological research to be covered in Chapter 2.

*Who are the psychologists who do research?* What training is needed to conduct psychological research, and how do the requirements vary among countries? What proportion of research psychologists are men and what proportion are women, how does this vary by country and by region of the world, and what are the implications of the large numbers of women in psychology relative to the numbers in other sciences? The amount of psychological research varies greatly among countries and regions; what are the facts about this distribution, and what are some of the causes of the inequalities? How has the growth in numbers of psychologists occurred in different countries and regions, and what are likely future trends? These questions are examined and discussed early in Chapter 2.

*How do psychologists keep in touch with research in psychology and related disciplines done in their own countries and in other parts of the world?* Many regular publications with national and international distribution publish research and reviews of research; information about the annual numbers of psychological publications and of databases and abstracting services is given in Chapter 2. National psychological organizations hold regular meetings at which members present and discuss research. International organizations bring together national societies (e.g., the International Union of Psychological Science) or individual investigators (e.g., the International Association of Applied Psychology; the Interamerican Society of Psychology; the International Council of Psychologists, the Society for Psychotherapy Research); some of these international organizations are described in Chapter 2. International congresses provide occasions for investigators from many parts of the world to present and discuss their research.

*What financial support and social recognition does psychological research obtain, and how does this vary among countries and regions of the world?* The amounts of financial support vary greatly, as the data presented in Chapter 2 show. Even in the countries with the most support, psychologists, like other scientists, see much more that could be accomplished if more adequate support were available. Esteem and social recognition for psychologists also vary greatly among countries, as examples will show. In part, these grow with the length of time that psychological science has been established in the country, and they are also affected by cultural traditions and the levels of academic training required to be a psychologist in different countries.

After Chapter 2, we turn to this final main question: *How do psychologists investigate behavior and experience?* To answer this question, Chapters 3 to 9 present examples of current psychological research in different fields. Chapter 3 takes up some questions of cognitive psychology: How do we learn and remember? Chapter 4 presents research on a related question: What processes in the brain enable us to remember? Chapter 5 examines parenting and child development and shows how comparative research conducted in different cultures (cross-cultural studies) enables investigators to find what aspects of development are common across cultures and what is specific to certain cultures. Chapter 6 discusses research on visual perception: How do we see and interpret the world around us? Chapter 7 asks how behavior affects health and longevity, because many of the major causes of illness and early mortality are related to behavior. Chapter 8 considers international research to test the processes and effectiveness of different kinds of psychotherapy. Finally, Chapter 9 considers psychological methods of assessment: the assessment of personality, of intelligence, of aptitudes, and of many different aspects of behavior and experience. Methods of assessment are both results of psychological research and methods for further research. They qualify as research methods because in some studies individuals are assigned to groups on the basis of assessments, and in many studies the effects of different conditions or of experimental treatments are measured by assessments of different groups of subjects. Research in many other major areas could have been described; these are given only as examples.

Methods of research in psychology differ widely depending on the questions being studied. The methods span a wide range including the following: case studies; systematic observations and descriptions of behavior; surveys of knowledge, beliefs, and attitudes; the use of questionnaires and tests; and formal experiments designed to test specific hypotheses. Sophisticated statistical procedures and the use of powerful computers now permit assessments of interactions among many variables and precise determinations of causal sequences. Cross-cultural studies are being undertaken with increasing frequency in collaborative efforts to find and understand what is common to human beings around the world and what aspects of behavior reflect the effects of cultural determinants. Examples of all of these types of methods can be found in the following chapters. Because behavior is inherently variable, many psychologists have worked hard to devise or adapt methods that will permit relatively clear descriptions and relatively full understanding of behavior and experience; such methodological concerns and advances are described and discussed in several of the following chapters.

Research methodology continues to advance in every field of psychology. In Chapter 8 on research in psychotherapy, Beutler and Machado describe the distinct stages through which that field has progressed. Case analysis was the main method used through the first three decades of this century. This, Beutler and Machado state, "was confined largely to intensive descriptions and analyses of individual cases, accompanied by elaborate theoretical formulations to explain the observations" (p. 227). The late 1940s and the 1950s saw the emergence of descriptive assessment, which replaced the earlier "uncontrolled single case analyses with investigations of several individuals at once (i.e., group designs), therapist observations with systematic and quantitative measurement, and complex or metaphysical explanations with more parsimonious formulations" (p. 228). By the late 1970s, there was a concerted effort "to develop experimental methods that would provide more control over the actual procedures used [in psychotherapy] and more systematic measurement both of what comprised the application of clinical theories and of the resulting therapeutic outcomes than had previously existed" (p. 230). The development of methodological advances led to the current period of controlled experimentation on psychotherapy, and Beutler and Machado describe several of these experiments in their chapter. They suggest that psychotherapy research appears to be entering a further stage of complex, programmatic, and collaborative studies, which they also describe.

Formal experimentation was adopted in many fields of psychology long before it entered research on psychotherapy. Chapter 3, on human learning and memory, recounts how the German psychologist Hermann Ebbinghaus showed in 1885 how to measure learning and memory, which opened a large field to experimental research. And even earlier than that, there was experimental research in perception, as indicated in Chapter 6 on visual perception.

Often, the same topic of research is investigated by different methods, and these can be used to cross-check the findings. Thus, a review of research methods used in presentations on developmental psychology at annual conventions of the Japanese Psychological Association from 1978 to 1984, showed that about 40% of the reports were based on experimentation, 36% on surveys, 16% on observation, 4% on case studies, and 3% on cross-cultural methods (Omura, 1990, p. 220). Chapter 4, on research on the neural mechanisms of learning and memory, describes the use of both neuropsychological studies of patients with various types of brain damage and formal experiments with animal subjects in which precise methods are used to modify the activity of particular regions of the brain during memory formation. The human case studies and the formal experiments with animals complement each other and are leading to a fuller understanding of the roles of particular brain regions in learning and memory formation.

## Conclusion

This book will enable the reader to become acquainted with modern psychological science and, especially, its basis in research. For those who have not been following the development of psychological science, its broad scope, its varied research methods, and its exciting prospects will be a revelation. Even for those who are well acquainted with psychology in their own country, the variety of the findings, emphases, and conditions of psychological research around the world will offer many surprises.

# References

Binet, A. (1896). Psychology of prestidigitation. *Annual report of the Board of Regents of the Smithsonian Institution, 1984* (pp. 555–571). Washington, DC: U.S. Government Printing Office.

Casti, J. L. (1991). *Searching for certainty: What scientists can know about the future.* New York: Morrow.

Druckman, D., & Bjork, R. A. (Eds.). (1991). *In the mind's eye: Enhancing human performance.* Washington, DC: National Academy Press.

Druckman, D., & Swets, J. A. (Eds.). (1988). *Enhancing human performance: Issues, theories, and techniques.* Washington, DC: National Academy Press.

Hyman, R. (1989). The psychology of deception. *Annual Review of Psychology, 40,* 133–154.

Irvine, J., Martin, B. R., & Isard, P. (1990). *Investing in the future: An international comparison of government funding of academic and related research.* Aldershot, England: Edward Elgar.

Jastrow, J. (1900). *Fact and fable in psychology.* Cambridge, MA: Riverside Press.

Lüer, G. (1990). Psychology as reflected by the proceedings of its scientific association. *German Journal of Psychology, 14,* 275–290.

National Science Foundation. (1988). *Profiles—Psychology: Human resources and funding* (NSF 88–325). Washington, DC: Author.

Omura, A. (1990). Japan. In G. Shouksmith & E. A. Shouksmith (Eds.), *Psychology in Asia and the Pacific: Status reports on teaching and research in eleven countries* (pp. 207–238; RUSHAP Series on Occasional Monographs and Papers No. 34). Bangkok: UNESCO.

Rosenzweig, M. R., & Holtzman, W. H. (1985). The International Union of Psychological Science (IUPsyS). *International Journal of Psychology, 20,* 753–781.

Shouksmith, G., & Shouksmith, E. A. (Eds.). (1990). *Psychology in Asia and the Pacific: Status reports on teaching and research in eleven countries* (RUSHAP Series on Occasional Monographs and Papers No. 34). Bangkok: UNESCO.

United Nations Development Programme. (1990). *Human development report 1990.* New York: Oxford University Press.

United Nations Development Programme. (1991). *Human development report 1991.* New York: Oxford University Press.

# Appendix: The Main Fields of Psychological Research

*Clinical* psychology is both a scientific and an applied field concerned with the application of psychological principles and knowledge to problems of adjustment and emotional well-being. It attempts to discover methods that improve the diagnosis, treatment, and prevention of emotional and behavioral disorders.

*Cognitive* psychology is concerned with the "higher" mental processes, including thinking, reasoning, and decision making; learning and memory; perception; and attention. Unlike traditional experimental psychology, it does not hesitate to use mental terms and constructs.

*Comparative* psychology involves the study of the differences in behavior of different species, undertaken to yield insight into the mechanisms or evolution of behavior. This term is often used for all animal psychology even if it is not undertaken to make comparisons among species.

*Counseling* psychology applies results of psychological research to provide guidance on practical personal problems such as vocational choices, problems in studying, and coping with the stresses of everyday life. (It is sometimes called *counseling and guidance.*)

*Developmental and gerontological* psychology studies the processes and changes—emotional, attitudinal, and cognitive—that take place in people at different ages. "Developmental" often stresses the first 20 years, during which changes are rapid, but many investigators have adopted a life-span approach.

*Educational* psychology studies methods of teaching and learning and psychological problems that arise in school settings, and applies such knowledge to improving teaching and learning.

*Experimental* psychology includes those topics that are firmly based on laboratory experimentation. It includes such areas as learning, memory, perception, and motivation. Cognitive psychology now occupies some of the same field.

*Industrial/organizational* (or *personnel–organizational*) psychology studies work and the working environment, including environmental and organizational factors, and applies knowledge to improving productivity and satisfaction at work.

*Personality* psychology studies the traits that characterize an individual over a relatively long period.

*Physiological* (biological) psychology studies the biological mechanisms of behavior, as well as interactions between behavioral and biological processes.

*Psychometrics* measures individual differences in behavior or personality; a similar term is *mental testing,* which includes the assessment of personality, the evaluation of intelligence, and the measurement of attitudes.

*Quantitative* psychology stresses the formulation and evaluation of quantitative methods (mathematical, statistical, scaling) for psychological research and applications.

*School* psychology studies the school as a social situation and focuses on social interactions that occur as teachers and others try to promote the intellectual, social, and emotional development of children.

*Social* psychology studies the behavior of the individual in groups, including social interaction and the influences of people on each others' behavior.


Brief discussions of these fields appear in encyclopedic dictionaries of psychology. Textbooks exist in each of these fields. Reviews of research in these fields appear regularly in the *Annual Review of Psychology.*

# CHAPTER 2

# Resources for Psychological Science Around the World

Mark R. Rosenzweig

T his chapter surveys the resources that are necessary to accomplish research in psychology, and it investigates the extent to which such resources are available. Primordial are the human resources—the highly trained specialists who design, carry out, and evaluate psychological research. Such scientists are distributed quite unequally among the fields of psychology and around the world, as we will see. Much modern psychological research also requires technological resources: Examples include computers to present stimuli, record responses, tabulate data, and perform statistical tests; video cameras to record responses for detailed study and scoring; electrophysiological apparatus to record and analyze potentials from the nervous system, muscles, and skin; and many other kinds of experimental apparatus. Both human and technological resources require funding for many reasons: to train research personnel, to pay the salaries of investigators and their staffs, to acquire and maintain research apparatus, to acquire and maintain animal subjects, to establish and gain access to databases, to prepare and publish reports of research, and to pay many other expenses of research. To the extent that available knowledge permits, this chapter surveys the financial resources available for psychological science in different parts of the world. Psychological organizations, journals, and databases are important because they enable psychologists to make their own research known and to keep in touch with research done in their own countries and in other parts of the world; some of these organizational resources are also described in this chapter.

In the international survey on psychological research conducted in 1991 by the International Union of Psychological Science (IUPsyS), representatives of psychological organizations around the world identified the main obstacles in their countries to achieving a satisfactory amount of high-quality research. Insufficient financial support was the obstacle named most frequently. Lack of sufficient numbers of highly trained investigators was another obstacle cited for many countries. Lack of social recognition for psychological research was mentioned by some national representatives.

In order to consider both the resources available for psychological research and obstacles to carrying out this research, we will discuss several key questions in this chapter (these questions were stated more fully in Chapter 1):

- Who are the psychologists who do research?
- What financial support does psychological research obtain, and how does this vary among countries and regions of the world?
- What organizational resources enable psychologists to make their own research known and to keep in touch with research in psychology and related disciplines done in their own countries and in other parts of the world?
- What social recognition does psychological research gain, and how does this vary among countries and regions of the world?

Before trying to answer these questions, we should acknowledge that many of them cannot be answered at present with the accuracy and detail that we would wish for a scientific inquiry. This is true in spite of the cooperation of psychologists from 38 countries in responding to the IUPsyS questionnaire. The countries with national member organizations in IUPsyS and the countries from which questionnaires were returned are shown in Table 1 (p. 20); because several of the analyses in this chapter differentiate between developing and industrialized countries, according to United Nations categories, the countries are shown under these categories in the table. Information about how the survey was conducted is given in the Preface, and the text of the questionnaire is given in the Appendix.

The lack of adequate information on these questions is true of the sciences in general, on both the national and the international level.[1] In the face of the frequent gaps in

---

[1] *In many cases, the national psychological societies do not have the information requested by the IUPsyS questionnaire, even about their own members. The secretary general of one national psychological association, apologizing for giving only partial*

data, we will do our best to provide more information than is available elsewhere and to be as accurate as possible, while noting the limitations of our sources.

# Who Are the Psychologists Who Do Research in Countries Around the World?

### Numbers and Training of Psychologists and of Psychological Researchers

The total number of psychologists in the world in the period from 1988 to 1991 appears to be well over 500,000 according to data from the IUPsyS survey and other current sources, especially Sexton and Hogan (1992). A similar estimate made for 1980 (Rosenzweig, 1982) showed about 260,000, so the number of psychologists appears to have doubled in the last decade. In making these estimates, local definitions of *psychologist* were used; that is, the numbers include those who are considered to be qualified to call themselves psychologists in each country. The amount of training required differs greatly among countries. In the United States and Canada, most psychologists have a PhD degree, and the rest have master's degrees. In many other countries, four or five years of postsecondary education suffice, and in some countries, as little as three years of postsecondary training are considered enough. It should be noted that in the countries where three, four, or five years of postsecondary training are sufficient to qualify as a psychologist, most of the course work during those years is devoted exclusively to psychology and related disciplines, whereas in countries where advanced degrees are required to be a psychologist, training for the B.A. or B.S. degree includes a variety of disciplines, some of them with little or no direct relation to psychology.

To put the worldwide number of psychologists into perspective, let us consider comparisons with the number of physicians and the number of neuroscientists, because the work of those groups parallels that of certain groups of psychologists: health-service-provider psychologists and research–academic psychologists, respectively. The estimated number of psychologists is about one twelfth the number of physicians in the world, taking the number of physicians from data in the 1990 *Encyclopedia Britannica Book of the Year* (pp. 870–872). Just as it is difficult to define the number of psychologists, so it is

---

information, stated, "I am glad to inform you that we are going to use this questionnaire as a model to help us form a data bank." Another wrote, "We are still in the process of developing a database for all necessary information concerning what you have asked us in the survey." In some cases, respondents gave estimates with a question mark attached.

**TABLE 1**

Countries Having a National Member in the IUPsyS as of Spring 1991, Classified by Level of Development

| Developing countries | Industrialized countries |
|---|---|
| Argentina* | Australia* |
| Brazil* | Belgium* |
| China* | Bulgaria* |
| Colombia* | Canada* |
| Cuba | Czechoslovakia* |
| Dominican Republic | Denmark* |
| Egypt* | Finland* |
| Hong Kong* | France* |
| India* | Germany* |
| Indonesia* | Hungary* |
| Iran | Israel* |
| Korea | Italy |
| Mexico* | Japan* |
| Nicaragua | Netherlands* |
| Nigeria* | New Zealand |
| Pakistan* | Norway |
| Panama* | Poland |
| Philippines* | Romania |
| South Africa* | Spain* |
| Turkey* | Sweden* |
| Uruguay* | Switzerland* |
| Venezuela* | United Kingdom* |
| Zimbabwe* | United States* |
| | USSR* |
| | Yugoslavia* |

**Note.** The classification is taken from the United Nations Development Programme (1990, p. 188).
*Country for which a questionnaire was returned in the 1991 IUPsyS survey.

not a simple matter to define the number of physicians, because there are wide variations around the world in the qualifying or certifying processes that permit individuals to represent themselves as physicians. At least, the World Heath Organization tries to institute standards for training and qualification of physicians, whereas no such international standardization exists for psychologists. The author of a chapter on psychology in Germany (Groebel, 1992) states that in 1984 in the Federal Republic there were only one ninth as many psychologists as physicians. In the United States at present, there are about two ninths as many psychologists as physicians. On the other hand, the number of psychologists in the world is almost 20 times the number of neuroscientists, as taken from the International Brain Research Organization's *IBRO Membership Directory 1991*. In this case, the number of neuroscientists is more comparable with the number of research psychologists, as we will see next.

### Numbers of Research Psychologists

About 62,000 to 82,000 psychologists around the world are engaged in research as their primary or secondary work activity, according to estimates based upon data obtained in the IUPsyS survey (Item 3.c) and on other current sources. These estimates involve problems of the definition and enumeration of psychological researchers. The worldwide total of psychological personnel is much larger than the number of researchers, but many individuals defined as psychologists are not, and could not be, engaged in research. They can, however, help to apply and to disseminate some of the findings of psychological research. Furthermore, among those involved in research, only some are engaged in research as their primary or secondary work activity.

When asked in the IUPsyS questionnaire (Item 3.b) to give the numbers of psychologists with various levels of earned degrees (B.A., B.S., or equivalent; M.A., M.S., or equivalent; PhD or equivalent), many countries did not list those with B.A. or B.S. degrees because in those countries it is considered necessary to earn an M.A., M.S., or PhD degree to conduct research or to practice psychology. Examples of such countries are Belgium, Canada, Finland, Israel, the Netherlands, Pakistan, Spain, and the United States.

Even within a single country, quite different estimates have been made of the number of research psychologists, as examples from the United States show. It is appropriate to consider these examples because approximately half of the psychological researchers in the world live in the United States, and several estimates and surveys have been made about them. The National Science Foundation (NSF; 1988) reported a total of 4,626,500 scientists and engineers employed in the United States in 1986; 253,500 of these were psychologists, and 20,600 of the psychologists had research and development as their primary work activity (Table 13, p. 100). The large total number of scientists included anyone who met two of the following three criteria: (a) an earned degree in science (including social science) or engineering, including B.A., B.S., or higher degrees; (b) employment in a science/engineering occupation; and (c) professional identification as a scientist or engineer, on the basis of total education and experience. When only those with doctoral degrees were counted, the NSF reported 419,100 employed scientists and engineers in the United States in 1987; 56,400 were psychologists (13% of the total), and 6,500 had research and development as their primary work activity (12% of the doctoral psychologists). The U.S. National Science Board (NSB; 1989) noted that "many faculty members who devote substantial time to R&D [research and development] often consider another activity (for example, teaching) to be their primary work activity," so the NSB tabulated those respondents who selected academic research R&D as either their primary or their secondary work activity (p. 115, Footnote 37). Including both primary and secondary activities resulted in doubling the count of doctoral psychologists involved in academic R&D, yielding a figure of 13,000 for 1987 (NSB, 1989, Table 5-18, p. 320). Allowing for research in nonacademic settings and for the involvement of master's level psychologists brings this figure to well over 20,000 American psychologists who do research as their primary or secondary work activity. An independent survey that largely corroborates but somewhat increases this estimate and that affords greater precision is discussed next.

The American Psychological Association (APA) conducted a major effort to take a complete census of psychologists in the United States in 1983, attempting to reach all of those with master's or doctoral degrees in psychology or who were working at an equivalent level (Stapp, Tucker, & VandenBos, 1985). On the basis of the survey, Stapp et al. concluded that there were 102,000 psychologists in the United States as of mid-1983; 29% of these psychologists had master's degrees, and 71% had doctoral degrees. Extrapolating to mid-1988, Sexton and Hogan (1992) arrived at a total of at least 125,000 psychologists in the United States; bringing this to mid-1992 yields about 145,000 U.S. psychologists. The APA survey also asked whether each respondent was "involved in" research activities. (Note that this is not the same as having research as one's primary activity, or even as the primary or secondary activity.) The responses showed 3.5% involved in research only, 15% involved in research and education (many of these being university professors), 3.9% involved in research and services, and 23% involved in research, education, and services. Thus, 46% of American psychologists overall reported being involved in research activities. Of those with doctoral degrees, 54% were involved in research activities, whereas of those with master's degrees, only 26% reported being involved in research (Stapp et al., 1985, Table 8, p. 1333). In an unpublished 1989 survey of APA members, 16,000 reported being engaged in research as their primary or secondary work activity; this was about 23% of the APA membership (not including students). If this percentage can be applied to the entire U.S. population of master's- and doctoral-level psychologists, it indicates about 35,000 U.S. psychologists engaged in research as their primary or secondary work activity as of mid-1992. To be prudent, we can propose the range of 30,000 to 40,000 U.S. psychologists engaged in research as their primary or secondary work activity.

In the IUPsyS survey, data on the numbers of psychologists engaged in research as their primary or secondary activity (Item 3.c) were furnished by 30 out of 38 national responses. Data were obtained from other sources for an additional 5 countries. From these data, it can be estimated that outside of the United States, there are about 37,000 psychologists engaged in research as their primary or secondary work activity; because of uncertainties in some of the estimates, we can give a range of 32,000 to 42,000. Most of these are psychologists with master's or doctoral degrees, although in a few countries the numbers given for researchers exceeded the numbers of those with master's or doctoral degrees. Thus, the worldwide total of research psychologists comes to about 72,000 (62,000 to 82,000).

For comparison, the number of neuroscientists in the world is about 27,000, as estimated from the *IBRO Membership Directory 1991*. As in the case of psychologists who do research, about half of the neuroscientists are in the United States (14,700 of 27,000 neuroscientists).

Internationally the modal degree for psychologists is the master's degree or its equivalent, and almost all programs of psychological training include courses in research methodology and in mathematical and statistical psychology; this is true for both undergraduate (tertiary) and graduate (master's and doctoral level) training. Theses based on research are usual requirements for master's and doctoral degrees in psychology. Thus, holders of master's and, especially, of doctoral degrees in psychology have considerable training and experience in research.

### Distribution of Research Psychologists Around the World

Human resources for psychological research are very unevenly distributed around the world, with the industrialized nations having over 20 times as many research psychologists per million population as do the developing nations. Fifteen industrialized nations and 15 developing nations provided figures for the total numbers of psychologists (questionnaire Item 3.a) and research psychologists (Item 3.c). As shown in Table 2, the overall data for the industrialized countries indicate about 347 psychologists per million population, with about 82 per million (22%) being research psychologists. If we consider only the 11 industrialized countries outside of eastern Europe, we see about 550 psychologists

**TABLE 2**

Numbers of Psychologists and of Research Psychologists per Million Population

| Area | No. psychologists per million population | No. research psychologists per million population | Research psychologists as percentage of total psychologists |
|---|---|---|---|
| Industrialized countries | | | |
| Outside of Eastern Europe (n = 11) | 550 | 124 | 22 |
| Eastern Europe (n = 4) | 83 | 27 | 32 |
| Total (N = 15) | 347 | 82 | 23 |
| Developing countries | | | |
| Outside of China | 191 | 6.9 | 3.5 |
| China | 2.4 | 1.0 | 42 |
| Total (N = 15) | 84 | 3.6 | 4.2 |

per million population and 124 research psychologists per million population. Comparable data for the 15 developing countries show about 84 psychologists per million population, but only 3.6 research psychologists per million: Only about 4% of the psychologists in the developing countries in our sample do research as their primary or secondary activity.

The differences between industrialized and developing countries in the numbers of psychologists and research psychologists would probably be even greater if we had a more complete sample. An indication of this can be found in facts about countries that have member organizations in the IUPsyS and those that do not. The *Human Development Report 1990* classified countries of over one million population as *least developed*, *developed*, or *industrial* (United Nations Development Programme, 1990, p. 188). Of the 30 least developed countries, not a single one has a member organization in the IUPsyS; of the 69 other developing countries, 23 (33%) have member organizations in the IUPsyS, whereas of the 30 industrial countries, 25 (83%) have member organizations in the Union.

The fact that the developing countries lack trained personnel of many kinds has been documented by the United Nations Development Programme (1990, 1991) and other sources. Now we can add to this their lack of psychologists and, especially, of research psychologists.

In general, the countries with large psychological communities (larger ratios of psychologists to population) are those where psychology started earlier and where the country has had relatively stable government and institutions. In an earlier publication (Rosenzweig, 1982, pp. 131–132), I speculated that the development of psychology in most countries might follow a familiar S-shaped model, with slow initial growth, then a period of rapid increase, and a final period of slow growth. But I noted that this might not hold in some countries for at least two reasons: (a) special political situations that could inhibit or even interrupt the development of psychology, and (b) cases in which changes in the roles of psychology would enlarge its scope and give rise to a new stage of growth after a plateau. The general model could be tested by attempting to relate, for various countries, the numbers of psychologists per million population to the date of initiation of modern psychology, as indexed by such events as the establishment of the first laboratory, the establishment of the first department or chair of psychology, and the founding of the first psychological society.

## Ratios of Male to Female Psychologists

Psychology, in many parts of the world, gives more opportunity and scope to women than do other sciences. Increasing the numbers of women in science and engineering is generally considered to be beneficial, both for women and for society, although some misgivings have been expressed about the high percentages of women psychologists in some countries and regions, as we will see shortly. Contrasting interpretations of the feminization of psychology will be presented.

Ratios of male to female psychologists come from the 1991 IUPsyS survey (questionnaire Item 3.a) and are also given in most of the chapters of Sexton and Hogan (1992). The ratios vary widely among countries, by degree level, and by occupation. Sexton and Hogan (1992, pp. 469–470) summarize by stating that in European countries, 53% of all psychologists are women; in South American and Caribbean countries, 70% are women; but overall in Asian countries, only 25% are women, although some Asian countries have high percentages of women. Furthermore, in some Asian countries, even though many women earn university baccalaureate degrees in psychology, they then become homemakers and do not work in psychology. Not only is the proportion of women psychologists large in most parts of the world, but it is increasing in most countries. Sexton and Hogan also point out that, as a group, women are less likely than men to be involved in research or in teaching at a university. Reflecting the lower involvement of women in research is the finding that in publications reported in *Psychological Abstracts* for 1975–1986, the authors were usually one or more men (62%); in only 15% were the authors one or more women, and in 23% the authors included both sexes (Coleman, Cola, & Webster, 1992).

Facts about sex representation among U.S. psychologists (from *Profiles—Psychology*, NSF, 1988) add detail to the picture: Among employed doctoral psychologists, women were 34% of the total in 1987. This was the largest percentage of women in any of the sciences in the United States (NSF, 1988, Table 5, p. 71), and the representation of women is increasing steadily. Male doctorates in psychology per year in the United States declined by 24% from 1977 to 1987, but female doctorates increased by 52%, so the overall number of doctorates increased slightly (p. 33). In 1986, women earned 69% of baccalaureate degrees in psychology, 69% of master's degrees, and 51% of doctoral degrees (pp. 31–33); by 1990 the percentage of U.S. doctoral degrees in psychology going to women had risen to 58 (Thurgood & Weinman, 1991). The proportions of men and women differ among different areas of psychology, as can be seen by the memberships of the divisions of the APA and by the numbers of recent doctorates. Among the 1990 U.S. doctorates, the ratio of women to men is clearly larger in the areas of educational (2.38), developmental (2.36), school (1.89), social (1.74), counseling (1.52), and clinical psychology (1.42); these include all of the health service provider fields but are not limited to them. The ratio of women to men is lowest in experimental (0.52) and industrial/organizational (0.75) psychology (Thurgood & Weinman, 1991, p. 57).

Many national leaders in the United States have been pointing with alarm to projected shortages of scientists and engineers during the next few decades and have been calling for programs to increase the recruitment of women and minorities to forestall the anticipated vacancies. A recent article on this topic (Brush, 1991) pointed to the relatively high proportions of women in the United States earning doctorates in psychology (36.0%), medical science (29.1%), biology (23.4%), and social sciences (21.2%), in contrast with the low percentages in engineering (3.1%), physics and astronomy (4.7%), environmental science (8.4%), and mathematics (8.7%). These figures came from the latest survey of employed doctoral scientists by the U.S. National Science Foundation. It would be worthwhile to compare for other countries as well the percentage of women in psychology with those in other sciences, but I have not seen such data. Brush attempted to analyze the obstacles and barriers to attracting women to do advanced work in engineering, physics, and mathematics. He did not, however, ask what attracts women to psychology, medicine, and biology. A study of this sort, including national differences in sex ratios in psychology, would be worth undertaking.

Some observers have voiced concern that psychology has become over-feminized in some parts of the world. Thus, Florence Denmark, an advocate of opportunities for women, speaking at the 1979 Interamerican Congress of Psychology in Peru, noted that female-typed occupations are devalued in most cultures, and warned that when large numbers of women enter previously male-dominated fields, the prestige of the field often drops (F. Denmark, personal communication, 1979). It is not clear, of course, that this will continue to be true, but it remains a concern for many. Thus, a French study of the employment of those who obtained degrees in psychology from 1984 to 1986 (Reyns & Verquerre, 1988) included the following observations:

> To a very large extent, those with university degrees in psychology are women ... 78% women, 22% men....
>
> After obtaining the baccalaureate from a lycée, it is mainly female students who go into university programs in psychology, probably because they think such studies are largely nonscientific and because of an incorrect understanding of the profession of a psychologist, according to which it favors the blossoming of feminine intuition. It is essential to give students realistic information so that they know about the scientific content of university studies in psychology and about the realities of professional psychology. The disparity between the proportions of women and men going into the profession of psychology is sure to have unfortunate consequences because it is common knowledge that professions that are mainly feminine are held in an unfavorable social and financial status that is usually difficult to improve (pp. 3–4; translation by Mark R. Rosenzweig).

A contrasting view is that the feminization of psychology is a consequence rather than a cause of the devaluation of psychology. That is, as various factors make psychology less attractive, some men leave the field and other men decline to enter it, thus creating opportunities for increased participation by women. The two factors may be combined in a positive feedback cycle, with devaluation of the field and feminization each stimulating the other. The APA set up in 1991 a Task Force on the Feminization of Psychology to collect data, study the situation, and propose a comprehensive action plan to respond to it.

### How Are Psychologists Deployed Among the Different Fields of Research?
The levels of research activity differ greatly among the different fields of psychology. This is shown both by ratings of research activity in the different fields and by the numbers of doctorates granted in these fields in the United States. Ratings of research activity were

made in the questionnaire sent in 1991 by IUPsyS to its national member organizations. It asked whether research activity in each of the 14 fields listed in the Appendix of Chapter 1 of this volume was high, moderate, or low (Item 1.a). A summary of the responses (Table 3) indicates that most of the respondents reported relative levels of activity within their own countries rather than absolute levels of activity on an international basis, and a few stated explicitly that the ratings referred only to relative activity within the country. The most active fields of research overall are social, educational, cognitive and clinical

**TABLE 3**

Relative Levels of Research Activity in Different Fields of Psychology, Based on the 1991 IUPsyS Survey (100 = maximum)

| Field | Industrialized countries (based on 20 responses) | Developing countries (based on 17 responses[a]) | Overall (based on 37 responses) |
|---|---|---|---|
| Academic/research fields | | | |
| Cognitive | 82 | 53 | 69 |
| Comparative | 20 | 12 | 17 |
| Developmental | 75 | 44 | 61 |
| Educational | 72 | 84 | 78 |
| Experimental | 75 | 34 | 57 |
| Industrial/organizational | 52 | 56 | 54 |
| Personality | 55 | 38 | 47 |
| Physiological | 58 | 28 | 45 |
| Psychometrics | 45 | 53 | 49 |
| Quantitative | 40 | 22 | 32 |
| Social | 78 | 78 | 78 |
| Mean | 59.3 | 45.6 | 53.4 |
| Health service provider fields | | | |
| Clinical | 60 | 69 | 64 |
| Counseling | 32 | 53 | 42 |
| School | 45 | 47 | 46 |
| Mean | 45.7 | 56.3 | 50.7 |
| Mean, all fields | 56.4 | 47.9 | 52.8 |

**Note.** The responses were quantified by giving each rating of "high research activity" a value of 2, "moderate research activity" a value of 1, scoring "low research activity" as 0, and setting the maximum possible score as 100. Identification of countries as industrialized or developing follows the classification of the United Nations Development Programme, 1990, p. 188.
[a]One of the 18 questionnaires from developing countries was too incomplete on this question to be used.

psychology. The least active field is comparative psychology, with quantitative also low.[2] The rankings are similar for industrialized and developing nations, indicating similar research interests around the world; the main exceptions are as follows: Developmental and experimental tied for third among the industrialized nations but scored below the mean among developing countries; counseling ranked at about the middle of the list in developing countries but second from the bottom among the industrialized nations; and cognitive, comparative, developmental, experimental, personality, physiological, and quantitative psychology all clearly showed higher scores among the industrialized than among the developing countries. Because there is much more research activity and many more research psychologists in the industrialized countries than in the developing countries, the overall world picture is closely approximated by the results for the industrialized countries.

Table 3 is set up so that the differences among the industrialized and developing nations can be examined in terms of two major areas of psychology, as defined by Howard et al. (1986): (a) the "traditional academic/research" fields, including comparative, developmental, educational, experimental, personality, physiological, psychometric, and social psychology, and (b) the "health service provider" fields, clinical, counseling, and school psychology. The academic/research fields (except for educational, industrial/organizational and psychometrics) scored higher among the industrialized countries, whereas the health service provider fields—especially consulting psychology—all scored higher among the developing countries. The mean level of research activity for industrialized countries was about 30% greater in the academic/research fields than in the health service provider fields; conversely, for the developing countries, the mean level of research activity was 23% higher in the health service provider fields than in the academic/research fields.

The questionnaire also provided space to enter additional fields beyond the 14 fields named, but only a few responses added other fields, so the listing appears to be appropriate for most countries.

Another item in the questionnaire (1.b.) asked whether there are fields of psychological research that are characteristic of the country and that tend to differentiate it

---

[2] Even the field that ranks relatively lowest in research activity—comparative psychology—nevertheless shows quite a bit of research in many countries and regions. Comparative has always been part of psychology in North America, and there are journals and textbooks in the field. The International Society for Comparative Psychology has members around the world, has a journal, and is an affiliate of the IUPsyS.

from other countries. Most countries did not name a special field that their psychology emphasizes, or they named only fields included in the list of main fields, but the following are some that named other fields: Japan mentioned the psychology of Zen and other eastern systems; Hong Kong, Chinese psychology; Turkey, immigration studies in social psychology; Colombia, experimental analysis of behavior; the United Kingdom, cognitive neuropsychology; Yugoslavia, self-management; and four countries mentioned cross-cultural psychology (India, Indonesia, Israel, and South Africa). So although most psychologists are working on the same main areas of psychology around the world, some psychologists in certain countries are investigating topics of special local or regional interest.

The numbers of psychologists who do research in different fields do not reflect a deliberate policy or specific assignments but rather occur as the sum of individual choices. When asked whether there is a national plan or set of priorities for research in psychology (Item 2), only one respondent said yes.

The relative strengths of research efforts among the main fields are changing, rather rapidly in some cases. When asked whether the numbers of psychologists active in research in the different fields have changed over the past 10 years and, if so, which fields have gained and which have lost (Item 4.c), most countries reported changes. Furthermore, the directions and amounts of changes correspond well to the degrees of activity reported in Item 1.a. For most fields, the overall changes in numbers of psychologists active in research were in the positive direction, and the fields for which the greatest numbers of countries reported positive changes were cognitive, social, educational, and clinical psychology. The only field to show an overall loss in the number of psychologists was comparative. Those fields that failed to gain significantly were personality, physiological, psychometrics, and quantitative.

Data from the United States are relevant here, both because the majority of the world's research psychologists live there and because published figures are available for the numbers of doctoral degrees awarded in most of these fields in 1977 and 1987 (see Table 4). On the other hand, it is clear that the data for the United States do not reflect the numbers or trends of doctorates in most other countries. The figures in Table 4 indicate for the United States the overall level of activity in the different fields as well as changes of emphasis over the 10-year period. It should be noted that the number of doctoral degrees granted in a field does not necessarily reflect the amount of research activity in that field, because many of the doctoral recipients in the United States do not continue in research but go into professional practice.

**TABLE 4**

Numbers of Doctoral Degrees Awarded in Certain Fields of Psychology in the United States in 1977 and 1987

| Field | 1977 | 1987 | % change, 1977 to 1987 |
|---|---|---|---|
| Academic/research fields | | | |
| Comparative | 22 | 9 | −59 |
| Developmental | 203 | 200 | −1 |
| Experimental | 337 | 146 | |
| Cognitive | — | 80 | |
| Experimental + Cognitive[a] | 337 | 226 | −33 |
| Industrial/organizational | 81 | 104 | 28 |
| Personality | 63 | 24 | −62 |
| Physiological | 132 | 69 | −48 |
| Psychometrics & quantitative | 19 | 22 | 16 |
| Social | 202 | 133 | −34 |
| Total, academic/research fields | 1,059 | 787 | −26 |
| Men | 687 | 373 | −46 |
| Women | 372 | 414 | 11 |
| Health-service-provider fields | | | |
| Clinical | 936 | 1,154 | 23 |
| Counseling | 269 | 485 | 80 |
| School | 148 | 93 | −37 |
| Total, health service provider fields | 1,353 | 1,732 | 28 |
| Men | 854 | 799 | −6 |
| Women | 499 | 933 | 87 |
| Ratio of numbers in academic/research fields to those in health-service-provider fields | 0.78 | 0.45 | −42 |
| Men | 0.81 | 0.47 | −42 |
| Women | 0.74 | 0.44 | −41 |
| General and other fields | | | |
| Educational | 136 | 89 | −35 |
| Psychology, general | 262 | 336 | 28 |
| Psychology, other[b] | 179 | 154 | −14 |
| Grand Total | 2,989 | 3,098 | 4 |
| Men | 1,902 | 1,446 | −24 |
| Women | 1,087 | 1,652 | 52 |

**Note.** Data are from the National Science Foundation, 1988, Table 27. Reprinted by permission.
[a]The survey did not use the category of "cognitive" in 1977, so the table includes the combined category of "experimental + cognitive" for comparability in both periods.
[b]The "other" category includes new and emerging subfields such as health psychology and psychology and the law.

Table 4 shows that the largest number of doctorates in the United States was in clinical psychology (37% of the total in 1987), with a gain of 23% in the number of doctorates from 1977 to 1987. The next largest number of doctorates was in counseling (16% of the degrees), which showed the largest relative gain over the decade: 80%. The large numbers of doctorates in clinical and counseling in the United States stand in contrast with many other countries that have very few doctorates in these fields because the doctorate in those countries is an academic/research degree. Industrial/organizational psychology and the small fields of psychometrics and quantitative also gained in the numbers of U.S. doctorates over the decade. The other fields all lost in their shares of U.S. doctorates, with the greatest relative losses in personality, comparative, and physiological psychology. (Again, these losses do not represent the case in Europe and perhaps elsewhere outside of North America.) The changes in numbers of American doctorates in the different fields over the period from 1977 to 1987 do not correspond very well to the reported changes in research activity in these fields internationally. The changes in the United States can also be examined in terms of the two major areas of psychology: the "traditional academic/ research" fields and the "health-service provider" fields. The traditional academic/research fields accounted for 35% of U.S. doctorates in psychology in 1977, but the proportion fell to only 25% in 1987. The health provider fields already accounted for 45% of the doctorates in 1977, and this rose to 56% in 1987.

## The Growth of Practice and the Decline of Academic/Research Psychology

A striking feature in the development of psychology in many industrialized countries, from the 1950s on, has been the growth of practice in the health-service-provider areas and the relative decline of the traditional academic/research areas. This has been discussed extensively in regard to the United States, but it is also true of many other industrialized countries, including Australia, Canada, Finland, Germany, Norway, Portugal, and Spain. Many developing countries also show a concentration of psychologists in areas of practice that can contribute to national development, including health provision. As Sexton and Hogan (1992, p. 472) point out, in many developing countries social needs demand a concentration on practical issues, and there is a lack of funding for research. Such developing countries that show a strong emphasis on application and practice include Argentina, Brazil, Cuba, the Dominican Republic, Hong Kong, India, Mexico, the Philippines, South Africa, Turkey, Uruguay, and Venezuela. Some implications of this shift in balance between the health-provider specialties and the academic/research areas will be discussed in this chapter.

*Obtaining Legal Recognition for the Practice of Psychology*
In keeping with the shift to practice, there has been a movement to obtain legal status for the professional practice of psychology, including, especially, counseling and psychotherapy, but also such services as the assessment of abilities and the provision of industrial/ organizational services. The quest for legal status is intended, on the one hand, to protect the public by ensuring that persons who represent themselves as psychologists have the necessary training and professional experience, and, on the other hand, to protect psychologists and psychology by preventing people without adequate training and experience from representing themselves as psychologists. Such people have often made unreasonable claims and have not had the training necessary to perform psychological functions and services. Starting in the United States in the 1940s, the movement to gain legal protection for the title "psychologist" soon became international. Many countries now have legal protection for the title, and campaigns to achieve this goal are being pursued in many parts of the world.

The IUPsyS and the International Association of Applied Psychology cosponsored an international symposium on the professional and legal status of psychologists in 1982 (Rosenzweig, 1983). In the symposium, the status of psychology in 11 countries was described, some with full legal recognition of professional psychologists (Brazil, the German Democratic Republic, Hungary, Norway, South Africa, Spain, the United States), one with partial recognition (Netherlands), one with social recognition but without legal status (the United Kingdom), and some without any legal status (France, Ireland). The symposium was the outcome of a survey by the French Psychological Society, which was attempting, in cooperation with several other organizations of French psychologists, to obtain legal recognition for the professional status of psychologists. This was finally obtained in a law of 1985, which was put into effect through regulations of 1990.

In Belgium, the question of legal protection for the title of psychologist has still not been settled (Richelle, Janssen, & Brédart, 1992). The Belgian Federation of Psychologists, founded in 1979 and coordinating the activities of 15 associations of university-trained psychologists, has been working to achieve this objective for a decade. One of the major problems is that some people are considered by Belgian law to have an "acquired right" to call themselves psychologists even though they are not university trained. As long as the title of psychologist is not defined legally, it is proving difficult for the Belgian Federation to work out the definitions of *clinical psychologist* and *industrial psychologist* in negotiations with the relevant government ministries.

In Austria, the situation of legal status is complicated (Guttmann & Etlinger, 1992): The use of the title "psychologist" is regulated by law, but the use of the adjective "psychological" is not, so anyone can offer "psychological counseling" or other "psychological" services. But neither the registered psychologist nor the self-declared psychological counselor can offer "therapy"; Austrian law stipulates that therapy, including psychotherapy, is reserved for physicians.

### Benefits and Costs of Legal Recognition

Where legal recognition has been achieved, it has brought both benefits and costs. On the positive side, it has helped to meet the growing demand for mental health services, and it has fostered a large growth of professional positions in psychology. This is in contrast with the situation in some countries, where psychology is not recognized legally and where large numbers of people with university degrees in psychology are not employed or are employed in other fields (e.g., Germany). The large numbers employed in psychology where it is recognized legally has, in turn, increased demand for psychological training. In the United States and some other countries where professional training includes training in the scientific bases and methods of psychology, this has meant an increase in the number of faculty positions in all areas of psychology. Without the growth in applications of psychology, the discipline might have remained largely academic and relatively small, like the related discipline of anthropology. The involvement of psychologists in psychotherapy and in health psychology has also led to many new questions that demand research, as is shown in Chapters 7 and 8 of this volume.

There have also been costs associated with the growth of psychological practice and its legal recognition. Legal recognition for the practice of psychology, especially in health-related areas such as psychotherapy, has tended to fix in public opinion the idea that psychology deals principally with psychotherapy. One result has been that many psychologists engaged in research now tend to avoid the title "psychologist" and to identify themselves with their fields of research and call themselves by such titles as "neuroscientists," "cognitive scientists," and "human factors engineers"; they also tend to affiliate with organizations in those fields in addition to, or in place of, psychological organizations. The fact that many students of psychology will take up health-related occupations has tended to orient psychological curricula in that direction, and institutions that accredit psychological training programs emphasize preparation for health-provider services. The rapid growth in the number of psychological practitioners has led to strains between the traditional academic/research groups and the health-service-provider groups within some national psychological associations. An example of this is the American

Psychological Association, where the discontent of many academic/research members in the 1980s led to the formation of the American Psychological Society (APS) in 1988. The APS, devoted to academic/research interests, attained a membership of over 12,000 by 1991, demonstrating a large constituency for these interests. Nevertheless, many APS members remain members of the APA, and the APA actively fosters academic/research interests as well as professional practice and the public interest functions, so American psychological science now has two large national organizations to promote its interests. Other countries have handled these tensions in other ways. For example, the Australian Psychological Association has the Division of Scientific Affairs and the Division of Professional Affairs.

## Concerns About Insufficient Numbers of Psychological Researchers

The number of psychological researchers is increasing on a worldwide basis, but relatively less among the industrialized than among the developing countries. Twenty-six of the 38 responses to the IUPsyS questionnaire (Item 4.b) reported increases over the last decade. Only one gave an unambiguous report of a decrease in the number of psychological researchers. It is worth separating the responses of industrialized and developing nations to this question. Eight of the 10 countries reporting "the same" were industrialized countries; so were the two countries giving qualified indications of increases, the one reporting "decrease," and the one not responding to this question. This indicates that in about half of the industrialized countries, the development of psychological research may have reached a plateau; this stands in striking contrast to the large increase in the overall number of psychologists. However, all but two of the developing countries that returned questionnaires reported increases over the last decade in the numbers of psychologists engaged in research.

As for the numbers of students getting degrees in psychology (Item 4.a), 31 of the 38 countries reported an increase over the last decade. This included 15 of the 20 industrialized countries and 16 of the 18 developing countries that responded. Thus, there are many students in the pipeline, but it is not known how many of these will go into research in psychology.

Are there enough psychological researchers to take care of the tasks that confront them? Some relevant information came out in responses to the following question in the IUPsyS survey (Item 9):

> Major obstacles or barriers exist in every country to achieving a satisfactory amount of high-quality psychological research. These may include too few highly trained research psychologists, insufficient financial support, lack of recognition for psychological research, and so on. What do you consider to be the main obstacles in your country?

The most frequently named obstacle was financial, as I will discuss later, but 17 of the 38 respondents complained that their country has too few highly trained research psychologists. Ten of the 18 developing countries named this obstacle, but so did 7 of the 20 industrialized countries. Psychologists from developing countries commented that there were "too few trained psychologists; too few full-time research psychologists," that there was a "lack of critical mass of research psychologists who are visible to the public," and that they felt isolated. One stated, "There are few researchers [in my country] who could be regarded as qualified and well-versed with the intricacies of research. Majority of the researchers are poor in research methodology and have little insight of research design and superficial knowledge of statistics. . . ."

Two respondents from prosperous industrialized countries made the following comments: "Too few highly trained (PhD and Postdoctoral) researchers. Mechanisms for encouraging such have not been in place. . . . the dispersal of researchers, leading to a lack of critical mass of researchers in particular geographic areas." "Very few psychologists are employed to undertake research only. . . . Most of us make research *and* teaching *and* administration of an institute/faculty/university."

Even though the United States has a relatively large number of psychological researchers, some reviewers are worried by the decline in the research/academic areas:

> The expansion in the health-service-provider specialties is a significant achievement in meeting the growing demand for mental health services. However, the accompanying decline in the traditional academic/research areas may be cause for alarm, as may the proliferation of practitioner programs, which has eroded psychology's overall ranking in the national scientific community as a producer of scientists from high-quality programs.
>
> What will it mean if psychology forsakes or is perceived to forsake its scientific side in the rush to provide health care? Is this related to its apparent loss of appeal to undergraduate men. . . ? Does it presage an overall decline in the prestige of the profession? . . . These questions and more, raised by the data presented here, demand careful consideration of the directions taken by psychology. . . ." (Howard et al., 1986, p. 1326)

It does not seem possible at present to make a definitive assessment of this problem because different surveys, using different methods, yield rather different results. Thus, the National Research Council surveys of new doctorates concerning their "planned employment" showed a downward drift of about 6% from 1980 to 1990 in those who planned research as their primary or secondary activity. On the other hand, APA surveys of work activities of new doctorate recipients in the United States showed a steep drop from 1981 to

1986 in those reporting any involvement in research: from about 1,600 individuals (60% of the total) to about 1,300 (46%). Reporting these findings, Pion (1991, p. 245) stated that this trend demonstrates that psychology needs to be concerned about whether it will be able to maintain a strong research presence and advance its knowledge base.

In the Epilogue to their *International Psychology: Views From Around the World,* Sexton and Hogan (1992) stated concerns related to those of Howard et al. (1986) about the shrinkage in the number of researchers in the United States:

> The shift from psychology as a scientific discipline to one dominated by practice has been occurring for decades. Nevertheless, the dramatic shifts of recent years have the potential for drastically altering the discipline. A unique feature of psychology, even as an applied specialty, has been its research base. Few applied disciplines can claim the rigorous scientific training that was, and perhaps still is, the hallmark of the PhD trained psychologist. Even though the usual goal of the individual student may be to engage in private practice only, that student is still likely to have extensive training in research methodology and statistics. But there are decreasing numbers of psychologists with the interest and special background to provide such training. If there are too few psychologist–researchers to replenish that base, the training will eventually erode and, with it, the special strength of the psychologist–practitioner will likewise diminish. The result, inevitably, would be a psychology without a science. (p. 476)

Psychology is not alone among the sciences to feel the threat of declining numbers of researchers. Atkinson (1990) spelled out this problem for the natural sciences in the United States and called it a crisis in the making. But psychology and the social sciences suffer from particular problems of secondary education in recruiting students for research, as pointed out by a Task Force of the National Science Foundation (1991): Secondary schools in the United States, and in most other countries, do not reflect current research in psychology or the social sciences, so students do not become aware early of the possibility of careers in research in these fields. Nor do secondary schools expose students to the kinds of mathematics needed for psychological and social science research (e.g., statistics, probability, the use of linear models).

The International Council of Scientific Unions (ICSU) called for study of this problem in the following resolution passed by its General Assembly in 1990:

> We live in an era of unprecedented progress in science but the attraction of science to the younger generation seems to be lessening in some countries. Where these statistics are available they point to the danger of insufficient human resources in science and

technology as the 21st Century opens. ICSU should examine, together with other concerned scientific bodies, the magnitude of this problem. (Marton-Lefèvre, 1990, p. 48)

The secretary general of the ICSU therefore wrote in early 1991 to both its scientific unions and its national members to ask whether this problem has been found to occur in their union or country and, if so, what activities are being undertaken in relation to this problem and what specific role the ICSU might play in this area. This appeal by the ICSU reveals the lack of data on this important question. The present survey is, in part, a response of the IUPsyS to the ICSU's appeal for information.

# What Financial Support Does Psychological Research Obtain?

Inadequate funding for research is a problem for psychologists just as it is for most scientists, but psychologists in most countries find themselves with even worse problems than do most other scientists. The problem of inadequate funding for psychological research is the major concern of most of the representatives of psychological organizations who took part in the 1991 IUPsyS survey. Nevertheless, only 9 of the replies from 20 industrialized countries and only 4 of the 18 from developing countries were able to furnish specific information about the amount of research funding for psychology in their own countries (Item 5.a). The combination of concern and lack of information makes it worthwhile to discuss this question in some detail here.

The ways in which psychologists obtain funding for their research and the amounts they obtain differ greatly around the world. In many countries (e.g., Germany, Japan, Nigeria, Turkey, the United Kingdom), universities supply a large part of the funds available for research. In some countries (e.g., Cuba, France, the former Soviet Union), much psychological research is done in governmental research institutes by career governmental investigators. In a few countries (e.g., Australia, Canada, the United States), much of the money to support research is obtained by individual investigators or by small groups of investigators in the form of grants awarded on a competitive basis by agencies of the national government or by private foundations. In many cases, a combination of these systems is used in the same country.

Although the systems of allocating research support differ, psychologists around the world complain that funding for their research is inadequate. For most countries, however, it is even harder to obtain precise data about funding than to obtain data about human resources for psychological research. Published sources are available, but for only a few of the main industrialized countries. To obtain the information necessary for policy decisions, the Advisory Board for the Research Councils (United Kingdom) and the National Science Foundation (United States) undertook a study to obtain information about research support by several of the main industrialized nations. Information helpful for our survey is contained in their report, *Investing in the Future: An International Comparison of Government Funding of Academic and Related Research* (Irvine, Martin, & Isard, 1990).

Reports of the funding of research use the following major categories: *basic research, applied research,* and *development.*[3] Research can also be assigned to one of the three following categories according to the method of funding by governmental agencies (we will see that countries differ in their preferred methods of funding): (a) academic research financed by general university funds supplied by governmental agencies; (b) academic separately budgeted research, that is, specific academic research projects or programs that are financed separately; and (c) academically related research, that is, government-funded research carried out in a variety of organizations that should be included for adequate international comparisons because, although formally outside of the higher education sector, they are nevertheless closely linked to academic research or they undertake activities that are similar to those that are the responsibility of universities in many other countries.

Throughout the decade of the 1980s, the industrialized nations of France, the Federal Republic of Germany, Japan, the United Kingdom, and the United States spent 2% to 3% of their gross national products on research and development (R&D), but the percentage of the R&D budget allocated to various purposes varied greatly among these countries.[4]

## Funding for Academic Research in Six Industrialized Countries

Table 5 presents information on the amounts spent in 1987 on academic and academically related research by six industrialized countries for a few academic fields, including

---

[3]*Definitions of these categories are as follows:* Basic research *has as its objective a fuller knowledge or understanding of the subject under study, rather than practical applications.* Applied research *is directed toward gaining the knowledge or understanding necessary for determining the means by which a recognized and specific need may be met.* Development, *in the context of research and development, is the systematic use of the knowledge or understanding gained from research directed toward the production of useful methods, systems, or devices. This categorization also varies to some extent among countries. For example, in China one distinguishes among "basic," "applied basic," and "applied" research; in this system, basic research is done without any thought of application, applied basic research is done with the hope that the results will find application, and applied research is directed toward application of the findings.*

[4]*As of 1985, the United States spent about 12% of its R&D budget on basic research, Japan about 13%, Germany about 18%, and France about 20% (National Science Board, 1989, Table 4-21, p. 288). Health received 12% of the 1987 R&D budget of the United States, 4.3% in the United Kingdom, 3.6% in France, 3.2% in Germany, and 2.4% in Japan (National Science Board, 1989, Table 4-22, p. 289).*

psychology (data from tables in Irvine, Martin, & Isard, 1990). The total amount spent on academic and academically related research for all sciences and engineering is also shown in this tabulation. The amounts allocated for psychology range from 2.5% of the country's total for academic and academically related research in science and engineering (the Netherlands) down to 0.5% (France), with a median of 1.3%. The allocations for psychology range from 41% of the total for social sciences (the United States) down to 11% (Japan), with a median of 24%. To permit comparison of allocations for psychology with those for a physical science, Table 5 includes the amounts for chemistry. The allocations for psychology range from 36% of that for chemistry (United States) down to 6% (France), with a median of 26%.

The total expenditure for academic and academically related research for science and engineering is about 9% greater in the United States than in the other five industrialized countries together, although the population of the United States is about 78% of the total of the other five countries. The disparity in expenditures for psychology between the United States and the other countries is striking: The total of $220 million for the United States is 59% greater than the total of $138 million for psychology in the other five countries together. This disparity appears to be in keeping with the large number of doctoral and research psychologists in the United States in comparison with other countries, as was noted earlier in this chapter.

The ways in which different nations allocate funds for academic research vary, as Table 5 shows. Four of the countries supplied money chiefly in the form of general university funds (GUF). The United States, however, gave funds mainly in the form of academic separately budgeted research (ASBR), usually in the form of research grants. And France supported mainly academically related research (ARR) carried out in laboratories outside of the higher education sector; these are mainly "grands organismes" such as the Centre National de Recherche Scientifique and the Institut National de Santé et de Recherche Médicale.

All of these quantitative comparisons should be taken with some caution because of difficulties in obtaining accurate and comparable information from different countries, as stated by the authors of the international study *Investing in the Future* (Irvine et al., 1990). These authors caution their readers about a number of problems in obtaining adequate and comparable data. For example, information about allocations of general university funds among different fields is based on out-of-date formulas in some countries. Also, the expenditures for each country were converted to U.S. dollars using "purchasing power parity" (PPP) exchange rates calculated by the European Organization for

## TABLE 5

Amounts Spent by Six Industrialized Countries in 1987 on Academic and Academically Related Research in a Few Fields of Science (amounts in millions of U.S. dollars)

| Type | Psychology | Total social sciences | Chemistry | Total sciences & engineering |
|---|---|---|---|---|
| United States | | | | |
| GUF | 58.5 | 242.5 | 81.1 | 2,257 |
| ASBR | 161.6 | 289.3 | 449.2 | 9,614 |
| ARR | 0.1 | 2.3 | 81.9 | 1,914 |
| Total | 220.2 | 534.1 | 612.2 | 13,784 |
| % of total sci. & eng. | 1.60 | 3.87 | 4.44 | — |
| Federal Republic of Germany | | | | |
| GUF | 20.4 | 110.9 | 161.0 | 1,774 |
| ASBR | 6.6 | 22.7 | 46.5 | 678 |
| ARR | 10.9 | 38.1 | 52.8 | 1,098 |
| Total | 37.9 | 171.7 | 260.3 | 3,551 |
| % of total sci. & eng. | 1.07 | 4.83 | 7.32 | — |
| Japan | | | | |
| GUF | 19.4 | 82.9 | 81.6 | 1,860 |
| ASBR | 5.1 | 17.7 | 15.5 | 797 |
| ARR | — | 19.7 | 1.6 | 324 |
| Total | 24.5 | 120.3 | 98.7 | 2,981 |
| % of total sci. & eng. | 0.82 | 4.00 | 3.31 | — |
| France | | | | |
| GUF | 9.0 | 38.2 | 77.1 | 804 |
| ASBR | 3.3 | 54.6 | 101.5 | 916 |
| ARR | 2.7 | 38.6 | 66.9 | 1,202 |
| Total | 15.0 | 131.4 | 245.5 | 2,922 |
| % of total sci. & eng. | 0.51 | 4.50 | 8.40 | — |
| United Kingdom | | | | |
| GUF | 30.3 | 105.8 | 98.6 | 1,160 |
| ASBR | 5.8 | 36.5 | 33.1 | 563 |
| ARR | 5.1 | 3.2 | 26.1 | 725 |
| Total | 41.2 | 145.5 | 157.8 | 2,448 |
| % of total sci. & eng. | 1.68 | 5.94 | 6.45 | — |
| Netherlands | | | | |
| GUF | 14.4 | 53.3 | 41.2 | 466 |
| ASBR | 5.4 | 22.1 | 9.6 | 161 |
| ARR | — | 4.2 | 0.2 | 162 |
| Total | 19.8 | 79.6 | 51.0 | 793 |
| % of total sci. & eng. | 2.50 | 10.04 | 6.43 | — |

**Note.** Data are from tables in Irvine, Martin, & Isard (1990). Reprinted by permission. GUF = general university funds; ASBR = academic separately budgeted research; ARR = academically related research carried out in laboratories outside of the higher education sector.

Economic Cooperation and Development, but not all economists believe that the PPP rates are applicable to R&D expenditures.

In addition to the cautions expressed by Irvine et al. (1990), it should also be noted that although academic and academically related research accounts for most of the research in psychology, it does not account for all of the research in the field. Thus, the National Science Foundation (1988) reported the following figures for the support of research in psychology in the United States in 1986: (a) federally financed R&D expenditures at universities and colleges: $118 million; (b) R&D expenditures at universities and colleges: $180 million; and (c) federal obligations for basic research of $150 million and for applied research of $201 million, for a total of $351 million for basic and applied research in psychology in 1986. Note that this last figure is much larger than the federally financed and total R&D expenditures at universities and colleges. It is also much larger than the total of $220 million given in Table 5 for academic and academically related expenditures for research in psychology in the United States in 1987. Thus, it should be kept in mind that the amounts given in Table 5 represent only a portion of the total support for research in psychology.

U.S. federal obligations for basic and applied research in psychology were larger than for any social science and amounted to three quarters of the total for all social sciences (economics, sociology, anthropology, and others; see Table 6). This was true despite the fact that there are only half as many doctoral psychologists with academic research as their primary or secondary activity as there are social scientists doing academic research (National Science Board, 1989, p. 320). Thus, on the average, the individual psychologist doing

**TABLE 6**
U.S. Federal Obligations for Basic and Applied Research in Certain Fields, 1987 (thousands of dollars)

| Type | Psychology | Social sciences | Chemistry | Total sciences |
|---|---|---|---|---|
| Basic research[a] | 150,287 | 131,480 | 464,253 | 7,799,038 |
| Applied research[b] | 215,097 | 352,054 | 231,755 | 6,034,319 |
| Basic + applied research | 365,384 | 483,534 | 696,008 | 13,833,357 |
| Percentage of total | 2.6 | 3.5 | 5.0 | — |

[a]From National Science Foundation, 1988, Table 31.   [b]From National Science Foundation, 1988, Table 33. Reprinted by permission.

academic research received about 50% more support than the individual social scientist doing academic research. On the other hand, the amount of support for academic research psychology was only half of that for chemistry, despite the fact that there are 15% more academic doctoral research psychologists than chemists. Thus, the average psychologist doing academic research received only about 45% of the support that the average chemist doing academic research received. Psychology accounted for less of the total allocation for basic academic research (1.9%) than for applied academic research (3.6%); it received 2.6% of the amount for basic and applied research combined.

The U.S. responses to the IUPsyS survey showed, for 1990, about $450 million in U.S. federal funds to support psychological research and an estimated additional $40 million from private foundations. Considering these amounts and the estimated number of research psychologists in the United States, the figures suggest a mean annual allocation per research psychologist of approximately $14,000. Of course, there is a wide scatter around this mean, with some psychologists receiving much more and many receiving no federal or private foundation funding at all for their research.

**Funding for Psychology in a Broader International Perspective**

Looking beyond the six countries of the study by Irvine et al. (1990), we find that some industrialized countries report very little support for psychological research. Here, for example, is a statement from New Zealand: "Government support for research in psychology is virtually non-existent. Most universities provide their own research funds for minor amounts from block grants. Even extensive Doctoral projects, however, are beyond the resources of most of these local funds. Thus ... research in psychology in New Zealand is severely hampered through lack of funding" (Shouksmith & Shouksmith, 1990, p. 446).

In most developing countries, the situation is even worse. In many of them, there is no specific national allocation for research in psychology; the only available funds come from universities, and there is not much of that. The following are some statements by respondents from developing countries to the IUPsyS survey:

> The only source of support for psychological research is the general research fund given to each university or research institute. This is usually not much, and everybody struggles to get a bit of it. Because psychologists are few compared to other groups [in our country], relatively little money is spent on psychological research.... The conference budget for my department last year was $80—not enough for one person to attend a conference.

> There is no special allocation of government's funds for Psychology.

There is no amount earmarked for psychological research.... The Project of Development in Basic Sciences of the Ministry of Education and Culture does not include psychology among the fields in which to develop research.

Another respondent from a developing country noted that the lack of funds for psychological research in his country is, in part, a self-fulfilling prophecy: Psychologists refrain from requesting funds because they are unlikely to receive any, and the government does not allot funds for psychological research because they receive so few requests and see so little being done.

Two Turkish psychologists (Basaran & Sahin, 1990) give a vivid picture of the situation:

Funded research [is] an exception among Turkish psychologists. The majority of the projects are supported by the personal means of the researcher. The salaries in the universities are low, an equivalent to 300 US dollars for a full-time associate professor, and have even been lower in the last decade, which prohibits the allocation of a substantial share to a project. The purchase of material, equipment and services through university resources is usually limited or disappointing....

This lack of support inevitably leads to severe limitations in the selection or treatment of research topics, often accompanied by painful conflicts on the part of the researcher. The choices seem to be either to give up cherished issues or to be content with a[n] ... inadequate treatment of the problem at hand. The cost of [such methods as] longitudinal studies, surveys requiring large representative samples, and, especially, experimental studies relying on precision instruments, remain beyond the financial resources of psychologists.

Combined with a heavy teaching load and a struggle to maintain high standards in teaching and research, the deprivation from research support taxes—sometimes cruelly—the endurance of the young academician. A fresh Ph.D. from the United States, with all the curiosity and commitment, faces a period of unpleasant resocialization....

At the time of writing this report, a total of 13 researchers (not projects) received some support from university funds, plus an additional 11 from non-university agencies. ... In personal contacts, we have learned that the total amount of support, when divided by the number of individuals in the project, amounts to an equivalent of about 700 US dollars. (pp. 24–25, quoted by permission)

It should be noted that, in spite of financial obstacles and insufficient numbers of trained psychologists, many developing countries have at least a few outstanding psychological investigators who overcome barriers and produce research of high theoretical and practical value. International congresses of psychology have featured the contributions of some of these investigators, and some of them have been elected to the national academies of sciences in their countries. These investigators pave the way for their compatriots. The IUPsyS has made it a high priority to find ways to promote psychological research in developing countries and is seeking ways to expand these efforts.

Whether their country is developing or industrial, most respondents to the IUPsyS survey (Item 9) named insufficient financial support as the chief obstacle to achieving a satisfactory amount of high-quality psychological research. Of 38 responses, 29 named insufficient financial support as a major obstacle, and one named a lack of convertible currency; 20 put financial problems as their first or only obstacle, and only 7 did not mention it. When asked to compare the financial support for psychology with that for other fields of science (Item 5.e), 24 of 38 respondents said "worse," 11 said "about the same," and 2 did not reply to this question; only one said "better." One of the respondents answering "about the same" qualified this by adding, "worse than the natural and technological sciences, better than the humanistic sciences," and the same could probably be said for many other countries as well. Clearly, psychologists in most countries believe not only that psychological research gets inadequate financial support, but that it is being treated less well than are other sciences. This perception is almost the same in the industrialized countries and the developing countries.

Some data on the relative treatment of psychology and other sciences is available for the United States. In constant dollars (i.e., allowing for inflation), the total of federal and nonfederal expenditures for academic R&D in all science fields increased by 65% from 1976 to 1987 (National Science Board, 1989, Appendix Table 5-9, p. 309). During the same period, expenditures in constant dollars for psychological research increased by 28%, for physical sciences by 94%, and for mathematics and computer science by 233%, whereas for social sciences they rose by only 1% (National Science Board, 1989, Appendix Table 5-9). The constant-dollar allowances for psychology thus showed a modest increase during the decade from 1976 to 1987, but the share of psychological research in the total science budget declined during this period from 2.36% to 1.84%—a drop of 22% in psychology's share of the total. Meanwhile, the social sciences declined from 7.95% of total science expenditures to 4.87%—a fall of 39% in their share of the total. Also, federal funding for psychological research fluctuated markedly from the late 1960s to the late 1980s, so there were periods of substantial gain and periods of major loss. For behavioral and social sciences combined, federal support in constant dollars reached a peak in 1978;

the level of support in 1987 was 30% below this peak and 25% below the level of 1972. The fluctuations in support make it hard to plan, and they create an unfavorable climate for research. In a study prepared for the American Psychological Association, Uebersax and Ferguson (1989) issued the following warning: "The lack of an adequate base of support for psychological research may have a vicious circle quality—if adequate funding is not available, the quality of research may suffer, and the field may appear less capable of addressing relevant social concerns. This, in turn, may lower public confidence in the discipline, making it more difficult to obtain societal resources for research" (p. 44).

The need for greater support of research in the behavioral and social sciences was spelled out in a detailed report of the National Research Council (NRC), the action arm of the National Academy of Sciences: *The Behavioral and Social Sciences: Achievements and Opportunities* (Gerstein, Luce, Smelser, & Sperlich, 1988). NRC reports, it should be noted, are reviewed and evaluated with great care for both accuracy and policy implications before being accepted for publication. The analyses in this report were made for psychology along with the social sciences, but several sections referred exclusively or mainly to psychology. After showing the achievements and potentials of these fields, the report concluded by advocating an increase of about 30% in federal expenditures for the behavioral and social sciences over the next few years. Detailed recommendations for increased support were made under the following headings:

(a) *Human resources.* Increased availability of predoctoral and postdoctoral research fellowships to encourage talented scientists in careers oriented to research.

(b) *Technological resources.* "Technological resources available to most researchers in the behavioral and social sciences have lagged badly behind needs except at a few sites. The lag has been particularly acute with respect to neuroimaging and the more diversified and specialized laboratory equipment used in research on behavior, as well as the recent upgrading of standards for animal care." Also, the "requirement for more capable computers and the development of specialized software (as well as the acquisition of more sophisticated general-purpose software systems)" (p. 247).

(c) *Data resources.* Upgrading and expanding extended data collections that are a significant feature of behavioral and social sciences research.

(d) *Investigator-initiated grants.* "The average size and duration of grants for small-group investigator research in most areas must be increased ..." (p. 249).

For those interested in this topic, it would be worthwhile to read the entire report.

Other countries with large psychological communities are also suffering from insufficient funding of psychological research. For example, in the United Kingdom funding for research has been cut for most fields of science and appears uncertain. This makes it impossible to maintain the former high level of research productivity and makes it difficult to attract students to careers in research. There is also a serious problem of brain drain of professors and researchers from the United Kingdom. In Australia, government policy is channeling financial support into the natural sciences, engineering and technology, and mission-oriented research associated with industry. Psychology is not faring well under this policy and is getting a much smaller share of the national research budget than is the case in most industrialized countries. In Canada, funding has not kept pace with the growth of the field or with the costs of psychological research. The Canadian psychological community finds itself vulnerable to losing productive investigators to better salaries and better research funding in the United States. In Germany, the tasks of absorbing and supporting psychological investigators from the former German Democratic Republic pose formidable financial and other problems that are still hard to envisage.

Thus, across the world, the financial picture for psychological research needs much improvement. Even in most of the industrialized countries, it lags behind the support for other sciences and does not allow psychological research to achieve its potential. And in most of the developing countries, the dearth of support for psychological research does not permit it to contribute as it should to the growth of the country and the development of its people. A further reflection of the need in developing nations is seen in responses to questionnaire Item 10, which asked what other activities the respondent would like to see the Union undertake to foster psychological research. Ten of the 18 developing countries mentioned the desirability of obtaining financial support, most of them either from the Union or through the Union; so did 2 of the 5 eastern European countries, but none of the other 15 industrialized countries. A hopeful indication is that in many countries, governmental scientific organizations contribute major financial support for psychological research.[5]

Another hopeful indication came from the responses to the question whether financial support for psychological research in each country increased, remained the same, or

---

[5]Some examples of agencies that support psychological research are the following: The Australian Research Grants Scheme, the Canadian National Research Council and the Natural Science and Engineering Research Council of Canada, the Colombian Colciencias, the Deutsche Forschungsgemeinschaft, the Egyptian Ministry of Scientific Research, the French Centre National de Recherche Scientifique, the Indian National Science Academy and the Indian National Institute of Mental Health and Neurosciences, the Japan Science Council and the Japan Society for the Promotion of Science, the Mexican Sistema Nacional de Investigadores, the Netherlands Organization for Scientific Research, the Norwegian Research Council for Science and the Humanities and the Norwegian Council for Research in Technology and Science, the South African Centre for Science Development of the Human Sciences Research Council, the Swedish Medical Research Council, the Swiss National Science Foundation, the U.K. Department of Education and Science and the Royal Society, and many U.S. agencies, including the National Science Foundation and the National Institute of Mental Health.

decreased over the last 10 years (Item 5.c). Eighteen replied "increased," 9 "the same," 7 "decreased," and 4 left the item blank. A few who replied "increased" noted that the increase only kept up with inflation or that the increase was less than that for other sciences. Thus, almost half of the responses noted an increase over the last decade and only one fifth reported a decrease, but responses to other items indicated that whatever increase occurred was usually inadequate.

There are indications, although not strong, that the available support is shifting among fields of psychology. When asked if such shifts have been occurring in their country (Item 5.d), 19 respondents said "yes," 11 replied "no," and 8 gave no response. Most of the reports of changes came from the developing countries (11 of the 19 affirmative responses, and only 3 of the 11 negative responses). Overall, the main gains reported were in cognitive, social, industrial/organizational, and educational psychology. This ranking of fields corresponds well with the directions of shifts reported above in the numbers of investigators active in different fields (Item 4.c; see p. 30), although the changes in support are weaker than the changes in human resources.

# How Do Psychologists Keep in Touch With Research in Psychology and Related Disciplines?

Major ways of learning about research in psychology are through meetings of psychological associations, through reading articles in psychological journals and other publications, and through on-line searches in computer databases. I will discuss these in turn.

### Psychological Organizations: National, Regional, and International

Almost from the start of psychological research, investigators from different laboratories and institutions began to meet to discuss their research. This soon led to the formation of various organizations to foster such meetings and to encourage research. By 1881, psychologists were discussing the need for an international meeting, and the first International Congress of Psychology took place in Paris in 1889. Subsequent International Congresses of Psychology have taken place every 3 to 5 years, with gaps caused by the two world wars. Since 1951, these Congresses have been organized under the auspices of the IUPsyS, and since 1972 they have taken place every four years. The most recent International Congresses of Psychology (Leipzig, 1980; Acapulco, 1984; Sydney, 1988) have each attracted about 4,000 participants. (For a brief history and list of International Congresses of Psychology, see Rosenzweig and Holtzman, 1985a, 1985b). National governments recognize the value of such scientific congresses and often contribute financial support to them.[6] An unusual level of governmental recognition was the fact that the XXIV International Congress of Psychology in Sydney in 1988 was an official bicentennial activity of the Australian government. As well as supporting the organization and running of international congresses of psychology, many governmental organizations provide travel grants to participants and delegates to such congresses.

### National Psychological Organizations

National organizations to promote psychological research were formed in some of the leading industrialized nations before the First World War (see Table 7). In the 1920s, China, India, and Japan formed national psychological associations. By 1940 there were still relatively few such societies, but the following years saw a major increase. The IUPsyS, formed in 1954 with 11 national organizations as charter members, encouraged the formation of national societies and their adhesion to the Union. By the end of the 1950s, most industrialized countries had a national psychological association, and so did several developing nations. The formation of national societies continues in developing countries, and the IUPsyS continues to attract new member societies. Among the countries included in Table 7, the median year for the establishment of a national psychological society was 1947 for the industrialized countries and 1956 for the developing countries. As a qualification, it should be noted that this table includes only recognized national societies; in some countries, psychological societies existed earlier than shown here, but they were not organized on a national scale.

### The International Union of Psychological Science (IUPsyS)

The Union is the international voice and representative of psychological science. It is a body whose members are organizations—either (a) national societies or associations of psychology or (b) national academies of sciences or similar organizations. The IUPsyS cannot have more than one national member organization per country, as is the rule for international unions. The IUPsyS has a national member organization from almost every country in which psychology is organized in a regular and stable way (and from a few in

---

[6]*Examples of national science organizations that have contributed support to international congresses of psychology are the following: Canada, National Research Council; Japan, Science Council of Japan and Japan Society for the Promotion of Science; Mexico, Consejo Nacional de Cienca y Tecnologia; the United Kingdom, Department of Education and Science and the Royal Society; the United States, National Science Foundation and National Institute of Mental Health.*

## TABLE 7
Years When Certain National Psychological Associations Were Founded

| Year | Industrialized countries | Developing countries |
| --- | --- | --- |
| 1892 | United States | |
| 1901 | France, United Kingdom | |
| 1904 | Germany | |
| 1908 | | Argentina |
| 1910 | Italy | |
| 1921 | | China |
| 1925 | | India |
| 1926 | Japan | |
| 1928 | Hungary | |
| 1934 | Norway | |
| 1939 | Canada | |
| 1943 | Switzerland | |
| 1945 | Australia[a] | Brazil |
| 1946 | Netherlands | Korea |
| 1947 | Belgium, Denmark | |
| 1948 | Poland | Egypt |
| 1949 | | South Africa |
| 1950 | Yugoslavia | |
| 1951 | | Mexico |
| 1952 | Finland, Spain | |
| 1953 | Austria | Uruguay |
| 1954 | Iceland | Peru |
| 1955 | Sweden | Colombia |
| 1956 | | Turkey |
| 1957 | Soviet Union | Venezuela |
| 1958 | Czechoslovakia, Israel | |
| 1960 | | Indonesia |
| 1962 | | Philippines |
| 1963 | Greece | |
| 1965 | Romania | |
| 1968 | | Hong Kong, Iran, Pakistan |
| 1969 | Bulgaria | |
| 1970 | Ireland | |
| 1971 | | Zimbabwe |
| 1975 | | Dominican Republic, Paraguay |
| 1979 | | Singapore |
| 1981 | | Nicaragua |

Note. The classification of countries as industrialized or developing follows that of the United Nations Development Programme, 1990, p. 188.
[a]Australian Branch of the British Psychological Society; replaced in 1966 by the Australian Psychological Society.

which the organization no longer fulfills those criteria). New national members are elected to the IUPsyS every year or two.

The IUPsyS assures the continuity of the International Congresses of Psychology by entrusting the organization of each International Congress to a national host committee and by maintaining a close liaison with the organizing committee. The Assembly of the Union meets at each Congress; it is the legislative body and final authority of the Union. Among its other activities, each Assembly chooses the host country for the Congress to be held eight years later. The countries that have member organizations in the IUPsyS are listed in Table 8. The names and addresses of the member organizations are given from time to time in the Union's journal, the *International Journal of Psychology* (most recently in 1988, Volume 23, pp. 231–243). From the formation of the Union until 1985, all of the member organizations of the Union were national psychological societies or associations. The Statutes of the Union were changed in 1984 to make it possible for a national member to be a national academy of sciences or similar organization. At present, three such organizations are members: the U.S. National Academy of Sciences; the Canadian Research Council; and the Royal Society of London. When an academy of sciences or similar organization joins an international union, it usually sets up a national committee to effectuate its membership (e.g., the U.S. National Committee for the International Union of Psychological Science). Certain other national academies of sciences have also set up national committees for psychological science: Australia, Belgium, Denmark, South Africa, and Sweden. The financial support of the IUPsyS comes principally from the dues of its member organizations. For more on the history, organization, and activities of the IUPsyS, see Rosenzweig and Holtzman (1985a, 1985b, in press).

As Table 8 shows, IUPsyS belongs to both the International Council of Scientific Unions (ICSU) and the International Social Science Council (ISSC), and it has consultative status with UNESCO. The ICSU is the apex of international scientific bodies. Its members are 20 international scientific unions and 68 national academies of science or similar national organizations. The ICSU formulates international scientific policy, aids developing countries in scientific projects and education, promotes free circulation of scientists and free collaboration among scientists, and fosters large interdisciplinary efforts such as the Man and Biosphere Program and the International Geosphere–Biosphere Program. The ICSU provides IUPsyS with some project grants.

When the ISSC was founded by UNESCO in 1952, the IUPsyS was one of its four charter members. Since then, 10 other international organizations have joined the ISSC,

**TABLE 8**
National and International Organizations of Psychology

| Organizations affiliated with the IUPsyS | The International Union of Psychological Science (IUPsyS) | International organizations to which the IUPsyS belongs |
|---|---|---|
| International or regional organizations whose members are individuals and whose aims are similar to those of the IUPsyS can request affiliation with the IUPsyS. Current affiliates are the following: | As is the rule for international unions, the IUPsyS has national organizations as its members, not more than one per country. The IUPsyS has member organizations in 48 countries: Argentina, Australia, Belgium, Brazil, Bulgaria, Canada, China, Colombia, Cuba, Czechoslovakia, Denmark, Dominican Republic, Egypt, Finland, France, Germany, Hong Kong, Hungary, India, Indonesia, Iran, Israel, Italy, Japan, Korea, Mexico, Netherlands, New Zealand, Nicaragua, Nigeria, Norway, Pakistan, Panama, Philippines, Poland, Romania, South Africa, Spain, Sweden, Switzerland, Turkey, U.S.S.R., U.K., U.S.A., Uruguay, Venezuela, Yugoslavia, Zimbabwe. | International Social Science Council. Charter member, 1952. |
| International Association of Applied Psychology | | International Council of Scientific Unions. Elected 1982. |
| Interamerican Society of Psychology | | The IUPsyS has consultative status with UNESCO. |
| L'Association de Psychologie Scientifique de Langue Française | | |
| International Council of Psychologists | | |
| International Association for Cross-Cultural Psychology | There are many other national organizations of psychology, both in these countries and in other countries. | |
| European Association of Experimental Social Psychology | | |
| International Society for Comparative Psychology | The IUPsyS assures the succession of International Congresses of Psychology and publishes the *International Journal of Psychology* and various directories. It is the international voice of psychological science. | |
| International Society for the Study of Behavioral Development | | |

and there are also associate member organizations. The ISSC is responsible for two international centers: the European Center for Research and Documentation in the Social Sciences (Vienna) and the International Center for Intergroup Relations (Paris). The IUPsyS cooperates with the ISSC and its member organizations in international issue groups, in special committees, and in a number of UNESCO-sponsored projects such as advanced research seminars and the exchange of young scientists, especially from developing countries. The ISSC provides the IUPsyS with an annual subvention and project grants, both taken from annual funding to the ISSC from UNESCO.

International or regional organizations whose members are individuals and whose aims are similar to those of the IUPsyS can request affiliation with the IUPsyS. The current affiliates are shown in Table 8. The International Association of Applied Psychology holds an international congress every four years, alternating with the Congresses of the IUPsyS, so that one or the other occurs every two years. In each year when either of these groups holds an international congress, the *Annual Review of Psychology* has an article about psychology in the host country. The International Council of Psychologists works to increase communication among psychologists throughout the world. It has members in about 75 countries, and it holds an annual international meeting, often in proximity to an International Congress of Psychology (IUPsyS) or to an International Congress of Applied Psychology. Some regional organizations to promote psychological science are also listed in the left column of Table 8.

Even though the IUPsyS can have only one national member per country, many countries have a number of psychological societies. In some cases, after a society for psychological science was formed in a country, another society was formed later to foster professional rather than scientific goals. This has occurred in Germany, Belgium, Finland, and Egypt, and probably in other countries as well. The opposite situation has also occurred. For example, in the United States psychologists who thought that the American Psychological Association was neglecting scientific interests formed the Psychonomic Society in 1960 and the American Psychological Society in 1988. In several cases, the large size of a society has led more specialized groups to break off to concentrate on promoting research in a particular area of psychology. Japan was able to give a total count of its psychologists from the memberships of 17 different national societies to whom it sends a newsletter, using a nonoverlapping mailing list. Many large national psychological societies have also set up specialized divisions for members interested in special topics or fields (46 divisions in the case of the American Psychological Association!).

Many countries have active national psychological organizations that promote research in many ways, especially by holding national conventions annually or biennially at which research reports are presented and discussed and by publishing scientific journals to disseminate the results of research. Other ways in which national psychological organizations encourage and aid research are shown in Table 9, drawn mainly from responses to the IUPsyS questionnaire (Item 8).

Some national psychological organizations are not very active in promoting research, for various reasons. They may not have enough highly trained and well supported psychologists to make a critical mass of researchers. Limited support for psychological research may not provide the funds to publish a research journal or to attend scientific meetings, especially in a country with a large geographic area. A national society with a large proportion of health-service-provider members may not devote sufficient attention to research. Some of these organizations may find in Table 9 feasible ways in which they could be more active in promoting research.

Even some long-established national associations no longer fulfill their functions, as Dalal (1990) reported about the Indian Psychological Association:

> In spite of its long history, the present state of the Association is far from satisfactory. ... It has lost its national character and is no longer regarded by many as representative of Indian Psychologists. ... The poor health of the Association is reflected in the irregular publication of the *Indian Journal of Psychology*. The quality of the published articles has deteriorated over the years and is in no way reflective of the quality of research being done in India. Many serious minded scholars are concerned about this state of affairs and are thinking in terms of forming an alternative body. (p. 113)

Most national psychological organizations are run completely or almost completely by volunteers, usually professors who also have many other responsibilities and who cannot be expected to devote much time and effort to the psychological organization. Relatively few national societies have an office with a professional staff. Thus, the secretary general of a Western European national society apologized for being late in returning the IUPsyS questionnaire, which was very well filled out, and gave the following explanation: "Nobody but professors of psychology can answer the questionnaire. Several professors of psychology did their best to answer with special administrative requests to the National Fund for Scientific Research which had only some of the figures. We have no competent secretary in this field. We sometimes are at the edge of refusing to undertake such work, but we have done it right for IUPsyS."

**TABLE 9**

Activities Undertaken by National Psychological Associations to Foster Research
(as reported in responses to the 1991 IUPsyS survey)

Activities undertaken by most national associations:
- Hold a national convention, in most cases annually or biennially.
- Publish journal(s).
- Organize symposia, workshops.

Activities undertaken by several national associations:
- Give prizes for excellent research and for scientific contributions.
- Have a Division of Scientific Affairs.
- Advocate and lobby for financial support of research by government.
- Publish a newsletter.
- Give financial support for research.
- Support travel by young scientists to the International Congress of Psychology.
- Issue news releases about psychological research and the recognition it receives.
- Hold workshops and seminars for science writers and journalists to inform them about newsworthy psychological research.
- Give prize(s) for excellent science reporting.

Activities undertaken by one or a few national associations:
- Set up a task force to set science agenda.
- Coordinate research projects.
- Publish thesis abstracts.
- Publish a list of publications of members.
- Give financial support for research projects.
- Support thesis research.
- Offer fellowships for doctoral candidates.
- Give an annual prize for best thesis.
- Support the preparation of applications for research support.
- Publish a bulletin listing sources of research support.
- Give a prize for excellent research published in the association's own journals.
- Send faculty abroad for doctoral programs and research.
- Circulate information about ongoing research.
- Provide continuing education for members.
- Provide information about research to legislators and their staffs.
- Support graduate programs.
- Establish a specialized research center.
- Cultivate public relations.
- Collaborate with the National Academy of Sciences or a similar organization.
- Collaborate with the National Fund for Scientific Research or a similar organization.
- Nominate experts for government research councils.

To facilitate communication among psychologists around the world, the IUPsyS is now preparing a worldwide directory of psychological organizations (d'Ydewalle, in press). The IUPsyS issued international directories of psychologists in 1958, 1966, 1980, and 1985, but the number of psychologists has now become too great to continue this series. The new directory will include not only psychological societies but also psychology departments and psychology laboratories.

## Psychological Publications and Databases

Psychological science benefits from a wealth of publications that report its research. The large number of these publications makes it necessary to have specialized abstracting and review services to help investigators, instructors, and students become aware of publications of interest to them. It also poses problems of access: Libraries even in wealthy countries have difficulty acquiring all of the materials their users request, and the problem is much more severe in most of the developing countries.

How many contributions to psychological science are published annually? Publications of psychological research occur in many forms, including: articles in scholarly journals and chapters in scholarly books; monographs; technical, laboratory, and university reports; manuals; and textbooks. The annual number of items added to the American Psychological Association's PsycINFO database, which includes mainly articles from journals of high scientific standards in both English and other languages, plus the annual number of books and book chapters, comes to a total of about 60,000 publications in psychological science. This does not cover all of the kinds of research publications, so it is undoubtedly understated. Furthermore, there are certainly many valuable contributions in journals that do not meet PsycINFO standards for such reasons as irregular appearance or not seeking independent evaluations of manuscripts. Even if we acknowledge that it is an underestimation, it is intriguing to note that the figure of 60,000 is not far from my completely independent estimate of the number of psychologists worldwide who do research as their primary or secondary activity. This suggests that the average psychological researcher publishes about one research report per year in a journal of high scientific standards or as a book chapter.

The output of psychological publications is so large that it is difficult, if not impossible, to find and read all of the publications that are relevant to one's field of research. International lists of journals are given annually by *Ulrich's International Periodicals Directory*. Although extensive, these listings are far from complete. Coleman et al. (1992) examined *Ulrich's International Periodicals Directory* (27th ed., 1988–89) and found 1,064 publications under the heading of "psychology," but this was reduced to 558 "bona fide" psychology journals if one eliminated cross-listed items, irregular and free items, and newsletters and proceedings of conferences. They also reported that *Psychological Abstracts* for 1988 surveyed over 1,300 periodicals in psychology and related fields, so it had a broader coverage than the psychology listing in *Ulrich's Directory*. A chapter by VandenBos (1992) describes the APA knowledge dissemination program, and it offers the estimate that APA publications reach almost 300,000 individuals and institutions worldwide. To help psychologists keep up with the flood of published research, several services and publications have been organized, and some of the chief ones are mentioned below.

*Psychological Abstracts* (*PA*), started by the American Psychological Association (APA) in 1927, gives brief, nonevaluative summaries of journal articles in psychology and related disciplines. *PA* draws its abstracts from the PsycINFO database, produced by the APA; this is a computerized file of over 700,000 references (as of spring 1990) that has been cumulated since 1967 and is updated monthly. The PsycINFO database includes abstracts of articles from over 1,300 journals published in 28 languages and from about 50 countries; it tries to include only articles from journals with high scientific standards. The database also covers technical reports and dissertations; it includes about 20% more material than is published in *PA*. Since 1988, *PA* has been limited to summaries of articles that appeared in English, and it contains about 35,000 summaries per year. The computerized PsycINFO database continues to include summaries of articles that appeared in languages other than English, and the APA Publications and Communications Board is considering having *PA* resume publication of abstracts of articles that appear in other languages. This would encourage publication in other languages and would help to disseminate knowledge about research that appears in other languages. During the period from 1987 to 1989, PsycINFO added about 48,000 records per year, 90% of these from English-language items. The APA also publishes several specialized computer databases.

*PsycBOOKS* is a series recently begun by the APA to abstract books and book chapters in the way that *PA* covers articles. The first volume included material published from 1987 to 1989. It is estimated that about 30% of the publications in psychology are in books and book chapters. Adding this to the number of items in the PsycINFO database indicates a total of about 60,000 publications in psychological science per year. *PsycBOOKS* was merged into *PA* beginning in January 1992.

The *Annual Review of Psychology*, begun in 1950, appears in an annual volume of about 20 chapters. Each chapter provides a critical evaluation of recent findings and theoretical advances in a particular field of research. Some topics appear each year, some every second year, and some less frequently, depending on the amount of research in the field.

*Contemporary Psychology*, which first appeared in 1956, is a book-review journal published by the APA. Many other psychological journals include book reviews among their rubrics.

*Current Directions in Psychological Science*, a new type of journal that began bimonthly publication by the American Psychological Society in February 1992, furnishes succinct reviews of major lines of contemporary research on topics throughout the fast-growing areas of behavioral science. It is intended to alert and introduce psychologists to significant developments in subdisciplines that may be remote from their own.

An overview of German journals of psychology was provided by Becker (1984). The *German Journal of Psychology*, published since 1977 under the auspices of the German Psychological Society and the IUPsyS, provides English-language abstracts of German-language contributions selected for high scientific quality, as well as review articles in English of subjects of research in German-language laboratories and institutions.

A German-language psychology database is the Zentralstelle fuer Psychologische Information und Dokumentation, located at the University of Trier. It tries to cover completely and nonselectively the German-language publications in psychology, and it furnishes abstracts translated into English to the PsycINFO system.

Services that abstract psychological publications that appear in French, German, Russian, and languages of Eastern Europe are described briefly by Brozek and Hoskovec (1992). While commending the APA for continuing to explore ways of covering the non-English literature, Brozek and Hoskovec propose that adequate coverage will require sustained international collaborative efforts.

English has been the primary language of publication of psychological research since the time of the First World War, and this trend continues to accelerate. English was the language of 90% of the publications reported in *PA* during 1975–1986, when *PA* was publishing abstracts of non-English as well as of English-language items (Coleman et al., 1992). Even when publications by authors from the United States were not counted, well over half of the publications were in English. The facts that more than half of all psychological researchers are native speakers of English and that English is the main language of scientific congresses make it increasingly less attractive to publish in languages other than English; one's prospective audience is definitely curtailed. This poses an additional handicap to developing and maintaining productive communities of psychological researchers in countries where English is not in active use even among well-educated people. Some measures have been taken to help overcome some of these problems. For example, some journals, such as the Union's *International Journal of Psychology (IJP)*, publish in more than one language; the *IJP* publishes articles in both English and French and publishes abstracts of its articles in both languages. The editor of *IJP* helps many contributors from developing countries put their manuscripts into publishable form. Some English-language journals (for example, *Psychotherapy Research*) evaluate manuscripts written in French or German and translate into English those that are accepted for publication. More needs to be done to help psychological journals in many countries to remain viable, in order to encourage research and the recruitment of young psychologists in those countries.

Gaining access to the research literature of psychology remains a problem for psychologists around the world, and especially in most developing countries. Library budgets are limited—severely and increasingly so in most countries—and there is widespread concern that libraries are not keeping up with the growth of psychological science as they make their allocations among the disciplines. For this reason, the U.S. organization of Chairs of Graduate Departments of Psychology set up a task force in 1991 to investigate how budgets are allocated to behavioral science in libraries of research universities. Similar inquiries in other countries would be worthwhile to undertake.

## Recent Attempts to Devise National Plans for Research in Psychology

There has been little overall planning or setting of priorities for psychological research at the national level, but there are indications that this is beginning to change on the part of both psychological organizations and governmental agencies. This change may reflect both growing maturity of national psychological organizations and recognition on their part that planning may help to obtain (or maintain) financial support from governmental agencies. It may also reflect growing recognition within governmental agencies of the values of psychological research.

Only one national psychological association reported the existence of a national plan for psychological research in response to the 1991 IUPsyS survey (Item 2); that was an eastern European country. Nine other national responses, however, volunteered the information that efforts are under way to devise a plan or set of priorities or that plans already exist in some agencies or for some fields of psychology. Seven of these nine additional responses came from industrialized countries. Further information on this subject might have been furnished if the survey questionnaire had asked for it.

As an example, such a programmatic effort has been undertaken in the United States, where the American Psychological Society convened three successive "psychology summit meetings" of representatives from over 60 national psychology and psychology-related organizations. These meetings led to a Human Capital Initiative program that targets six critical contemporary problems in which psychological science can help: mental and physical health, the aging society, drug and alcohol abuse, schooling and literacy, worker productivity, and violence in society (National Behavioral Science Research Agenda Committee, 1992). (Note that most of these six priority areas can be put under one of the three main rubrics of the United Nations Development Programme, mentioned on p. 2.)

Much of the current work of this sort attempts to foster research that will increase basic knowledge and understanding of major problem areas—"mission-oriented basic research" (Featherman, 1991)—rather than applied research that aims directly at finding solutions to these problems. The hope is to work toward eventual social benefits by inducing agencies to invest in mission-oriented basic research and by encouraging investigators to concentrate in such areas. Adoption of such programs or sets of priorities may lead to productive concentration on particular areas of research, but the benefits may be accompanied by costs such as limiting support for important initiatives in other areas.

## Recognition of the Scientific Status of Psychology

Plato wrote, "What a country honors will flourish there." Obtaining recognition of the scientific achievements of psychological research and of the scientific status of psychology is both a reward for psychological investigators and one of the conditions that fosters further achievements. Failure to obtain recognition for the scientific status of psychological research retards the further advancement of that research. For example, whether a group of psychologists in a university obtains the space and facilities necessary for their research depends in part on the scientific value that university authorities place on psychological research. The 1991 IUPsyS survey showed that psychological science is increasingly valued and is gaining many signs of esteem. When asked in the IUPsyS questionnaire to identify barriers to accomplishing psychological research (Item 9), only 9 responses out of 38 named a lack of recognition for psychological science. One of these responses from a developing country cited as a major barrier "a general view of psychology as a humanistic, literary, philosophical, qualitative, intuitive discipline rather than as a science."

The IUPsyS questionnaire also asked whether recognition of psychological research in the respondents' countries was increasing, remaining the same, or decreasing (Item 6.d). Twenty-six of the 38 responses stated that recognition is increasing; only one reply said "decreasing," but one reply from a developing country left the item blank, commenting, "It cannot decrease because there has been [so] little recognition." There was no clear difference between replies to this question from developing and industrialized countries. The one region that did not report an overall increase was eastern Europe, with one report of "increasing," three of "remaining the same," and the only report of "decreasing." It should be noted that several reports of "increasing" were qualified as "moderate," "slowly," or "slightly." One report of "increasing" was qualified by the statement, "but not enough to improve funding." Thus, there is clearly still room for improvement in the recognition of psychological science.

### Evidence for the Scientific Contributions of Psychologists

A brief review of how and where psychological research is being recognized may not only be of interest, but some psychologists may be able to put it to good use. A fuller treatment of this topic appeared in an article by Rosenzweig (1991), who gave 20 kinds of evidence of the recognition of the scientific nature of modern psychology. The following are 10 kinds of the evidence for the recognition of scientific contributions by psychologists:

*Psychologists have been elected members of the national academies of science or similar organizations in many countries.* For example, the 1991 membership list of Section 52 (Psychology) of the National Academy of Sciences of the United States (NAS) shows 72 psychologist members, of whom 8 are Foreign Associates (National Academy of Sciences, 1991). The first psychologist to be elected to the NAS was James McKeen Cattell in 1901; the second was William James in 1903. The Royal Society also began electing psychologists to Fellowship early in this century, one of the first being William H. Rivers in 1908. Psychologists are also members of at least 21 similar organizations, according to the IUPsyS survey (Item 6.a) and other sources (see Table 10). Table 10 also shows 13 countries in which psychologists are not elected to the national academy of sciences or a similar organization, according to the IUPsyS survey. The table reveals that most of the industrialized nations in our sample elect psychologists to their national academies of science, whereas over half of the developing nations in our sample still do not.

## TABLE 10
Membership of Psychologists in National Academies of Sciences and
Similar Organizations

| Academies of science and similar organizations to which psychologists are elected | Countries in which psychologists are not elected to an academy of science or similar organization |
|---|---|
| *Industrialized countries* | |
| Australian Academy of Science | France |
| Austrian Academy of Sciences | Israel |
| Royal Belgian Academy of Sciences, Letters, and Fine Arts | Spain |
| Bulgarian Academy of Sciences | |
| Royal Society of Canada | |
| Czechoslovak Academy of Sciences | |
| Royal Dutch Academy of Sciences | |
| Finnish Academy of Science and Letters | |
| Hungarian Academy of Sciences | |
| Science Council of Japan | |
| New Zealand Royal Society | |
| Royal Swedish Academy of Sciences | |
| Swiss Academy of Sciences | |
| Academy of Sciences of the U.S.S.R. | |
| Royal Society of London | |
| National Academy of Sciences, U.S.A. | |
| Yugoslav Academy of Art and Science | |
| *Developing countries* | |
| Chinese Association for Science and Technology | Argentina |
| Colombian Academy of Sciences | Brazil |
| Egyptian Academy of Scientific Research and Technology | Hong Kong |
| Indian National Academy of Science | Nigeria |
| Mexican Academy of Scientific Research | Pakistan |
| Philippine National Academy of Science and Technology | Panama |
| | South Africa |
| | Turkey |
| | Uruguay |
| | Zimbabwe |

**Note.** This table is not exhaustive but contains information available at the time of the preparation of this book.

The question of membership in an academy of sciences is complicated by the fact that some of the national academies include a wider range of disciplines than is indicated by the term *science* or *natural sciences* in English; some are academies of *Wissenschaft* or knowledge. The case of Belgium is instructive in this regard. Its Royal Academy has separate sections for sciences, letters, and fine arts. In 1982, one psychologist was a member of the science section and three were in the letters section. Then, after the IUPsyS was elected to the ICSU in 1982, the three psychologists in the letters section were invited to join the science section.

In some of the countries that do not elect psychologists to their academy of sciences, psychologists are elected to academies of social sciences or to academies of moral and political sciences (e.g., France, Spain). (To complete the picture, it should be noted that some countries, such as Germany and Indonesia, do not have an academy of sciences to which members are elected.)

*The IUPsyS is a member of the ICSU along with 19 other scientific unions.* The ICSU is the apex of international scientific organizations and undertakes such international programs as the International Geophysical Year, the Man and Biosphere Program, and the International Geosphere-Biosphere Program of the 1990s. The IUPsyS and the International Union of Microbiological Societies were elected in 1982, the latest unions to be elected to the ICSU.

*Some national members of the IUPsyS are national academies of science or similar organizations; all national members are dedicated to the development of psychological science.* As noted earlier, three national members of the IUPsyS are the NAS, the National Research Council of Canada, and the Royal Society of London. The NAS formed the U.S. National Committee for IUPsyS (USNC/IUPsyS) to implement its membership in the IUPsyS. At the request of the Japanese Psychological Association, the Science Council of Japan expressed willingness to represent the Japanese psychological community in the IUPsyS, but this has not worked out for technical reasons within the psychological community. Some other national academies of science have established national committees for psychology (e.g., Australia, Belgium, Denmark, South Africa, and Sweden).

As established by the NAS, the purposes of USNC/IUPsyS are as follows:

(a) to effect appropriate participation in all activities of the IUPsyS through the NAS–NRC, which adheres to the IUPsyS on behalf of the scientists of the United States;
(b) to promote the advancement of the science of psychology in the United States and throughout the world. (Rosenzweig & Flattau, 1988, p. 371)

All national members of the IUPsyS, most of which are psychological associations or societies, subscribe to the main aim of the IUPsyS, as stated in its statues: "the development of psychological science, whether biological or social, normal or abnormal, pure or applied" (Rosenzweig & Holtzman, 1985b, p. 765).

*Research in psychology demonstrates its scientific nature.* Chapters 3 to 9 of this volume will provide abundant evidence of this. The *Annual Review of Psychology,* founded in 1950, reviews scientific advances in the main areas of psychological research according to a regular plan of rotation; each annual volume includes about 20 chapters.[7]

*Much psychological research is done in laboratories, and over 60 laboratories of psychology date back to the 19th century.* Many of the early laboratories were the institutional focus for the emergence of psychological science in a given university or country. The founding of laboratories led, in many intellectual communities, to the recognition in the last century of psychology as an experimental science.

*Psychologists show a keen interest in experimental design and statistical methodology and have made many contributions to these fields.* In many interdisciplinary research groups, psychologists are chiefly responsible for research design and statistical tests because of their training in these topics. In the APA, Division 5 is the division of Evaluation and Measurement; it includes 1,390 members, according to the 1991 *APA Membership Register.* The Psychometric Society, founded in 1935, includes about 1,000 members. The journal of the Society, *Psychometrika,* also founded in 1935, contains, as stated on its inside cover, "articles on the development of quantitative models for psychological phenomena and on quantitative methodology in the social and behavioral sciences, including new mathematical and statistical techniques for the evaluation of psychological data, and the application of such techniques." Other journals in this field are the *British Journal of Mathematical and Statistical Psychology* (founded in 1947) and the *Journal of Mathematical Psychology* (founded in 1964). Each volume of the *Annual Review of Psychology* includes one or more chapters on research methodology.

---

[7]*A few additional references for books that document the scientific nature of psychology are the following:* Stevens' Handbook of Experimental Psychology *(1988, 2nd ed., Atkinson, Herrnstein, Lindzey, & Luce, Eds.);* The Behavioral and Social Sciences: Achievements and Opportunities *(1988, Gerstein, Luce, Smelser, & Sperlich, Eds.);* Traité de Psychologie Expérimentale *(1963–1981, 9 vols., Fraisse & Piaget, Eds.);* Traité de Psychologie Cognitive *(1990, 3 vols., Bonnet, Ghiglione, & Richard, Eds.);* Handbuch der Psychologie *(1958–1983, Lersch et al., Eds.). Textbooks in specialized areas of psychology (e.g., perception, cognition, biological psychology, social psychology) also serve to show its scientific status. A six-volume series edited by Koch (1959–1963),* Psychology: A Study of a Science, *evaluated and depicted psychology as a science in terms of its methodologies, findings, and conceptualizations.*

*Psychologists have been awarded many prizes for their scientific accomplishments.* Although there is no Nobel Prize in psychology, psychologist Roger W. Sperry was awarded the Nobel Prize in Medicine or Physiology in 1981, and Herbert A. Simon was awarded the Nobel Prize in Economic Sciences in 1978. Several other Nobel Prizes have been awarded in areas of research in which psychologists are active. In a recent textbook of physiological psychology (Rosenzweig & Leiman, 1989), the subject index included a heading for "Nobel Prize laureates" and listed 10 laureates in addition to Sperry.

The IUPsyS questionnaire asked (Item 6.b) for examples of official recognition or prizes; the following are a few examples. In the United States, psychologists are included among the awardees of the National Medal of Science. The Universidad Nacional Autonoma de Mexico started awarding prizes for scientific research in 1985, and one of the first of these prizes was given to a psychologist in 1986. Over the past decade, a number of psychologists have become recipients of the Order of Canada, the highest civilian award made by the government of Canada. Several Egyptian psychologists have received the State Prize of Egypt, the highest award of the Supreme Council of Culture, accompanied by a medal presented by the president of the country. The NAS of the United States annually gives the Troland Research Award in experimental psychology, named in honor of research psychologist L. T. Troland. The NAS also gives an annual award for scientific reviewing, and some of the recipients have been psychologists.

*Some psychological research is displayed in exhibits or even in whole exhibitions at museums of science and technology.* The largest such display, occupying over 1,000 square meters, opened in 1991 at the Ontario Science Centre, Toronto, Canada. Beginning in 1992, the Association of Science–Technology Centers will circulate a travelling version to other museums of science and technology in Canada and the United States, starting with the Smithsonian Institution in Washington, DC and the exhibition has been requested by some museums in Europe. This travelling psychology exhibition has been in preparation since 1986 as a joint project of the Ontario Science Centre and the APA, with major funding by the NSF of the United States.

Other science and technology museums have or have had exhibits on psychological research prepared in collaboration with psychologists, for example, the exhibition on memory at the Exploratorium in San Francisco (1988). Psychologists have had a long history of displaying psychological phenomena and also of gathering data at museums and fairs, probably the first being Francis Galton at the International Health Exhibition of 1884 (Perloff & Perloff, 1977). Other pioneer psychologists who had scientific displays at fairs were Raymond Dodge at the Chicago World's Fair in 1890; Joseph Jastrow at the World Columbian Exposition in Chicago, 1893; and Hugo Münsterberg and Robert S. Woodworth at the St. Louis World's Fair of 1904 (Perloff & Perloff, 1977).

*In some countries, the scientific research of psychologists is reported frequently in the news media.* The IUPsyS questionnaire (Item 6.c) asked which of the following terms best represents the frequency with which major newspapers in each country report on psychological research: *daily, at least once a week, at least once a month, a few times a year, almost never,* or *never.* For the 18 developing nations and for the 5 Eastern European countries that responded to the survey, the modal response was "a few times a year." For the 15 other industrialized nations, most responses were "at least weekly" or "at least monthly."

Frequent coverage of psychological research is shown in the indexes of such newspapers as the *New York Times* and the *Washington Post* in the United States and the *Times* and the *Guardian* in the United Kingdom. In the *New York Times*, some research in psychology is reported in the Tuesday science section, some in the Thursday health section, and some in the regular news pages. Articles from the *New York Times* are reprinted in hundreds of other newspapers throughout the English-speaking world. A collection of articles on psychology written by one journalist for the science section of the *New York Times* has appeared recently (Goleman, 1991).

Occasional special television series report psychological research. An early example was the eight-part series "The Mind of Man" (Calder, 1970), produced in 1970 by the British Broadcasting Corporation in collaboration with U.S. National Educational Television, Sveriges Radio, and Bayerischer Rundfunk. This series was written by Nigel Calder, a British science reporter, and was based on visits to laboratories of psychologists and investigators in related fields in eight countries around the world. A current example is the 26-part television series "Discovering Psychology," made available to U.S. Public Broadcasting Stations in the fall of 1990 (Kent, 1990; Moses, 1990).

Each number of *The Psychologist*, the monthly journal of the British Psychological Society, has sections titled "Media Watch" and "On the Air." "Media Watch" reports and comments on recent coverage of psychology in the press and on radio and television, and "On the Air" gives advance information about programs in which psychologists are to appear. The British Psychological Society, the APA, and the American Psychological Society all make systematic efforts to inform the media and science journalists about news of psychological research. The Colegio Official de Psicologos in Spain and the APA give annual prizes to journalists for the best reporting on psychological topics.

Both the benefits and the limitations of science reporting were emphasized in a recent report by an NSF task force (NSF, 1991):

> Science journalists, in both print and broadcast media, are an important conduit for conveying an awareness of science and information about the sciences into the public consciousness. But within the media the "science beat" is generally viewed as a sideline, falling outside the mainstream of important topics. Science journalists themselves are often trained poorly, if at all, in the subjects upon which they report. Thus, their reporting is often superficial, sometimes inaccurate, and their rapport with scientists far from perfect. Especially in the social sciences, it is common for journalists to believe they understand the subject matter and therefore to approach it cavalierly, when in fact the nature and purposes of these sciences today are not generally well understood by lay people. Nevertheless, the scientific enterprise needs science journalists to help convey its importance, its challenges, and its achievements to the public upon which it depends for support. (p. 75)

Therefore, both individual psychologists and psychological organizations have much to do to encourage adequate and accurate coverage of psychological research.

*Dictionary definitions of psychology in several countries of North America and Western Europe reflect general usage in defining psychology as a science.* These definitions testify to widespread acceptance of this status. In part, this acceptance is probably due to some of the facts mentioned in the points stated above. The following are a few examples of such definitions.

*The Oxford English Dictionary* (2nd ed., 1989):

> 1.a. The science of the nature, functions, and phenomena of the human mind (formerly also of the soul). . . .
>
> c. In mod. usage, the signification of the word has broadened to include (a) The scientific study of the mind as an entity and its relationship to the physical body, based on observations of the behaviour and activity aroused by specific stimuli; and (b) The study of the behaviour of an individual or of a selected group of individuals when interacting with the environment or in a given social context. So *experimental psychology*, the experimental study of the responses of an individual to stimuli; *social psychology*, the study of the interaction between an individual and the social group to which he belongs. (Vol. 12, p. 766)

*The Random House College Dictionary* (1984): "1. the science of the mind or of mental states and processes. 2. the science of human and animal behavior" (p. 1068).

The Larousse French dictionaries show a transition in definitions around 1960. The *Nouveau Petit Larousse Illustré* (1952) still defined psychologie as "partie de la philosophie qui traite de l'âme, de ses facultés et de ses opérations." But the *Grand Larousse Encyclopédique* (1963, Vol. 8, p. 887) defined it as "science des faits psychiques" and went on to mention specialties, including comparative psychology, experimental psychology, and psychometry.

The *Grand Larousse de la Langue Française* goes further: "2. A partir du XIX^e s., étude scientifique des faits psychiques (activité mentale, mémoire, affectivité, perception, sensation) en vue d'établir des lois qui les régissent, envisagée selon des modalités diverses par les différentes théories ou doctrines ...," and it mentions some specialties, including "Psychologie expérimentale ou empirique," which uses laboratory experimentation, tests, and so forth; "Psychologie de comportement ou de réaction ... (Syn. Béhaviorisme)"; and "Psychologie objective" (Vol. 6, p. 4756).

## Pleas for More Adequate Data

A lack of adequate and internationally comparable data is evident at several points in this chapter. Psychology is not alone in the inadequacy of its social statistics. The United Nations Human Development Reports of 1990 and 1991 make pleas for improving the statistics of human development: "... for investing at least as much in the production of social data as has been invested in the production of economic statistics. Otherwise ... it would continue to be extremely difficult to ... integrate economic and social concerns in the design, monitoring, and review of development efforts, policies, and programmes" (United Nations Development Programme, 1991, p. 100). Similarly, psychology needs better data to plan and monitor its progress. For example, are data being gathered that will enable us to answer such questions as the following? Are enough young researchers being recruited to maintain (if not increase) the current volume and level of psychological research? Is the disparity of psychological research efforts between developing and industrialized countries increasing or decreasing?

Steps to improve the availability of data about psychological science could be taken by several kinds of readers of this volume. These include members, officers, and staff of national psychological associations, as well as officers and staff of organizations such as the following: national academies of sciences and similar organizations, agencies that grant funds for research, regional and international science associations, and international organizations such as the United Nations, UNESCO, and the World Health Organization. Guides for some of the kinds of data that should be gathered in a comparable way around the world can be found in the 1991 IUPsyS questionnaire (Appendix) and in the presentations and discussions in this chapter. International efforts in this direction could make a future survey far more revealing and helpful in orienting and monitoring the growth of psychological science.

## Summary and Conclusions

The large numbers of psychologists who teach, practice, and do research make them major, worldwide professional and scientific resources. They contribute to the main components of human development: health, knowledge, and standard of living. There are over half a million psychologists in the world, as defined by local standards, according to the survey undertaken in 1991 by the IUPsyS. Comparison with previous data shows that the number has doubled in the last decade. A new finding from the survey is that about 70,000 of these psychologists do research as their primary or secondary activity. There do not appear to be earlier data from which to measure a change in the number of researchers over the last decade. Most countries reported an increase, but half of the industrialized countries reported no increase in researchers over the last decade. Most of the research psychologists in the world have doctoral (PhD) or master's degrees or their equivalents. To provide some comparative figures for professionals and scientists in related disciplines, there are about 6 million physicians and about 27 thousand neuroscientists in the world, as of 1991.

Human resources for psychological science are located preponderantly in the industrialized countries; the lack of research psychologists in developing countries is a major factor in the relatively low amount of psychological research accomplished in those countries. In the industrialized countries, there are about 82 research psychologists per million population; in the developing countries with a national organization in the IUPsyS, there are only about 3 or 4 per million. A more complete sample of developing countries would probably show an even greater disparity. Survey responses from over half of the developing countries stated that a lack of highly trained psychologists was a barrier to accomplishing sufficient research in those countries; similar statements came from one third of the industrialized countries in the sample. Furthermore, there is concern in some of the industrialized countries about the growing shift of psychology from a scientific discipline to one dominated by health-provider practice. For these reasons, efforts to recruit research psychologists are needed in most countries, and especially in the developing nations.

Psychology, in many parts of the world, provides more opportunity and scope for women than do other sciences, but there is concern in some parts of the world about over-feminization of the discipline and about its decreasing appeal to men.

The level of research activity and the number of research psychologists differ greatly among fields of psychology (Table 3). The most active fields of research, on a worldwide basis, are social, educational, cognitive, and clinical psychology; the least active are comparative and quantitative. Most of the traditional academic/research fields scored higher in relative research activity among the industrialized than among the developing countries, whereas the health-provider fields scored higher in relative research activity among the developing nations.

Most responses to the 1991 survey showed a lack of detailed knowledge of national financial resources for psychological research, but four fifths of the responses stated that insufficient funding is a major obstacle to conducting sufficient amounts of research. Better knowledge of funding resources for psychology should be a goal for most national psychological organizations to help them set policies and campaigns to improve research productivity. When asked to compare financial support for psychology with that for other fields of science, two thirds of the responses said "worse," and only one said "better." This evaluation was largely borne out by a major study of the funding of academic and academically related research for the main academic fields, including psychology, in France, Germany, Japan, the Netherlands, the United Kingdom, and the United States, but large national differences in the adequacy of funding were also shown. The amounts allocated for psychology range from 2.5% of the country's total for academic and academically related research in science and engineering (the Netherlands) to 0.5% (France), with a median of 1.3% (Table 5). Clearly, psychological research has achieved much better support in some industrialized countries than in others.

In both industrialized and developing countries, there is concern that many psychologists do not apply for research funding because of the low chances of obtaining it. The lack of demand then provides a justification for governments to continue to supply inadequate funding. Those psychologists who submit strong, well-prepared requests for research funding and who campaign to increase funding help to assure the future development of the discipline.

National, regional, and international institutions and organizations aid psychologists to diffuse research and to keep in touch with research. International congresses of psychology have taken place since 1889, and national governments often provide financial support for them. National psychological organizations exist in all industrialized countries and in many developing countries. The formation of national psychological associations has occurred at an increasing rate since the 1940s. These associations foster research in many ways, as shown in Table 9; national associations may find in Table 9 feasible additional ways to encourage research.

A variety of publications and databases aid the diffusion of psychological research; a few of the main ones are named in this chapter. The annual number of articles on psychological research in journals of high scientific standards, plus books and book chapters on psychological research, provides an index of research productivity; it totals at least 60,000. Inadequate library acquisitions impair the diffusion of psychological information in many countries, especially developing countries.

A lack of recognition for psychological research was named as a major obstacle to accomplishing psychological research by one quarter of the responses in the 1991 survey; two thirds of the responses said that recognition for psychological science is increasing. Ten kinds of evidence for the scientific contributions of psychologists are given in this chapter; these include the election of psychologists to national academies of sciences or similar organizations in most industrialized countries (but in few developing countries); the election of the IUPsyS to the ICSU; scientific prizes given to psychologists; research accomplishments of psychologists, as reported in various handbooks, textbooks, and review publications, and as reviewed in Chapters 3 to 9 of this volume; displays of psychological research in museums of science and technology; reports of psychological research in newspapers, and dictionary definitions of psychology as a science. Many national and international psychological organizations make deliberate efforts to foster recognition of the scientific achievements and status of psychology; other psychological organizations can find in this chapter examples of ways in which they can work toward this goal. In particular, those countries with relatively poor levels of financial support for psychological research are usually those that accord only meager recognition to psychological research. As well as campaigning directly for improved financial support, psychological organizations should strive to improve recognition for the scientific accomplishments and status of psychological science. This can also aid in recruiting young scientists to the field.

The evidence for the scientific contributions of psychologists provides further justification for the point made in Chapter 1 concerning the classification of psychology among the sciences. Therefore, psychologists should urge wider adoption of the practice that already exists in several countries and universities of either classifying psychology in a class of its own, between the biological and the social sciences, or recognizing psychology as a science that overlaps the biological, behavioral, and social science categories.

# References

Atkinson, R. C. (1990). Supply and demand for scientists and engineers: A national crisis in the making. *Science, 248,* 425–429.

Basaran, F., & Sahin, N. (1990). Turkey. In G. Shouksmith & E. A. Shouksmith (Eds.), *Psychology in Asia and the Pacific: Status reports on teaching and research in eleven countries* (RUSHAP Series on Occasional Monographs and Papers, No. 34, pp. 7–41). Bangkok: UNESCO.

Becker, J. H. (1984). German-language psychological journals: An overview. *German Journal of Psychology, 8,* 323–344.

Brozek, J., & Hoskovec, J. (1992). Abstracting psychological literature, especially non-English, in the 1990s. *International Journal of Psychology, 27,* 100–109.

Brush, S. G. (1991). Women in science and engineering. *American Scientist, 79,* 404–419.

Calder, N. (1970). *The mind of man.* New York: Viking.

Coleman, S. R., Cola, P., & Webster, S. (1992). Characteristics of history-of-psychology literature, 1975–1986. *International Journal of Psychology, 27,* 110–124.

Dalal, A. K. (1990). India. In G. Shouksmith & E. A. Shouksmith (Eds.), *Psychology in Asia and the Pacific: Status reports on teaching and research in eleven countries* (RUSHAP Series on Occasional Monographs and Papers, No. 34, pp. 87–138). Bangkok: UNESCO.

d'Ydewalle, G. (Ed.). (in press). *International directory of psychological organizations.* Hove, East Sussex, England: Erlbaum.

Featherman, D. L. (1991). Mission-oriented basic research. *Items, Social Science Research Council, 45,* 75–77.

Gerstein, D. R., Luce, R. D., Smelser, N. J., & Sperlich, S. (Eds.). (1988) *The behavioral and social sciences: Achievements and opportunities.* Washington, DC: National Academy Press.

Goleman, D. (1991). *Psychology updates: Articles on psychology from the New York Times.* New York: Harper-Collins.

Groebel, J. (1992). Psychology in the Federal Republic of Germany. In V. S. Sexton & J. Hogan (Eds.), *International psychology: Views from around the world* (2nd ed.; pp. 159–181). Lincoln: University of Nebraska Press.

Guttmann, G., & Etlinger, S. C. (1992). Psychology in Austria. In V. S. Sexton & J. Hogan (Eds.), *International psychology: Views from around the world* (2nd ed.; pp. 35–45). Lincoln: University of Nebraska Press.

Howard, A., Pion, G. M., Gottfredson, G. D., Flattau, P. E., Oskamp, S., Pfafflin, S. M., Bray, D. W., & Burstein, A. G. (1986). The changing face of American psychology: A report from the Committee on Employment and Human Resources. *American Psychologist, 41,* 1311–1327.

International Brain Research Organization. (1991). *IBRO membership directory 1991.* London: Pergamon Press.

Irvine, J., Martin, B. R., & Isard, P. (1990). *Investing in the future: An international comparison of government funding of academic and related research.* Aldershot, England: Edward Elgar.

Kent, D. (1990). Psychology telecourse, premiering this fall. *APS Observer, 3*(5), 24–25.

Koch, S. (Ed.). (1959–1963). *Psychology: A study of a science* (Vols. 1–6). New York: McGraw-Hill.

Marton-Lefèvre, J. (Ed.). (1990). *International Council of Scientific Unions: Reports of 23rd meeting of the General Assembly, 1–5 October 1990, and 27th and 28th meetings of the General Committee, 1 and 4 October 1990.* Paris: International Council of Scientific Unions.

Moses, S. (1990, May). Stay tuned for fall TV series on psychology. *APA Monitor*, 42–43.

National Academy of Sciences of the United States of America. (1991). *Members' directory.* Washington, DC: Author.

National Behavioral Science Research Agenda Committee. (1992). Human Capital Initiative: Report of the National Behavioral Science Research Agenda Committee. *APS Observer, 5,* 1–33.

National Science Board. (1989). *Science and engineering indicators—1989.* Washington, DC: Author.

National Science Foundation. (1988). *Profiles—psychology: Human resources and funding* (NSF 88–325). Washington, DC: Author.

National Science Foundation. (1991). *Adapting to the future: Report of the BBS [Biological, Behavioral, and Social Sciences] Task Force looking to the 21st century* (NSF 91–69). Washington, DC: Author.

Perloff, R., & Perloff, L. S. (1977). The fair: An opportunity for depicting psychology and for conducting behavioral research. *American Psychologist, 32,* 220–229.

Pion, G. M. (1991). Psychologists wanted: Employment trends over the past decade. In R. R. Kilburg (Ed.), *How to manage your career in psychology* (pp. 229–246). Washington, DC: American Psychological Association.

Reyns, S., & Verquerre, R. (1988). L'insertion professionelle des psychologues. *Psychologues et psychologies, 99,* 2–28.

Richelle, M., Janssen, P., & Brédart, S. (1992). Psychology in Belgium. *Annual Review of Psychology, 43,* 505–529.

Rosenzweig, M. R. (1982). Trends in development and status of psychology: An international perspective. *International Journal of Psychology, 17,* 117–140.

Rosenzweig, M. R. (1983). Professional and legal status of psychologists [papers from 11 countries]. *International Journal of Psychology, 18,* 569–602.

Rosenzweig, M. R. (1991). The scientific status of psychology. *International Journal of Psychology, 26,* 514–530.

Rosenzwieg, M. R., & Flattau, P. E. (1988). The U.S. National Committee for the International Union of Psychological Science. *International Journal of Psychology, 23,* 367–375.

Rosenzweig, M. R., & Holtzman, W. H. (1985a). The International Union of Psychological Science (IUPsyS). In K. Pawlik (Ed.), *International directory of psychologists* (4th ed., pp. 3–10). Amsterdam: North-Holland.

Rosenzweig, M. R., & Holtzman, W. H. (1985b). The International Union of Psychological Science (IUPsyS). *International Journal of Psychology, 20,* 753–781.

Rosenzweig, M. R., & Holtzman, W. H. (in press). The International Union of Psychological Science (IUPsyS). In G. d'Ydewalle (Ed.), *International directory of psychological organizations.* Hove, East Sussex, England: Erlbaum.

Rosenzweig, M. R., & Leiman, A. L. (1989). *Physiological psychology* (2nd ed.). New York: Random House/ McGraw-Hill.

Sexton, V. S., & Hogan, J. (Eds.). (1992). *International psychology: Views from around the world* (2nd ed.). Lincoln: University of Nebraska Press.

Shouksmith, G., & Shouksmith, E. A. (Eds.). (1990). *Psychology in Asia and the Pacific: Status reports on teaching and research in eleven countries* (RUSHAP Series on Occasional Monographs and Papers, No. 34) Bangkok: UNESCO.

Stapp, J., Tucker, A. M., & VandenBos, G. R. (1985). Census of psychological personnel: 1983. *American Psychologist, 40,* 1317–1351.

Thurgood, D. H., & Weinman, J. M. (1991). *Summary report, 1990: Doctorate recipients from United States universities.* Washington, DC: National Academy Press.

Uebersax, J., & Ferguson, L. (1989). *ADAMHA and NIH research grants to psychologists* (RAND Publication Series N–3031–APA). Santa Monica, CA: RAND Corporation.

*Ulrich's international periodicals directory.* (1988–89). (27th ed., Vols. 1–3). New York: Bowker.

United Nations Development Programme. (1990). *Human development report 1990.* New York: Oxford University Press.

United Nations Development Programme. (1991). *Human development report 1991.* New York: Oxford University Press.

VandenBos, G. R. (1992). The APA knowledge dissemination program: An overview of 100 years. In R. B. Evans, V. S. Sexton, & T. C. Cadwallader (Eds.), *The American Psychological Association: A historical perspective* (pp. 347–390). Washington, DC: American Psychological Association.

# CHAPTER 3

# Human Learning and Memory: A Cognitive Perspective

Lars-Göran Nilsson

T he scientific study of human learning and memory has a history of a little more than 100 years. Much has happened during that time, the problems posed now are different than those of a century ago, many new methods have been developed, and the theories recently formulated are more sophisticated. Some of these changes took place during the early years of this period, but there is no doubt that the main progress has been made during the past few decades. This chapter will focus on these later developments after a brief introduction of some historical landmarks of the field.

## Some Historical Notes

The German psychologist Hermann Ebbinghaus was the first to demonstrate that learning and memory can be measured. In his ground-breaking 1885 book, *Über das Gedächtnis*, he described how he, as the constructor of the study materials, the experimenter, and the sole subject, spent several hours each day over a 2-year period learning these materials and testing himself on how much he remembered.

*The preparation of this chapter was supported by a grant from the Swedish Council of Research in the Humanities and Social Sciences.*

The study materials that he constructed were nonsense syllables of consonant–vowel–consonant combinations, such as XUT, GEX, and VIP. Sometimes, often among researchers primarily interested in more applied work, Ebbinghaus's fame has been attributed solely to the invention of such syllables. Such comments have been expressed, at times, in a rather belittling tone alluding to the artificial nature of this material. It was commonly believed among these critics that real words, sentences, or stories would be more suitable to measure "real" memory. Their verdict was that the kind of memory that is measured by means of nonsense materials must be nonsensical too.

These critics forgot or ignored Ebbinghaus's reason for using these syllables in his experiments. He invented these syllables as study materials because he was interested in exploring how new memories were formed and how they deteriorated over retention intervals of varying length. He conducted many experiments to determine how variables that he thought were crucial would affect learning, retention, and forgetting. However, Ebbinghaus's main contribution to the science of learning and memory was not the empirical finding per se; we will therefore not be dealing with these here. His main contribution was that of methodological inventiveness. In addition to the construction of nonsense syllables to study new memories, there were a couple of inventions of long-standing quality.

Ebbinghaus's most basic methodological creation was the study/test procedure. This procedure is now so basic and self-evident that some might call it trivial, but no one before Ebbinghaus had the insight to invent this method. It simply requires that the subject study certain material in the form of equivalent items; the subject is then tested on how much he or she remembers of the material studied. This procedure forms the basic foundation of a memory experiment and constitutes even today the model for how an experiment in human learning and memory should be conducted.

Another good example of Ebbinghaus's methodological inventiveness is the measure of savings. The first step in this procedure is to study a list of items to complete mastery. Some time later, when the subject fails to remember any of these items, he or she is asked to relearn them. The difference between the number of trials it takes to relearn the items and the number of trials it took to learn them originally is the savings measure. More precisely, the savings measure is computed as follows:

$$\frac{O-R}{O} \times 100,$$

where O stands for the number of trials for original learning and R stands for the number of trials for relearning. For example, if 10 trials are required for original learning and 6 trials for relearning, the amount of savings is 40%,

$$\frac{10-6}{10} \times 100 = 40.$$

This measure, developed more than a century ago, is of particular interest because it has recently been used to shed light on a kind of memory that does not require a conscious recollection of the study episode. This is called *implicit memory* and will be discussed later.

The fact that Ebbinghaus constructed his own study items, served as the experimenter, used himself as the subject, and analyzed the data on his own might deserve a brief comment with respect to the need for rigorous control in experimental work. To say the least, Ebbinghaus was very careful at all stages of his work. After having constructed a large pool of nonsense syllables, he selected randomly from this pool the items to be included in his learning lists. When he was ready to start an experiment, he randomly selected each list to be used in each experiment. He then began to recite each list at a fixed rate until he was able to recite the whole list by heart without any error. He rigidly avoided any attempt to seek meaningful associations between syllables, and he was careful always to test himself at exactly the same time of day. In his method of savings, he was careful to start relearning a list that he was sure he could no longer recite.

One critical feature of Ebbinghaus's work and the research tradition built on his work is thus the strong emphasis on experimental control in a laboratory setting. As such, this work has been very compatible with the theoretical orientation of behaviorism that dominated psychological research in North America from the beginning to the middle of this century. In this tradition, the main emphasis was on learning rather than on memory. Simple forms of learning like classical and operant conditioning were explored using various species of animals as subjects. Attempts were then made to apply the basic principles demonstrated in this research domain to human learning; it was these attempts in particular that showed a strong similarity to the research approach initiated by Ebbinghaus. In fact, the verbal learning research carried out in North America from, say, the 1930s and for many years to come has often been referred to as the Ebbinghaus tradition. Alternative research traditions of human learning and memory during this time had a much more pragmatic orientation (e.g., that of Bartlett in Great Britain and the Gestalt

psychologists in Germany). It should be mentioned that a glimpse of this historical difference in the orientation of memory research between North America and Europe can be
seen in a recent article by Banaji and Crowder (1989). The primary target for the criti-
cisms of these two American psychologists was the applied memory research reported in
the proceedings of two European conferences on practical aspects of memory.

Generalizations like this, that laboratory work has found its home in North America
whereas more applied work has been done in Europe, are of course risky, and I do not
want to overemphasize this rather crude impression. Certainly, applications of basic
learning principles to more complex and applied settings were made in North America as
well. Dewey, Thorndike, and other functionalistic psychologists in the 1930s and 1940s
are good examples of this. In recent years, the American psychologist Ulrich Neisser has
been one of the most well known and eager advocates of the "everyday memory approach." And there was of course basic research and theorizing going on in Europe too.
Semon in Germany is an excellent example of an early theoretician with important insights into issues of memory—insights about retrieval processes that were a bit too modern for his early-20th-century colleagues but that reappeared much later, during the late
1970s and early 1980s (see Schacter, 1986).

Semon's or Bartlett's work, or the work on human learning and memory by the
Gestalt psychologists, had a very limited influence on the mainstream verbal learning
tradition in the middle of the century. The behavioristic orientation dominated, and it
was against such theorizing that researchers in the field started to revolt at the end of
the 1950s.

# The Cognitive Revolution

In the late 1950s, a new theoretical orientation in the study of learning and memory began to emerge in both Europe and North America. Several factors were responsible for
this change in theoretical outlook; a profound dissatisfaction with the behavioristic
framework was possibly the main factor. To some extent, this dissatisfaction grew out of
applied research on psychological phenomena discovered during the war and soon after.
For example, it was discovered that persons who inspected radar screens for enemy air-
craft made surprisingly many mistakes, especially after having watched the screen for a
long period of time. To understand problems of this sort, researchers realized that concepts like *attention* and *processing capacity* were necessary. Because mentalistic concepts of this sort had had no place in behavioristic theory, the conceptual framework

needed to be broadened. However, many years went by before concrete theories including such mentalistic concepts were formulated.

## Short-Term Memory

In *Perception and Communication* by the English experimental psychologist Donald E. Broadbent (1958), a theory was proposed that contained concepts like *attention, capacity limitation, short-term memory*,[1] and *long-term memory*. This theory, called the *filter theory*, was proposed to account for phenomena like attention failures observed, for example, in radar operators and air traffic controllers during the war and after. In brief, the filter theory states that there are filters between the initial sensory process and the brain, which selectively blocks out unattended information from further processing to make possible a more complete processing of information to which the observer attends. On the basis of experimental data, Broadbent located the filters relatively early in the information processing sequence. The filter theory, which in its original form has been rejected, was crucial to modern research on attention and to the understanding of a person as an information processing system with limited capacity.

Broadbent's book is commonly regarded as one of the first signs of the emerging cognitive revolution. In addition to the specific concepts he proposed, Broadbent also made use of a whole new framework for conceiving the human mind. This framework later became one of the cornerstones of cognitive psychology. Inspired by the emerging computer technology of the 1950s, Broadbent proposed that attention, memory, and other types of cognitive processes could be regarded as flows of information through several hypothetical compartments, each of which was responsible for separate stages of processing. The well-known memory model of Atkinson and Shiffrin (1968) is a good example of the flow-diagram models that became popular ways of depicting conceptual frameworks of memory in the 1960s. Figure 1 outlines the basic features of the modal[2] short-term/long-term memory (STM/LTM) model such as the Atkinson–Shiffrin model.

The three separate compartments, according to such modal models, are as follows: a very short-lived sensory store with high capacity, a short-term memory store with

---

[1] For simplicity, the term short-term memory *will be used throughout this chapter, although* short-term store *is the correct term to use when referring to a hypothetical memory system, and* short-term memory *is used as a term for describing an experimental paradigm.*

[2] The term modal model, *discussed in Murdock (1974), means an average (prototypical) model. The meaning of "modal" is here derived from statistics: average = mean, median, mode.*

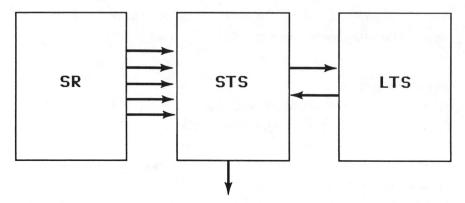

**FIGURE 1**    The main components of the modal model of short-term and long-term memory. (SR = sensory register; STS = short-term store; LTS = long-term store.)

limited capacity, and a high-capacity long-term store for the permanent storage of information. It is primarily the latter two subsystems that made a special impact on researchers in the field. This division of memory into separate compartments with different functions did not occur until the cognitive revolution; in the orthodox Ebbinghaus tradition, memory was conceived of as a unitary system.

Basically, the kinds of evidence in favor of a division of memory into short- and long-term components are as follows: (a) Some types of patients show deficits in long-term memory while short-term memory is intact; other patients show deficits in short-term memory with an intact long-term memory (this will be discussed further in Chapter 4). (b) Some memory tasks (e.g., free recall of unrelated verbal items) produce data that clearly indicate one short-term memory component and one long-term memory component. (c) Short-term memory relies primarily on acoustic or phonological coding, whereas long-term memory relies on semantic coding of the to-be-remembered information. (d) Short- and long-term memory differ dramatically with respect to capacity: Whereas the capacity of short-term memory is low, it is very high or possibly unlimited for long-term memory.

Another important hallmark in the early development of the new cognitive orientation of learning and memory research, parallel with and contemporary to Broadbent's research, was methodological rather than conceptual: the discovery of a method to measure short-term memory. Independently of each other, John Brown (1958) in England and

Lloyd and Margaret Peterson (Peterson & Peterson, 1959) in the United States proposed a technique that later became known as the Brown–Peterson method. The main features of this technique were first to present subjects with small amounts of information (e.g., three consonants or three words), then to prevent them from rehearsing this information, and finally to have them recall the information presented. Prevention of rehearsal was accomplished by backward counting: Subjects were instructed to count backward by threes from a given three-digit number (768, 765, 762, 759, . . . and so on) for as long as the retention interval lasted. This interval was varied systematically from 3 to 18 seconds by Peterson and Peterson (1959). The results showed a rapidly decreasing forgetting function: After 3 seconds subjects were, on the average, able to recall about only 80% of the information, and after 18 seconds the performance was as low as 10% of the information.

Such results by Brown (1958) and Peterson and Peterson (1959) suggested that short-term memory could be measured: This was the important discovery. However, on the basis of such results, it was also suggested that the duration of short-term memory could be determined. Later research showed this ambition to be futile because short-term memory could be of different durations: 20 seconds were suggested by some, 30 seconds by others, 60 seconds by still others, and so on in a never-ending story. The attempt to understand this variability led to a new approach.

**Levels of Processing**

Partly on the basis of these differences in results and related conceptual difficulties, Craik and Lockhart (1972) suggested a different framework for memory research than the one based on a flow of information through a series of memory compartments. This framework, referred to as the *levels-of-processing* view, provided the area with quite a different way of thinking about learning and memory. These authors proposed that the duration of short-term memory, and its claimed limitation in capacity, were not crucial to the matter of describing and understanding memory. Instead, they argued that the level to which information was processed was the major determinant of memory performance. Information that was processed to a shallow orthographic or phonemic level would be recalled to a much lesser extent than information that had been processed to a deep, semantic, or meaningful level. In a typical levels-of-processing experiment, subjects are instructed to make judgments for each item in the study list in relation to various orienting tasks. To accomplish a processing at a shallow orthographic level, a question is asked about the physical appearance of the word (e.g., "Is the word written in uppercase letters?"). An intermediate, phonemic encoding is attained by an orienting task about the sound of the word (e.g., "Does the word rhyme with _____ ?"). The deep, semantic encoding is accomplished by referring to the meaning of the word in the orienting task (e.g., "Does the word fit in the sentence: — — — ?").

This framework proposed by Craik and Lockhart (1972) had an enormous appeal to people working in the field of human learning and memory. It had an impact on practitioners in the field that few other frameworks have had; the levels-of-processing wave swept across the world of studies of learning and memory for many years.

However, there were also critics of the levels-of-processing view who stood up to declare their opinion. Baddeley (1978) was one of those who came up with well-thought-out arguments that left the field with considerable concern. His main arguments against the levels-of-processing notion were that (a) there is no adequate and independent measurement of the level to which the information is processed, (b) there is no evidence of a series of independent stages or processing, (c) there has to be a meaningful semantic encoding of information, although subjects are instructed to encode the information solely in terms of orthographic or phonemic encoding, and (d) the levels-of-processing view places too much emphasis on encoding, as opposed to retrieval.

In stating his first criticism, Baddeley (1978) argued that separate levels of encoding are an empty concept unless there is a reliable and independent measure of the level to which the processing has been carried out. The core of this criticism is that the levels-of-processing view easily becomes circular if there is no such independent measure. There is a risk of circularity, Baddeley claimed, in saying that everything that is well remembered is also encoded to a deep level, whereas that which is poorly remembered is poorly encoded. The only way to avoid this risk of circularity is to require independent measurements of the levels of encoding.

Regarding the second point of criticism, Baddeley claimed that the view of a series of stages was outdated, and he based this criticism on reading research rather than on memory research. Baddeley's argument was that reading studies have shown that processing goes on in parallel at several levels, feeding both from the shallow level to the semantic level and from the semantic to the nonsemantic orthographic and phonemic levels. Thus, information is not processed first at a visual–orthographic level, then at a level of phonological characteristics of the materials, and finally at a meaningful semantic level.

About the third point of his critique, Baddeley said that, by and large, the levels-of-processing view loses its elegance and importance if it can be claimed that the qualitative differences in processing are merely quantitative in nature. As long as meaningful words are used as the to-be-remembered materials, subjects would have to encode the meaning of the word in any case. Instructions about orthographic and phonemic encoding simply distract subjects from basing their encoding on semantic processing. Thus, the procedure used is not a true test of different levels of encoding. Rather, it is primarily a semantic encoding of all verbal information, which may or may not be disturbed by the instructions that the to-be-remembered information should be encoded orthographically or phonemically as well.

Finally, Baddeley also claimed that Craik and Lockhart (1972) missed the crucial phase of remembering when they argued that encoding of the to-be-remembered information is the primary process to take into account. Baddeley's argument was that retrieval processes cannot be left aside. He based this argument on the results of an experiment by Morris, Bransford, and Franks (1977), who demonstrated that performance depends on a relationship between encoding and retrieval: Semantic encoding produced a higher performance when tested the standard way in a recognition test. However, when the test required subjects to judge whether each test item rhymed with a word presented at study, Morris et al. were able to show that a previous encoding of phonemic features was superior to an encoding of semantic features.

On the basis of these results, the notion of "transfer-appropriate processing" was proposed as a central concept for understanding human memory. According to this view, the best encoding occurs when subjects are aware of the type of test that will follow. Transfer-appropriate processing was certainly acknowledged as a central concept when it was proposed by John Bransford at the end of the 1970s (Bransford, Franks, Morris, & Stein, 1979; Morris et al., 1977). However, its main impact came much later in relation to the distinction between explicit and implicit memory. This distinction will be dealt with in more detail later in this chapter.

It is probably fair to say that research on human learning and memory during the 1960s was dominated by research on short-term memory. To some extent, this approach came to an end as a result of the levels-of-processing view. Although Craik and Lockhart (1972) also acknowledged the need for short-term memory, in their framework they conceived of its role primarily as a means of encoding information.

**Working Memory**

A more active role for short-term memory was proposed by Baddeley and Hitch (1974) in their model of working memory. The aim of this model was initially the same as that of the levels-of-processing view of Craik and Lockhart (1972), namely to account for the problems that the STM/LTM models (e.g., Atkinson & Shiffrin, 1968) encountered. Several large problems persisted for such models even after levels-of-processing theories had been proposed: (a) The maintenance of information in a short-term store for a long period does not guarantee that it will transfer to long-term memory. (b) Short-term memory is not limited to acoustic processing, and long-term processing is not limited to semantic processing. (c) Patients who demonstrate a short-term memory deficit do not necessarily show a poor performance in long-term memory, which they should, according to the modal model (see Figure 1). (d) There are long-term recency effects. (e) Memory span tasks fail to disrupt short-term recency effects.

Rather than a single-unit short-term memory system, as in the modal model, Baddeley and Hitch (1974) proposed a multicomponent short-term store. These components are a central executive, a phonological loop, and a visual–spatial sketch pad. The role of the central executive is to control and supervise the two slave systems. One of these, the phonological loop, is assumed to be responsible for the processing of speech-based information, whereas the other, the visual–spatial sketch pad, is assumed to be responsible for forming and processing visual images. There is reasonably good agreement in the field that the model of working memory of Baddeley and Hitch can account for the problems that the modal model encountered.

In summary, then, short-term memory was one of the core concepts in the cognitive revolution that began at the end of the 1950s. Although short-term memory research is still being carried out, its focus and orientation is quite different now in the first years of the 1990s. The conceptualization of short-term memory is different, the pool of useful tools for investigating short-term memory is much broader, and the orientation of research based on the working memory model is much more applied and pragmatic than research based on the modal model and levels of processing. These latter two frameworks are in essence two extensions of the Ebbinghaus tradition, with its strong emphasis on experimental work in the laboratory.

Research on working memory has in fact returned to the practical problems that inspired Broadbent to formulate his filter model. The basic question asked by Baddeley and Hitch, when they started their short-term memory research, clearly reflects this state of affairs: What is short-term memory for? The answers that they and others have given to this question indicate that working memory in general, but the phonological loop in particular, plays an important role in language comprehension, in acquiring a vocabulary, and in learning to read.

Thus, a general pattern is beginning to emerge. Much of the European research on short-term memory is of a pragmatic and goal-oriented character. Research in the same field in North America has been more laboratory oriented, with the goal of testing a specific theory for understanding memory per se. This pattern is not meant to be generalized in an absolute sense. There are of course cases of research on short-term memory in Europe that have a clear Ebbinghaus flavor, and there are cases in North America in which the main contribution of knowledge is of an applied nature.

The separation of memory into short- and long-term memory brings us to the topic of the next section of this chapter, namely the separation of long-term memory into different subsystems.

# Memory Systems

### Episodic and Semantic Memory

Not long ago, long-term memory (or long-term store, to be correct) was conceived of as a unitary memory store. A couple of decades ago, however, Tulving (1972) suggested that we should rather talk about two forms of memory: *episodic memory* and *semantic memory*. Lately, other forms of memory have been added to these two, and it has become necessary to introduce a new approach to the study of memory: the classification of memory (Tulving, 1985). This section will deal with different memory systems and with the notion of classification.

The dichotomy proposed by Tulving in 1972 in terms of episodic memory and semantic memory was the first attempt to make explicit the basic difference between the memory of personally experienced events and the memory of general knowledge. Thus, episodic memory makes it possible to remember episodes or events from the personally experienced past. For example, to remember what one had for dinner last Sunday and to remember who the person was that one met at a party on July 14 last year are expressions of episodic memory. In fact, that one has to make a conscious recollection of the original event is a defining characteristic of episodic memory.

Semantic memory is the memory of general knowledge of the world. For example, to remember that Rome is the capital of Italy is an expression of semantic memory, or that NaCl is the chemical formula for regular table salt. Semantic memory can be conceived of as the source of the material needed for thought and reflection, and it goes beyond what can be immediately perceived. The utilization of information in semantic memory does not require a conscious recollection of the situation in which the information was acquired. The term *semantic memory* is a bit unfortunate because it may make one believe that it is limited to language and the meaning of words. This is not at all the case: Semantic memory is about general knowledge in the broad sense of the word, including language, semantics, and syntax.

## Other Systems

Episodic memory and semantic memory are sometimes collectively called *declarative memory* (e.g., Cohen & Squire, 1980) or *propositional memory* (Tulving, 1983).

Both episodic and semantic memory are cognitive systems, and so is a recently formulated concept for a separate memory system: the *perceptual representation system* (PRS; Tulving & Schacter, 1990). This form of memory is used for perceptual learning and for the identification of objects. In contrast with episodic memory, there is no need for a conscious recollection of the event when the critical information was acquired. For example, the perception of an object at a given occasion makes it "easier" to perceive the object at a later occasion in the sense that the time needed to see the object properly is shorter than the first time. The amount of information needed for successful identification the second time is also less as compared with the first time. The mechanism for this is called *perceptual priming*.

In contrast with episodic memory, semantic memory, and the PRS, a fourth proposed system is an action system rather than a cognitive system. It expresses itself in behavior rather than in cognitive responses. Perceptual–motor skills like walking or biking are examples of *procedural memory*. Like the PRS, it does not require a conscious recollection of a given situation when the response or the behavior was acquired. Conditioning of simple stimulus–response connections is another example of a situation in which procedural memory comes into play. In Cohen and Squire's (1980) terminology, procedural memory constitutes a contrast to declarative memory. At present, this terminology seems to be in a phase of transition such that the term *procedural memory* is being replaced by the term *nondeclarative memory*.

## The Classification of Memory

There are many ways in which memory systems can be classified. Tulving (1992) proposed five memory systems as being the basic components of memory. In addition to the four systems described earlier, Tulving included short-term memory as a separate system. Thus, his list includes procedural memory, the perceptual representation system, short-term memory, semantic memory, and episodic memory.

This ordering of the systems was aimed at reflecting the developmental sequence of the systems, with procedural memory being the earliest and episodic memory the latest. The systems are also supposed to be independent but interactive such that later systems are dependent on or supported by the earlier ones.

There are two main sources of evidence for the claim of separate memory systems. One kind of evidence comes from clinical data. Several authors (e.g., Cohen & Squire, 1980; Warrington & Weiskrantz, 1968) have demonstrated intact learning and memory for amnesic patients in tasks assumed to reflect procedural memory or the perceptual representation system. Some of the tasks used in demonstrating an intact procedural memory in amnesic patients are enhanced reading of a transformed script (Cohen & Squire, 1980), conditioning (Weiskrantz & Warrington, 1979), and learning complex puzzles such as the Tower of Hanoi (Cohen, 1984). The tasks used in demonstrating an intact perceptual representation system include various sorts of picture- and word-completion tasks. For example, Warrington & Weiskrantz (1968) first presented words like *cyclone*, and later presented the first three letters of each word (i.e., *cyc*____) with the instruction to say the first word that comes to mind when each word stem is presented. In tasks of this sort, amnesic patients perform as well as or almost as well as control subjects without any memory disorders. When episodic memory tasks (e.g., recall or recognition of previously studied material) are used, the performance of the amnesic patients is markedly lower than that of the control subjects.

The other type of evidence for the classification of memory into separate systems comes from experiments using persons without memory disorders as subjects. Demonstrations of functional dissociations and stochastic independence are such evidence. A functional dissociation is demonstrated when a given variable known to affect a certain task in one way is found to have no effect (single dissociation) or the opposite effect (double dissociation) on another task. For example, levels of processing are known to affect memory performance in a direct way by means of recognition or recall tests. However, when tested indirectly by means of perceptual identification, performance was not affected by levels of processing (Jacoby & Dallas, 1981). That is, the speed of identifying words presented tachistoscopically was not affected by whether the words had been encoded in a shallow phonemic or orthographic way or in a deep, semantically meaningful way.

LARS-GÖRAN NILSSON

Stochastic independence is demonstrated when two measures of memory prove to be statistically unrelated. A recently developed technique for demonstrating stochastic independence is the method of triangulation (Hayman & Tulving, 1989). In this method, subjects are first presented with a long series of words followed by a recognition test in which the same words, intermixed with distractors not previously shown, are presented along with the instruction to the subjects to say "yes" or "no" depending on whether they think they have seen each word at study. This recognition test, referred to as a *referential test*, constitutes a means to assess episodic memory. Half of the subjects are then given a cued recall test as another means to assess episodic memory. In this task, a fragment of each word from the study list is presented (e.g., for the word ASSASSIN the fragment might be __ SS __SS __ __) together with the instruction to use each fragment as a cue to try to remember a word that was presented at study. The other half of the subjects are presented with exactly the same fragments (i.e., __ SS__ SS__ __) but with a different instruction: For each fragment, the subject is instructed to say the first word that comes to mind. In these two tests, fragments from words previously not shown in the study list are also presented (distractors). This word fragment completion task is used as a means to assess the perceptual representation system. When the data from these three tasks of the triangulation method are subjected to statistical testing by means of Yule's Q (see Hayman & Tulving, 1989), the two episodic memory tasks (recognition and cued recall) show statistical dependence—and so they should if they reflect the same memory system. As expected, recognition and word fragment completion show statistical independence because they reflect two separate memory systems. This pattern of data holds true if the word fragment completion task can be arranged such that subjects do not use each fragment as a cue for remembering the words from the study list. If the subjects use the fragments in the completion task as cues for episodic remembering, the degree of dependence between the recognition test and the word fragment completion test increases because the same memory system is then used for both tasks.

The word fragment completion task is typically used not only to determine stochastic independence with the reference test but also to assess the perceptual representation system more precisely. This is accomplished by comparing the completion rates for those fragments that were presented as words at study for those fragments that were not presented as words at study. This difference, referred to as the amount of *priming*, is an expression of the function of the perceptual representation system.

For obvious reasons, this discussion of the classification of memory into subsystems has emphasized psychological variables and tasks. However, a multilevel approach is required to undertake a more ambitious classification of memory systems (see Tulving, 1992). The analysis of the psychological aspects of each system is not enough. It is necessary to combine such an analysis with various types of neurobiological analyses, for example from the point of view of neuroanatomy, neurophysiology, and neurochemistry. There are some insights within these domains that might easily be connected with functional data with respect to the localization of different forms of memory. Such biological aspects of memory will be dealt with in detail in Chapter 4.

Finally, it should also be mentioned that the classification of memory need not necessarily focus on structural subsystems of memory. Quite a different view is the one emphasizing different processes and a single, unitary memory system. This view has been a dominating one in memory research since the levels-of-processing view was proposed (Craik & Lockhart, 1972). Current versions of this general framework focus on the notion of "transfer-appropriate processing." For example, in relation to the recent interest in various completion tasks among students of memory, the distinction has been made between bottom-up processing and top-down processing (e.g., Roediger & Blaxton, 1987). In a recent publication, Roediger, Weldon, and Challis (1989) seemed to retreat from the hard line of a pure processing view to a more eclectic view of a combination of the memory systems view and the processing view.

The systems view and the processing view discussed are theoretically well specified. In contrast with both of these approaches, another theoretically neutral view has recently been proposed by Graf and Schacter (1985), who made the distinction between explicit and implicit memory. Explicit memory tasks refer to tasks that require a conscious recollection of the study episode. This is typical for the recall and recognition tasks referred to earlier as episodic memory tasks. Implicit memory tasks, on the other hand, do not require a conscious recollection of the study episode. Some of the tasks used for implicit memory research have already been mentioned in connection with the multiple systems view: word stem completion and word fragment completion. Other useful tasks in this category are perceptual identification and the method of savings originally developed by Ebbinghaus.

Thus, several useful tasks have been explored in the context of implicit and explicit memory research. This seems to be a valuable first step toward a more thorough task analysis, which would seem to be an important prerequisite for future progress in this field. Perhaps such an analysis should be a necessary prerequisite even for the more general topic of the classification of memory. This might in fact be one additional level in the multilevel approach proposed as being a necessary requirement for reaching further goals in the classification of memory.

## The Storage of Information

For a long time, memory has been conceived of as a receptacle—simply something in which information is dumped until the rememberer is ready to use it. Aristotle and Plato already conceived of memory as a spatial entity, and this spatial metaphor of memory storage was common among philosophers and memory researchers for many centuries thereafter. The long list of spatial metaphors of memory provided by Roediger (1980) is an expression of the general consensus of the organization of memory that seems to have dominated for many years. Even at the time of the emerging cognitive revolution the late 1950s and early 1960s, this view was a dominating one. The spatial metaphor still flourished for more years, and it was not until the late 1970s or early 1980s that one could notice a change in the conceptualization of the storage of information.

It is not easy to determine one single factor that caused the demise of the spatial metaphor. One likely candidate, however, for its declining popularity is the search metaphor so closely connected with the spatial view of memory. According to the search metaphor, retrieval requires that the information stored is thoroughly checked before a response can be given. Several basic issues were investigated in relation to the notion of memory search, for example, whether the search should be regarded as serial or parallel, and whether the search should be conceived of as exhaustive or self-terminating. These two issues and others were explored for many years without any sign of a reasonable resolution. Supposedly, this lack of a breakthrough discouraged people from pursuing this view any further. The suspicion that the basic question was inadequately addressed probably crossed the minds of many students of memory engaged in exploring the notion of storage.

An alternative to the view of storage as a receptacle for separable units of information localized in space began to emerge recently. Rather than considering separable memory traces as the units carrying information from encoding to retrieval, proposals were made that information is stored in a distributed way across many units. This approach is generally known as *parallel distributed processing* (PDP) or *connectionism*. The ideas embedded in this framework are new and often very technical, and indeed it is almost impossible to do justice to the complexity of PDP models in a limited space, but a few general remarks might be useful.

Although most of the basic ideas of this approach are new, it is interesting to note that the term *connectionism* has its roots in Thorndike's old general principles of learning. According to these principles, learning evolves by a series of steps of trial and error. Successive steps were assumed to create associative connections, some of which are rewarded and hence strengthened. Given, then, the first step of such a connection, there is an increased likelihood that the second step will occur, and so on for further pairwise steps.

In the framework of PDP models, the connections are those between units of the storage system (or neurons of the brain). In brief, it is generally assumed that aspects of the environment activate distributed units of the storage system and that the concurrent activation of several such interconnected units makes possible the perceptual experience of an event as well as, later, the recollection of this event. This notion of distributed units for storage is not new; it dates back to the findings, many years ago, of Karl Lashley (1929) showing that, rather than being located in one place, memories were distributed throughout an animal's brain.

These observations indicate that PDP models are part of the evolutionary development of a long and important tradition. Moreover, the exciting modeling work done in this framework demonstrates that the researchers in this field have come much further than their predecessors in understanding basic principles of learning. This can be seen, for example, in many expert systems that have been developed in recent years to perform complex diagnostic and problem-solving tasks (see the thorough introductory texts by McClelland & Rumelhart, 1986, and Rumelhart & McClelland, 1986, and perhaps also some critical views on connectionism and PDP models, e.g., Fodor & Pylyshyn, 1988).

## Processing

In addition to storage, encoding and retrieval are generally considered as the main phases in the act of remembering. Whereas encoding has been extensively investigated since Ebbinghaus began to explore memory, the nature of retrieval is less well known. With the exception of Semon's (1921) work earlier in this century, it was not until fairly recently that students of memory began exploring retrieval processes.

The concept of encoding refers to the hypothetical psychological process that follows perception. By means of an encoding operation, the information is transformed in such a way that it can be stored in memory and later retrieved when needed. Different events are encoded in different ways, leading to differences in the ease of retrieving the information. However, the same event can be encoded differently, leading to differences in the amount of information retrieved.

The levels-of-processing approach (Craik & Lockhart, 1972), discussed earlier, was formulated to account for this fact. As mentioned, levels-of-processing states that the amount of information retained is a function of how the information was encoded. A deep, meaningful encoding leads to better performance than a phonemic encoding, which in turn produces a higher recall or recognition score than a structural orthographic encoding. The theoretical reason for this, as stated by Craik and Lockhart, is that a deeper encoding produces a richer, more elaborate, or more distinctive memory trace than does a shallow processing.

What is it, then, that makes the memory trace more distinct after deep than after shallow processing? Although there is no single factor agreed upon to account for this result, attempts to reach a consensus converge on the notion of meaning. When information is encoded in a meaningful way, the information makes contact with the previous experience and knowledge of the person who is doing the encoding. More shallow processing, like rote rehearsal, does not facilitate such a contact with previous experience and knowledge.

A retrieval process is always triggered by some kind of stimulus information. This might be some other information that is presented externally. A picture, a word, a smell, or some other perceptual input are examples of such a stimulus. The triggering information can also be a specific question about some general fact or some previous experience. It is also possible for a thought, rather than some external information, to trigger the retrieval process. The term used for all such triggering instances is *retrieval information* or *retrieval cue.*

The mechanism generally assumed for the effectiveness of retrieval cues is that they somehow make contact with the stored information to be retrieved. There are several ways in which this contact between retrieval cues and stored information can be accomplished. One is the similarity between the cue and the memory trace. The most extreme form of similarity is complete identity, which is the case in a recognition situation: A word or a picture presented to a person might be identified as something that this person has seen before. In a recall situation, in which the person is supposed to produce the response, similarity is not a distinguishing factor. Rather, the cue presented to the person should have some contextual relation to the stored information. If the cue had been encoded together with the to-be-remembered information, this cue is typically bound to trigger a successful retrieval process, making it possible to respond with the information that is stored.

This latter case expresses a basic principle in remembering: the encoding specificity principle. This principle can be stated formally as follows: Encoding operations determine what is stored, and what is stored determines the effectiveness of retrieval cues (Tulving & Thomson, 1973). Research on this basic principle has recently brought about the observation of a remarkable regularity in the data from experiments studying the relationship between recognition and recall.

It is a commonsense opinion that recognition should be easier than recall. It should be easier to identify something as having been experienced earlier than to produce a response on the basis of a question or some other cue. In such a context, it was thus rather contraintuitive when Tulving and Thomson (1973) first demonstrated that subjects, under certain conditions, manage to recall information that they fail to recognize. This phenomenon is generally referred to as the phenomenon of recognition failure of recallable words. It is interesting because it is contraintuitive, it goes against the commonly held generation–recognition theory, and it may form the basis for an empirical law.

The generation–recognition theory states that there are two bottlenecks in recall and that only one of these affects recognition. Therefore, it should be impossible for subjects to recall information that they fail to recognize. The two bottlenecks in recall are (a) to generate a number of response alternatives from memory when the recall cue is presented, and (b) to decide which of these alternatives is the correct one to be given as a response. In recognition, only the latter of these is of interest because one crucial aspect of the experimental procedure in a recognition test is typically to present the response alternatives for the subject. Thus, it is only the decision process that should be critical in recognition. According to the generation–recognition theory, then, it is only recall that is penalized if the generation phase fails; that is, recognition should be possible even when recall is unsuccessful. If the decision process fails, both recognition and recall should be unsuccessful.

The recognition–failure paradigm developed by Tulving and Thomson (1973) involves the study of a series of cue–target word pairs (e.g., glue–CHAIR), followed by a recognition test of the right-hand member of each pair and a recall test in which the left-hand member of each pair is presented as a cue and the subject is supposed to respond with the right-hand member of the pair. When the results from such experiments are plotted as recall against recognition, there is a scatter of points depicting no apparent order and the correlation is low, about 0.20. However, when the data are rearranged to show the conditional probability of recognition given recall as a function of the overall recognition hit rate, a remarkable regularity appears. This rearrangement of the data is accomplished by means of a $2 \times 2$ contingency table involving a hit or miss on the two successive tests, recognition and recall. Table 1 presents a hypothetical example to illustrate this type of data analysis.

This table shows that subjects in this hypothetical experiment managed to recognize and recall 30% of all target items, and recognized but failed to recall 20% of the target items, for an overall recognition hit rate of 0.50. Subjects also failed to recognize, but managed to recall, targets in 15% of the cases, which gives an overall recall performance of 0.45. Finally, in 35% of the cases, subjects failed both to recognize and to recall the target items. The conditional probability of the recognition failure of recallable words in this case is then $^{15}\!/_{45}$ = 0.33. For various reasons that are unimportant in this context, it has become customary in this field of research to deal with the complement of this value (i.e., the probability of the recognition success of recallable words). In this case, this probability is $1 - 0.33 = 0.67$, or, computed directly from the values in the table, $^{30}\!/_{45} = 0.67$. Thus, the observed probability of the recognition success of recallable words, $p(Rn|Rc)$, in this hypothetical experiment is 0.67 for an overall probability of recognition of 0.50.

Almost all existing data points from experimental conditions that have used the recognition failure paradigm fit a mathematical function that was proposed by Tulving and Wiseman (1975). This function has the following form:

$$p(Rn|Rc) = p(Rn) + c[p(Rn) - p(Rn)^2]$$

The conditional probability of recognition success given recall is expressed by $p(Rn|Rc)$, and the overall recognition hit rate by $p(Rn)$. By means of a least squares analysis, Tulving and Wiseman (1975) were able to determine the value of the constant $c$

**TABLE 1**

A $2 \times 2$ Contingency Table of Recognition and Recall, Describing a Hypothetical Set of Data

| Recognition | Recall Hit | Miss | Total |
|---|---|---|---|
| Hit | 30 | 20 | 50 |
| Miss | 15 | 35 | 50 |
| Total | 45 | 55 | 100 |

to be 0.50, but their analysis was based on data points from only 40 experimental conditions. In a recent update of data from recognition failure experiments including data points from 255 conditions, Nilsson and Gardiner (1991a) found no reason to change the value of the constant $c$. It should be noted that the probability of recognition given recall in the equation is a predicted value according to the Tulving–Wiseman function, whereas the value computed on the basis of the $2 \times 2$ contingency table (see Table 1) is an observed probability of recognition given recall. In each experiment using the recognition failure paradigm, the observed and predicted values of recognition given recall were compared to determine the fit between the function and the data. The observed value of recognition given recall in the hypothetical example presented here (0.67) is slightly higher than what the Tulving–Wiseman function predicts. If the observed recognition hit rate in the hypothetical example (0.50) is entered into the equation, the resulting predicted value of recognition given recall is 0.63. Various statistical procedures can then be used to determine whether the observed and the predicted values are the same.

Although the vast majority of the data that has been obtained since Tulving and Wiseman (1975) presented their summary of recognition failure data conform with the function, some cases have been reported for which the data points deviate markedly from the Tulving–Wiseman function. These deviations were analyzed and discussed by Nilsson, Law, and Tulving (1988) and Nilsson and Gardiner (1991b). From these analyses it was concluded that deviations from the function occur for two reasons. One reason is that the cue–target word pairs are poorly integrated at the time of study. In this case, the context cue presented at the recall test becomes inefficient, essentially producing a case of free recall rather than the cued recall test that was intended. The second reason is that the retrieval information that can be extracted from the copy cue at the recognition test overlaps (partly or fully) with the retrieval information that can be extracted from the context cue presented at the cued recall test. This means that the context cue presented in the recall test was already functionally present in the recognition test. Thus, in this case the context cue does not provide any new retrieval information. Figure 2 summarizes the data from all published experiments to date that have used the recognition failure paradigm. The filled squares in this figure represent data from experimental conditions that fit the Tulving–Wiseman function, and the open circles represent data from experimental conditions that, on the basis of a critical ratio measure, have been found to deviate significantly from the function. The deviations above the function represent the two types of exceptions described above, whereas the two open circles below the diagonal are two aberrant negative deviations for which there is no reasonable explanation at present.

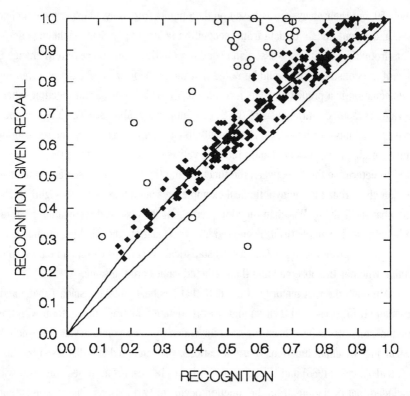

**FIGURE 2**   The probability of recognition given recall as a function of the probability of recognition. Filled squares represent data fitting the Tulving–Wiseman function; open circles represent deviations from it. (Adapted by permission from Nilsson & Gardiner, 1991b.)

After identifying the important and theoretically interesting exceptions above the function, the next step was to relate them to the regularity reported in all of the other recognition failure experiments. We proposed that the data at hand could now be formulated as an empirical law (Nilsson et al., 1988). This law, called the Tulving–Wiseman law after those who first described it, was formulated by Nilsson and Gardiner (1991b) as follows: *Recognition is largely independent of subsequent recall whenever the recall environment includes effective contextual cues that were absent in the recognition environment.*

"Empirical law" is here given the same meaning as in more mature sciences (Nilsson et al., 1988). That is, an empirical law "seems to summarize simply some fairly directly observed regularity, without attempting to provide a theoretical explanation for it" (Holton & Brush, 1973, p. 158). It is to be regarded as a major step in research on human learning and memory that such a law can be formulated despite all of the sources of variability in data that are typically present in psychological research.

To state an empirical law in psychology is apparently very controversial. Several critics have turned against the notion of this remarkable regularity, assuming that it has to be some kind of artifact. For example, Hintzman (1991) has recently argued that the regularity is an effect of mathematical constraints. Such constraints occur, according to Hintzman, whenever the recall score in an experimental condition is higher than the recognition score. The implication of Hintzman's argument is that there should be a fit to the function for those data that are subject to mathematical constraints, whereas for those data not subjected to mathematical constraints there should be deviations from the function. Gardiner and Nilsson (1991) and Tulving and Flexser (in press) have, however, demonstrated that the data pattern for experimental conditions subject to mathematical constraints is indistinguishable from that of those experimental conditions that are not subject to such constraints.

## Summing Up and Looking Ahead

Research on the cognitive aspects of human learning and memory has undergone a dramatic development since the days of Ebbinghaus. After Ebbinghaus's ground-breaking discovery that memory can be measured quantitatively, there was a steady but slow progress for many years. It was not really until the late 1950s and early 1960s that theories and methods of learning and memory began to undergo a more dramatic development in the realm of the "cognitive revolution." The highlights of the development of this field after this revolution were as follows. First came the conceptual framework of the modal model as expressed, for example, by Broadbent (1958) and Atkinson and Shiffrin (1968) and the methodological inventiveness that went along with this framework. Then came the opposition to the modal model on two fronts. One was the levels-of-processing framework developed by Craik and Lockhart (1972). This view had an enormous impact on the progress of the field by reorienting the focus of many memory researchers away from the view that information is transferred from one memory store to the next in a static fashion. The other main opposition to the modal model was the changed view of storage. Whereas the localized view of storage was commonplace among advocates of the modal model, a distributed view of storage is presently emerging in current theories of memory.

As the demise of the modal short-term memory model became more and more apparent after the opposition from the levels-of-processing view, there was a gap to be filled by a more active conceptualization of short-term memory. The working memory model of Baddeley and Hitch (1974) came along to fill this gap.

I have also mentioned the multiple systems view of memory of Tulving and others as a major hallmark of the development in modern memory research. Related to this view is the notion of the classification of memory, which, at present, at least in some quarters, seems to specify the following main components: procedural memory, the perceptual representation system, short-term memory, semantic memory, and episodic memory. This particular classification may very well change in the years to come, and other classifications may be proposed. But the important step already taken in this regard is that students of memory have begun to realize that terminology, nomenclature, and classification are as important in cognitive psychology as in other sciences; this approach has been too often neglected in memory research.

The possibility of the existence of an empirical law in human learning and memory constitutes another example of the fact that cognitive psychology, or at least some portions of the field, may share basic properties with the natural sciences. Time will tell how far one can go in claiming such a resemblance. However, what the notion of memory systems and the empirical law show is that cognitive psychology should probably be classified along with other biological sciences rather than with the social sciences.

It should be realized though that for this to happen, a closer relation should be sought with other biological disciplines. Important steps along this line have already been taken under the rubric of cognitive neuropsychology. Several patient groups in various research centers and clinics throughout the world are being investigated daily by cognitive neuropsychologists. Although cases of interaction between psychology and biology have occurred in the history of memory research, it has not been until very recently that this interaction has meant any basic exchange of theories.

The ultimate goal in understanding learning and memory would seem to be to bring together knowledge from psychology and several other disciplines. In the section of this chapter about the classification of memory, it was pointed out that a multilevel approach—involving at least neuroanatomy, neurophysiology, and neurochemistry, in addition to psychology—is needed to make such a classification meaningful. As we will see in Chapter 4, on the biological aspects of learning and memory, such integrations are already underway, and even more interdisciplinary research is yet to come.

# References

Atkinson, R. C., & Shiffrin, R. M. (1968). Human memory: A proposed system and its control processes. In K. W. Spence (Ed.), *The psychology of learning and motivation: Advances in research and theory* (Vol. 2, pp. 89–195). New York: Academic Press.

Baddeley, A. D. (1978). The trouble with levels: A re-examination of Craik and Lockhart's framework for memory research. *Psychological Review, 85,* 139–152.

Baddeley, A. D., & Hitch, G. (1974). Recency re-examined. In S. Dornic (Ed.), *Attention and performance VI* (pp. 647–667). Hillsdale, NJ: Erlbaum.

Banaji, M. R., & Crowder, R. G. (1989). The bankruptcy of everyday memory. *American Psychologist, 44,* 1185–1193.

Bransford, J. D., Franks, J. J., Morris, C. D., & Stein, B. S. (1979). Some general constraints on learning and memory research. In L. S. Cermak & F. I. M. Craik (Eds.), *Levels of processing in human memory* (pp. 331–354). Hillsdale, NJ: Erlbaum.

Broadbent, D. E. (1958). *Perception and communication.* London: Pergamon Press.

Brown, J. (1958). Some tests of the decay theory of immediate memory. *Quarterly Journal of Experimental Psychology, 10,* 12–21.

Cohen, N. J. (1984). Preserved learning capacity in amnesia: Evidence for multiple memory systems. In L. R. Squire & N. Butters (Eds.), *The neuropsychology of memory* (pp. 419–432). New York: Guilford Press.

Cohen, N. J., & Squire, L. R. (1980). Preserved learning and retention of pattern analyzing skill in amnesia: Dissociation of knowing how and knowing that. *Science, 210,* 207–210.

Craik, F. I. M., & Lockhart, R. S. (1972). Levels of processing: A framework for memory research. *Journal of Verbal Learning and Verbal Behavior, 11,* 671–684.

Ebbinghaus, H. (1885). *Über das Gedächtnis* [Memory]. Leipzig, Germany: Dunker. (Trans. by H. Ruyer & C. E. Bussenius, 1913, *Memory.* New York: Teachers College, Columbia University).

Fodor, J., & Pylyshyn, Z. (1988). Connectionism and cognitive architecture: A critical analysis. *Cognition, 28,* 3–71.

Gardiner, J., & Nilsson, L.-G. (1991, July). *On the psychological nature of the Tulving–Wiseman law.* Paper presented at the International Conference on Memory, Lancaster, England.

Graf, P., & Schacter, D. L. (1985). Implicit and explicit memory for new associations in normal and amnesic subjects. *Journal of Experimental Psychology: Learning, Memory, and Cognition, 11,* 501–518.

Hayman, C. A. G., & Tulving, E. (1989). Contingent dissociation between recognition and fragment completion: The method of triangulation. *Journal of Experimental Psychology: Learning, Memory, and Cognition, 15,* 228–240.

Hintzman, D. (1991, July). *Mathematical constraints and the "Tulving–Wiseman Law".* Paper presented at the International Conference on Memory, Lancaster, England.

Holton, G., & Brush, S. G. (1973). *Concepts and theories in physical science* (2nd ed.). Reading, MA: Addison-Wesley.

Jacoby, L. L., & Dallas, M. (1981). On the relationship between autobiographical memory and perceptual learning. *Journal of Experimental Psychology: General, 110,* 306–340.

Lashley, K. S. (1929). *Brain mechanisms and intelligence: A quantitative study of injuries to the brain.* Chicago: University of Chicago Press.

McClelland, J. L., & Rumelhart, D. E. (Eds.). (1986). *Parallel distributed processing: Explorations in the microstructure of cognition: Vol. 2. Psychological and biological models.* Cambridge, MA: MIT Press.

Morris, C. D., Bransford, J. D., & Franks, J. J. (1977). Levels of processing versus transfer appropriate processing. *Journal of Verbal Learning and Verbal Behavior, 16,* 519–533.

Murdock, B. B., Jr. (1974). *Human memory: Theory and data.* Potomac, MD: Erlbaum.

Nilsson, L.-G., & Gardiner, J. M. (1991a). *A data base of recognition failure studies from 1973 to 1991.* Unpublished manuscript.

Nilsson, L.-G., & Gardiner, J. M. (1991b). Memory theory and the boundary conditions of the Tulving–Wiseman law. In W. W. Hockley & S. Lewandowsky (Eds.), *Relating theory and data* (pp. 57–74). Hillsdale, NJ: Erlbaum.

Nilsson, L.-G., Law, J., & Tulving, E. (1988). Recognition failure of recallable unique names: Evidence for an empirical law of memory and learning. *Journal of Experimental Psychology: Learning, Memory, and Cognition, 14,* 266–277.

Peterson, L., & Peterson, M. (1959). Short-term retention of individual verbal items. *Journal of Experimental Psychology, 58,* 193–198.

Roediger, H. L. (1980). Memory metaphors in cognitive psychology. *Memory & Cognition, 8,* 231–246.

Roediger, H. L., & Blaxton, T. A. (1987). Retrieval modes produce dissociations in memory for surface information. In D. Gorfein & R. R. Hoffman (Eds.), *Memory and cognitive processes: The Ebbinghaus Centennial Conference* (pp. 349–379). Hillsdale, NJ: Erlbaum.

Roediger, H. L., Weldon, M. S., & Challis, B. H. (1989). Explaining dissociations between implicit and explicit measures of retention: A processing account. In H. L. Roediger & F. I. M. Craik (Eds.), *Varieties of memory and consciousness: Essays in honour of Endel Tulving* (pp. 3–41). Hillsdale, NJ: Erlbaum.

Rumelhart, D. E., & McClelland, J. L. (1986). *Parallel distributed processing: Explorations in the microstructures of cognition: Vol. 1. Foundations.* Cambridge, MA: MIT Press.

Schacter, D. L. (1986). *Stranger behind the engram.* Hillsdale, NJ: Erlbaum.

Semon, R. (1921). *The mneme.* London: George Allen & Unwin.

Tulving, E. (1972). Episodic and semantic memory. In E. Tulving & W. Donaldson (Eds.), *Organization of memory* (pp. 381–403). New York: Academic Press.

Tulving, E. (1983). *Elements of episodic memory.* Oxford, England: Oxford University Press.

Tulving, E. (1985). How many memory systems are there? *American Psychologist, 40,* 385–398.

Tulving, E. (1992). Concepts of human memory. In L. R. Squire, G. Lynch, N. M. Weinberger, & J. L. McGaugh (Eds.), *Memory: Organization and locus of change* (pp. 3–32). New York: Oxford University Press.

Tulving, E., & Flexser, A. (in press). On the nature of the Tulving–Wiseman function. *Psychological Review.*

Tulving, E., & Schacter, D. L. (1990). Priming and human memory systems. *Science, 247,* 301–306.

Tulving, E., & Thomson, D. M. (1973). Encoding specificity and retrieval processes in episodic memory. *Psychological Review, 80,* 352–373.

Tulving, E., & Wiseman, S. (1975). Relation between recognition and recognition failure of recallable words. *Bulletin of the Psychonomic Society, 6,* 79–82.

Warrington, E. K., & Weiskrantz, L. (1968). New method of testing long-term retention with special reference to amnesic patients. *Nature, 217,* 972–974.

Weiskrantz, L., & Warrington, E. K. (1979). Conditioning in amnesic patients. *Neuropsychologia, 8,* 281–288.

# CHAPTER 4

# Research on the Neural Bases of Learning and Memory

Mark R. Rosenzweig

A chapter such as this can offer only a sample from the rich array of studies on the neural bases of learning and memory. I will start with some examples of research to find the neural mechanisms of different categories of learning and memory and the brain regions particularly involved in these kinds of memory. The categories of memory considered are the following: (a) so-called declarative versus nondeclarative memories, or representational memories versus habits, and (b) short-term versus long-term memories. Both of these categories were described in Chapter 3. As will be discussed, the hippocampus is required for the formation of declarative or representational memories. The second main section of this chapter deals with research to test the law stated by the French psychologist Théodule Ribot in 1881 that when memories are impaired by various causes—including brain injury and disease—more recent memories are impaired more severely than are older memories. Recent research with animal subjects has provided strong support for this law but has also indicated certain qualifications that should be imposed on the law. The final section of this chapter touches on some attempts to apply research in this field.

Research by biological psychologists on the neural bases of learning and memory encompasses a broad scope: It investigates a wide range of problems, it studies learning and memory in a variety of human and animal subjects, and it uses a multiplicity of research techniques. Among the problems studied, this research attempts to find the neural bases of several different categories of learning and memory. In fact, research in biological psychology has helped to define some of the categories of learning and memory. Among the kinds of subjects studied are normal human subjects whose neural process of learning and memory are investigated by using noninvasive techniques to monitor brain activity and by testing the effects of pharmacological agents. This research also studies learning and memory in people whose brains have been damaged by injury or disease, and it tries to find which behaviors are impaired and which are spared, depending on the site(s) and kind(s) of brain damage. As well as studying learning and memory in human subjects, investigators in this field also use many species of animal subjects because of particular advantages of those species for investigating certain aspects of the mechanisms of learning and memory. These species include the familiar laboratory rats and mice, as well as nonhuman primates, but also include birds, such as chicks and pigeons, and invertebrates, such as the sea hare (*Aplysia*), fruitflies (*Drosophila*), and the millimeter-long roundworm (*C. elegans*). Techniques used, depending on the particular question being studied, include case studies of brain-injured patients, experiments involving stimulation or inactivation of brain regions, direct or indirect tests of memory, metabolic or electrophysiological measures of neural activity, neurochemical analyses of samples of neural tissue, and administration of chemical or pharmacological agents, either systemically or to specific sites within the nervous system.

Before starting to present this research, let me state a disclaimer about the role of biological psychology (or physiological psychology) in this field. This chapter presents mainly research done by psychologists because one of the main purposes of this book is to provide information about the kinds of research that psychologists do, but there is no intention to imply that the field of mechanisms of learning and memory is the exclusive domain of psychologists. It should be clear that although psychologists were the first to state many of the questions in this field, research on these topics is being done by a wide variety of neuroscientists, including neuroanatomists, neurochemists, and neurophysiologists. On many of these topics, psychologists are collaborating with other neuroscientists. In many cases, psychologists are using techniques borrowed from other neuroscience disciplines. The study of neural mechanisms of learning and memory is an interdisciplinary field in which, for over a century, many psychologists have played active roles.

# A Little History

Research by psychologists on the neural bases of learning and memory goes back at least to the 1880s. In 1881, Ribot issued his classic book *Les Maladies de la Mémoire* (see also the translation, *Diseases of Memory*, 1882). In that book, Ribot reviewed impairments of memory, drawing upon published sources and using the pathological cases to illuminate the basic processes of memory. Rereading his book today, one is struck by the many ways in which he anticipated the cognitive revolution. For example, Ribot emphasized memory as an active process, and he stressed the necessity of considering different kinds of memory. He regretted the fact that it was not possible to measure each kind to compare them; one could only estimate their relative strengths (Ribot, 1881, p. 110). And, as mentioned earlier, he stated the law that recent memories are more subject to impairment than are older memories—a formulation that is now called Ribot's Law.

Following Ribot's work, the Russian physician S. S. Korsakoff published an important paper in 1889 describing a form of amnesic syndrome that now bears his name. This is a kind of amnesia that is often associated with alcoholism. People suffering from Korsakoff's syndrome fail to recall many items or events of the past; if such an item is presented to them, or if they happen to recall it, they do not recognize it as familiar. Korsakoff's syndrome patients frequently deny that anything is wrong with them. They often show disorientation for time and place, and they may "confabulate," that is, fill a gap in memory with a falsification or a mislocated memory that they accept as correct.

Ribot's regret that it was not possible to measure memory was soon allayed when the German psychologist Hermann Ebbinghaus announced in 1885 his discovery of how such measurements can be done with verbal material. (Ebbinghaus's trailblazing work is reviewed briefly in Chapter 3, so it will not be taken up further here.) Once Ebbinghaus showed how learning and memory can be measured, experimental studies of learning and memory became a major field of psychological research.

In his monumental textbook of 1890, *Principles of Psychology*, William James did not yet have much experimental work on learning and memory to report, although he paid tribute to Ebbinghaus for being able to test experimentally between two opposed hypotheses and demonstrate that in learning a list of items, associations are formed not only between adjacent items, but also between nonadjacent items. James distinguished between "primary memory," now called "short-term memory," and "secondary memory," similar to what is now called "long-term memory," and I will later discuss the different neural mechanisms involved in these two kinds of memory. In addition to his chapter on memory, James also had in another part of his book a chapter on habit, which he obviously considered quite different from memory; this distinction foreshadowed the discovery of two different brain regions involved, respectively, in representational memory (or "declarative" memory) and habit (also called "procedural" or "nondeclarative" memory).

In 1900, Mueller and Pilzecker put forward the hypothesis, based on their research on verbal learning, that memory storage develops gradually after material is first acquired. Their perseveration–consolidation hypothesis has had a long influence.

Research on learning and memory was extended to animal subjects independently by the psychologist Edward L. Thorndike and the physiologist Ivan P. Pavlov. Thorndike demonstrated in his doctoral thesis (1898) how learning and memory can be measured in animal subjects, using cats, dogs, and chicks. Pavlov began systematic experiments on conditioning in dogs after 1900 and soon began to publish on this topic (Gantt, 1959, p. 169).

In 1902, American psychologist Shepard I. Franz opened a further line in this research: He sought to determine sites of learning in the brain by combining Thorndike's methods of training and testing with the technique of localized brain lesions. Franz later recruited Karl S. Lashley, and through Lashley many others, to productive careers of research on this problem.

# Neural Mechanisms of Different Categories of Learning and Memory

In this section, I will discuss research that indicates that different parts of the brain perform different kinds of memory functions. Research on this topic provided strong incentives to classify different types of memory. Research with human subjects on declarative versus nondeclarative memories is discussed in Chapter 3 (see p. 86); human research on short-term versus long-term memories is reviewed on pp. 79–85.

## Declarative Versus Nondeclarative Memories
### The Surprising Case of H. M.

Reports of a patient who appeared to lose his ability to form new memories after a brain operation have engendered much research and much controversy ever since the first account was published in 1957 by neurosurgeon W. B. Scoville and Canadian psychologist Brenda Milner. This patient is known by his initials, H. M. He had suffered from epilepsy since childhood, and unlike most people with epilepsy, his seizures could not be controlled by medication. His condition became progressively worse, and he had to stop work at the age of 27. The symptoms indicated that the neurological origins of the seizures were in the medial basal regions of both temporal lobes, so in

NEURAL BASES OF LEARNING AND MEMORY

1953 the neurosurgeon removed tissue in this region bilaterally, including much of the hippocampus. Similar operations had previously been performed without harmful effects, although less tissue had been removed than in this case. The operation quelled the seizures, but after recovery H. M. appeared to be unable to recall new material for more than brief periods. Most of his old memories were intact, although there was amnesia for most events that had occurred during the three years before the operation.

The following is one example of H. M.'s inability to learn new information, even with repeated practice. Six months after the operation, H. M.'s family moved to another house on the same street; when H. M. went out, he could not remember the new house and kept returning to the old one. Also, H. M. cannot remember the names or faces of people he met after the operation, although he recognizes people he knew before the operation. He retains a new fact only briefly; as soon as a distraction occurs, the newly acquired information vanishes. H. M. converses easily, and his IQ remains above average: 118 when tested in 1962 and in 1977, but declining to 108 in 1983 (Corkin, 1984).

H. M. recognizes that something is wrong with him because he has no memories of the last several years or even of what he does earlier in the same day. His description of this strange state of isolation from his own past is poignant:

> Every day is alone in itself, whatever enjoyment I've had, and whatever sorrow I've had. . . . Right now, I'm wondering, have I done or said anything amiss? You see, at this moment everything looks clear to me, but what happened just before? That's what worries me. It's like waking from a dream. I just don't remember. (Milner, 1970, p. 37)

After publication of the case of H. M., similar cases were reported that resulted not from brain surgery but from disease, and similar cases have undoubtedly occurred in the past but without being reported. Occasionally, the herpes simplex virus attacks the brain and destroys tissue in the medial temporal lobe, and this destruction can produce a severe failure to form new long-term memories, although acquisition of short-term memories is normal. Episodes of anoxia have been reported to have similar effects on the hippocampus and on memory. Rupture of the anterior cerebral arteries can also damage basal forebrain regions and cause amnesia.

### Research Inspired by "Hippocampal Amnesia"

H. M.'s memory deficit was ascribed by the investigators who studied his case to bilateral destruction of much of the hippocampus. They reached this conclusion because some earlier surgical cases that had not shown memory impairment had involved less damage to the hippocampus, although they shared with H. M. damage to more anterior structures, including the amygdala. Soon after publication of the case of H. M., investigators began to remove the hippocampus in experimental animals to try to define precisely the region involved, and then to study the mechanisms of formation of long-term memories. However, although some kinds of memories were impaired—especially spatial ones—generalized impairments of memory formation were not found in rats or monkeys after bilateral destruction of the hippocampus (Isaacson, 1972). Attempts to account for the discrepancy between the human cases of amnesia and the animal experiments focused on the kind of memory test used and on the particular brain structure(s) involved. Both lines of research proved productive.

What kinds of memory ability are lost in human amnesia, and what kinds of memory ability are retained? Further work with H. M. led to a progressive understanding of his impairment. An early observation led to the hypothesis that his memory impairment might be mainly restricted to verbal material and might not hold for motor learning; this case would not show up in animal subjects. This observation was made by Milner (1965), who presented a mirror-tracing task to H. M. (Figure 1). In this test, the subject looks at a geometrical figure and his hand in a mirror and tries to stay inside the double boundaries of the figure while tracing its contours with a pencil. At first, a person makes many mistakes because movements appear to be "backwards," but H. M., like most subjects, showed considerable improvement during a session of 10 trials. The next day, Milner presented the mirror-tracing task again. H. M. said he had no memory of it, even though he had helped set up the apparatus, but his performance was much better at the outset than on the first day. Over three successive days of testing, H. M. showed no sign of recognizing the test, but his performance demonstrated that he retained the improvement of the previous days. If an animal subject showed similar improvement of performance, we would have no doubt about its memory. We usually do not try to test animals for recognition memory, but this can be done, as discussed later.

Further findings indicated that the memory problems of H. M. and similar patients cannot be solely attributed to verbal materials. For one thing, such patients also have difficulty in reproducing or recognizing pictures and spatial designs that are not recalled in verbal terms. For another, although these patients have difficulty learning the specific content of verbal material, they can learn procedural or rule-based information about verbal material (Cohen & Squire, 1980).

Performance of H. M. on mirror-tracing task

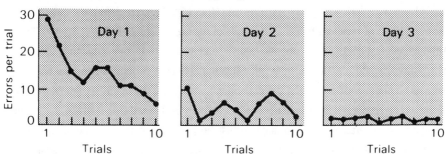

**FIGURE 1**   The mirror-tracing task, and learning by H.M. Top: H.M. attempts to trace the outline of a form, keeping his pencil within the double boundary, while observing the form and his hand in a mirror. A barrier prevents direct observation of hand and form. Bottom: The performance of H. M. over three successive days. The record shows both improvement within days (short-term memory) and retention from one day to another (long-term memory). (Data reproduced by permission from Milner, 1965; figure reproduced by permission from Rosenzweig & Leiman, 1989, p. 651.)

A brief look at this research will make the distinction clear. Subjects are asked to read successive sets of three moderately long words printed mirror-reversed, like the following:

əsoibnɒɹǫ　　　　　　  ƨuoiɔiɹqɒɔ　　　　　　  bəlǫǫɒɹbəd

The task is difficult, but subjects improve markedly with practice. No motor skill is involved but rather the ability to deal with abstract rules or procedures. If some words are used repeatedly in the training, normal subjects come to recognize them and to read them mirror-reversed more easily than words that have not been presented reversed. Patients with amnesia caused by brain injuries learn the skill of mirror reading well, so they are not handicapped in dealing with this verbal material, but they show significantly less learning of specific words than do normal subjects, and they do not recognize the task from one occasion to another. Thus, the important distinction is probably not between motor and verbal performances but between habits or rule-based information, on the one hand, and recognition memory or data-based information, on the other. In other terms, the patients learned *how*, but they did not learn *what*.

Even with verbal material, some investigators have found that amnesic patients show evidence of recall with special methods of testing (Warrington & Weiskrantz, 1968). Although confirming that the patients seemed to be unable to learn even simple lists of words after several repetitions, these investigators noticed a curious fact: As the patients were given one list after another, the experimenters began to recognize as familiar many of the wrong responses their patients produced. Analysis showed that many of the wrong responses were actually words from earlier lists in the experiment. Thus, memories for the words were being stored by the patients but were emerging at the wrong time. Further experiments showed that providing cues at the time of recall could substantially improve the performance of amnesic patients (Weiskrantz & Warrington, 1975). Weiskrantz and Warrington took this as evidence that the defect was more in retrieval than in the storage of memory and that amnesic subjects could be aided to overcome their deficits, at least in part. However, Graf, Squire, & Mandler (1984) showed that when normal subjects were instructed to use the cues to remember recently presented words, they always performed better than amnesic subjects. On the basis of further research, one can now generalize that the degree of deficit is a function of the nature of the method of testing for memory, so that with the same amnesic subjects, one can use a variety of tests, from those that reveal no deficit to tests that demonstrate total inability (Richardson-Klavehn & Bjork, 1988).

### The Impairment of Memory in Animals With Lesions of the Medial Temporal Lobe

At the same time that some investigators were finding that brain damage in human patients can impair some kinds of memory performance while leaving other kinds intact, other investigators were making similar findings with animal subjects; this allowed researchers to generalize more broadly about the classification of kinds of memory. It also permitted detailed studies of how particular brain regions are involved in memory. Reviewing research in this field, Hirsh (1974, 1980) suggested that normal, adult mammals can use both cognitive, contextual memory and stimulus–response (S–R) associative memory or habit, but mammals whose hippocampus has been destroyed are limited to S–R associations.

Building on the work of Hirsh, Mishkin and his colleagues used the terms *memories* and *habits* to label two mnemonic systems shown in two kinds of tasks with monkeys; these tasks revealed both developmental differences and different effects of brain lesions (Mishkin, Malamut, & Bachevalier, 1984). One of these tasks is called "concurrent learning of pairs of objects"; the other is called "delayed nonmatching to sample." Let us see, with the aid of Figure 2, how each task is performed. In both tasks, on a given trial a monkey is presented with a pair of easily discriminable three-dimensional objects on a special tray. During pretraining the monkey has learned that if it chooses and moves the correct object of the pair, it will find a reward (a raisin or a peanut) in a small well under the object. If it displaces the wrong member of the pair, it finds an empty well and does not receive a reward on that trial, so the monkey tries to learn which object of the pair is correct. Between trials, a screen is lowered between the monkey and the tray so that the monkey cannot see which well is baited for the next trial.

In the concurrent learning problem, indicated in the left half of Figure 2, a set of 20 pairs of objects is presented once a day, one pair at a time. One object in each pair has been chosen arbitrarily to be correct (for example the star in the first trial, as shown by the asterisk); that is, if the monkey displaces that object, it gains a reward. The same set of 20 pairs of objects is presented in the same order each day, but a given object may appear on the right or on the left, so the monkey must learn to respond to the identity of the object, not to its position. To improve its performance, the subject must retain information from one day to the next.

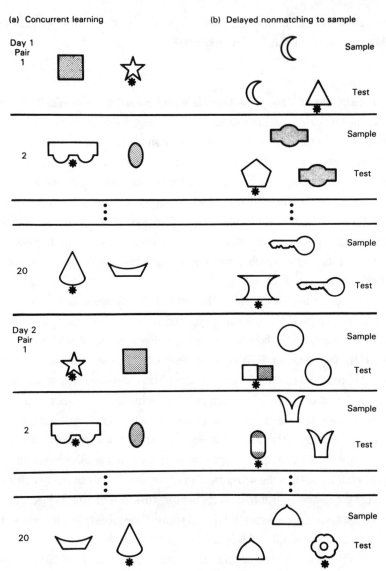

**FIGURE 2** Experimental designs for (a) concurrent discrimination learning and (b) delayed nonmatching to sample. The actual test objects are three-dimensional and more complex than illustrated here. The correct choice in each pair is designated by an asterisk. Note that in concurrent object discrimination (a), the same pairs of objects are presented in the same order each day. In contrast, the delayed nonmatching to sample test (b) uses new pairs of objects each day. (Figure reproduced by permission from Rosenzweig & Leiman, 1989, p. 643.)

In the delayed-nonmatching-to-sample problem, as indicated in the right half of Figure 2, the monkey is shown a sample object on each trial, and then, 10 seconds later, it is presented with a pair of objects, one of which is the same as the sample. The correct object of the pair is the one that does not match the sample (for example, the triangle on the first trial, as marked by the asterisk). As in the other task, the subject has 20 trials per day. In this task, however, each pair of objects is novel; that is, unlike the case of the concurrent learning problem, the objects used one day are not repeated on subsequent days. In this task, the monkey has to remember the sample object for only 10 seconds, although the task can be made more difficult by lengthening the delay between presentation of the sample and the pair of objects.

One of these two tasks turns out to be easy for even 3-month-old monkeys to learn, but the other is not solved with full proficiency before monkeys are 2 years old. Which one is easy for young monkeys to learn, and why? One of these tasks is possible for monkeys that have sustained bilateral lesions of the medial temporal lobe, but the other task is very difficult for such monkeys. Which task can the brain-lesioned monkeys still learn?

In the case of concurrent discrimination learning, monkeys form associations between the appearance of an object and the occurrence of reward. These associations gain in strength through repetition, even though the repetitions occur 24 hours apart. Monkeys can form such associations early in life, just as they can form conditioned responses early in life. They can also form such associations even after surgical removal of medial temporal lobe tissue. On the other hand, in the case of nonmatching to sample, the animal must form a "memory"—a representation of the sample—and then use this memory at the time of the test, deciding which object does not match the representation of the sample. The mature monkey forms this kind of representation rapidly and uses it skillfully, but young monkeys appear to be incapable of the representational aspect of the task. Also, lesions of the medial temporal lobe severely impair the ability of monkeys to perform the nonmatching-to-sample task, especially for delays longer than a few seconds, apparently because the brain-lesioned monkeys cannot form representational memories.

The contrast between the results of the two tasks is particularly important for the interpretation of the findings. Suppose we knew only that temporal lobe lesions impaired performance on the nonmatching-to-sample test. Then we could not be sure whether the brain lesions interfered with some aspect of the task other than memory: for example, the ability of monkeys to perceive and discriminate the objects, or the motivation of the monkeys to perform for rewards. But the excellent performance of brain-lesioned monkeys on the object-discrimination task demonstrates that medial temporal lobe lesions do not impair either object discrimination or motivation to perform, so the dissociation between effects on the two tasks strengthens the interpretation that lesions of the medial temporal lobe impair the ability to form representational memories. Much current research in memory, with both human and animal subjects, uses batteries of carefully chosen tasks to characterize performance and ability more completely than any single task could do (Richardson-Klavehn & Bjork, 1988).

Thus, results of more discriminating tests with amnesic patients and with animal subjects are converging. In both amnesic patients and animals with medial temporal lobe lesions, the formation of representational memories (also called *declarative memories*) is severely impaired, whereas the formation of other kinds of memories (called *habits*, or *procedural* or *nondeclarative memories*) remains essentially normal.

It should be noted that some observations have indicated that the object discrimination task may require more than nondeclarative memory. Human patients with severe temporal lobe amnesia cannot learn new object discriminations, and some investigators have found that monkeys with the hippocampal formation ablated cannot form such discriminations (Zola-Morgan, Squire, & Amaral, 1989). It is not yet clear whether the difference between the results of Mishkin et al. (1984) and those of Zola-Morgan et al. (1989) in this regard can be attributed to differences in the extent of the brain lesions, to differences in training and testing, or to other factors.

If representational or declarative memory is particularly related to processing in the hippocampus, can habits, or nondeclarative memories, be shown to depend on some other brain region or regions? Recently, a team of Canadian psychologists investigated this question by studying the performance of rats on two different tasks in the radial maze and making bilateral brain lesions either in an output tract from the hippocampus (the fimbria-fornix) or in the caudate nucleus (Packard, Hirsh, & White, 1989). On a task designed to require representational memory (the standard radial maze paradigm), lesions of the fimbria-fornix impaired performance, whereas lesions of the caudate nucleus did not. Another task was designed in which a single stimulus was consistently paired with the correct response; on this test, which involved habit formation, lesions of the fimbria-fornix did not impair performance, but lesions of the caudate did. Thus, the results demonstrated what is called a "double dissociation" of memory systems that involve the hippocampus and the caudate nucleus: Each brain region is required for one memory system but not for the other. Similar results showing the importance of the caudate nucleus for the formation of visual habits in monkeys have been reported by Wang, Aigner, and Mishkin (1990).

## Brain Sites in Amnesia

At the same time that some investigators were trying to resolve the apparent discrepancy between human patients and animal subjects by studying which abilities are lost and which are spared in amnesia, others were taking a different tack: They were critically examining whether the site of the lesion responsible for memory deficits like those of H. M. is in fact the hippocampus or some other structure in the limbic system. Some were also asking whether all cases of human amnesia involve the same brain site(s).

Within the temporal lobe, other sites besides the hippocampus have been implicated in memory formation. One is the temporal stem, the large fiber tract that carries the afferent and efferent connections of the temporal cortex and the amygdala but not of the hippocampus. Horel (1978) showed that transecting the temporal stem without harming the hippocampus severely impaired visual discrimination learning, and he proposed that the temporal stem must be intact if learning and memory storage are to occur. Another possible site is the amygdala (or amygdaloid complex), a body that lies within the temporal lobe just anterior to the hippocampus and that bridges between temporal lobe cortex and other brain structures, as does the hippocampus. Mishkin (1978) proposed that both the amygdala and the hippocampus must be destroyed in order to damage severely the capacity to form memories. To test between the hypotheses of Horel and of Mishkin, an experiment was designed with two kinds of surgical intervention and two tasks: The temporal stem was transected bilaterally in some monkeys, whereas both the amygdala and hippocampus were ablated bilaterally in others. The animals were tested both on a visual discrimination task and on delayed nonmatching to sample. The results provided another demonstration of double dissociation: Transection of the temporal stem impaired visual discrimination but did not affect ability on the memory task. On the contrary, combined ablation of the amygdala and hippocampus left visual discrimination unaffected but severely impaired the formation of memory (Zola-Morgan, Squire, & Mishkin, 1982). Further research has attempted to test whether both the amygdala and the hippocampus must be destroyed to impair severely the ability to form memories, or whether destruction of the hippocampus alone is sufficient to produce the amnesic syndrome. This question has not yet been resolved to the satisfaction of all investigators, and I will not go farther into it here; for additional review, see Rosenzweig and Leiman (1989, pp. 655–660).

A recent study used the noninvasive techniques of magnetic resonance imaging to obtain neuroanatomical information about two groups of patients with amnesia, in comparison with normal controls (Squire, Amaral, & Press, 1990). One group consisted of four patients with alcoholic Korsakoff's syndrome; they showed abnormally small mammillary nuclei that were barely detectable in most cases, but their temporal lobes, hippocampal formations, and parahippocampal gyri were of normal size. In contrast, a group of four non-Korsakoff amnesic patients showed a marked reduction in size of the hippocampal formation; the mammillary nuclei were significantly reduced in two of these patients but normal in the other two. The temporal lobe and parahippocampal gyri were of normal size. Thus, the neuroimaging technique can distinguish between patients with diencephalic and temporal lobe amnesias. The degree of reduction of the mammillary bodies or the hippocampal formation in the individual patients corresponded in general to the severity of their memory impairment as measured by the investigators, who used a battery of tests of memory and intelligence. Thus, quantitative neuroanatomical information can be related to quantitative scores of memory performance in living patients.

Although the hippocampus appears to be important to accomplish storage of long-term representational memories, it is clear that the hippocampus is not the site of storage. This is shown by cases such as H. M. because, although they are greatly impaired in storing new long-term representational memories, their preoperative memories are largely intact. This and other evidence has led some investigators to conclude that the earlier formed memories must be stored elsewhere in the brain, although other researchers (as in Chapter 3) prefer not to consider memory in spatial terms. Studies with both animal subjects and human patients indicate to neuroscientific investigators that regions of the cerebral cortex are sites of memory storage in mammals (Squire, 1987, pp. 114–123). In a recent study in Mishkin's laboratory, monkeys with bilateral lesions of the inferior temporal cortex (area TE) were impaired in both one-trial visual recognition memory and visual habits (object discrimination; Wang et al., 1990).

A patient who has been intensively studied in this regard cannot recall anything that has ever happened to him. This patient, known by his initials, K. C., has been studied by Canadian psychologist Endel Tulving and his collaborators (Tulving, 1989; Tulving, Hayman, & Macdonald, 1991; Tulving, Schacter, McLachlan, & Moscovitch, 1988). K. C. had a motorcycle accident that caused widespread damage to the cerebral cortex, especially in the left frontal-parietal and right parietal-occipital regions. He recovered general health and now seems normal in most ways, but he has no memories about his past, although he retains much knowledge from past learning. Thus, he converses easily and plays a good game of chess, but he cannot remember when he learned to play chess or from whom. He displays what is called "semantic," or general, impersonal knowledge but fails to show any "episodic," or personal, knowledge. Unlike H. M., whose past knowledge, both episodic and semantic, is largely intact, K. C. has lost his episodic knowledge, or at least his ability to access it, and he cannot acquire any new episodic knowledge, although he can acquire new semantic memories. Even though most current research on mechanisms of memory is experimental in nature, studies of exceptional cases such as K. C. are of obvious importance in testing and extending our concepts.

### Localizing Different Memory Processes in the Intact, Normal Human Brain

As noted in Chapter 3, Tulving (1992) has proposed that episodic memory is the latest of the memory systems to develop and that it depends on semantic memory. There is also some evidence that episodic memory is especially likely to be impaired by damage to the frontal lobes. Because it would be valuable to study in intact normal brains whether activity of particular brain regions shows specific associations with particular memory systems, Tulving undertook a study with Swedish neurophysiologists to find whether metabolic activity of different cerebral cortical regions in normal subjects differed according to whether they were recalling episodic or semantic memories (Tulving, 1989). The technique used to measure regional cerebral blood flow involved detecting very low levels of radioactivity from intravenously injected $^{195m}$gold. With this technique, a map of cortical blood flow could be obtained in less than 3 seconds—much greater temporal resolution than with previous techniques. Results are still preliminary, and not all subjects showed regional differences between retrieval of episodic and semantic memories, but a pattern did emerge in several subjects: Episodic retrieval was usually accompanied by a relatively greater degree of activation of the anterior regions of the cortex, and semantic retrieval was accompanied by a relatively greater degree of activation of the posterior regions. Further work of this sort may help to confirm a differential anatomical substrate for episodic and semantic memories, just as the work reported earlier showed that the hippocampus is necessary to accomplish storage of declarative but not of nondeclarative (procedural) memories. Finding such neuroanatomical correlates offers further support for the categorization of memory systems that emerged from behavioral psychological techniques.

This mutually supportive research in cognitive and in biological psychology offers testimony to the need for technological resources for such research. It was with special regard to research of this sort that a committee of the National Research Council of the

United States (Gerstein, Luce, Smelser, & Sperlich, 1988) made the following statement: "Technological resources available to most researchers in the behavioral and social sciences have lagged badly behind needs except at a few sites. The lag has been particularly acute with respect to neuroimaging and the more diversified and specialized laboratory equipment used in research on behavior, as well as the recent upgrading of standards for animal care" (p. 247).

## Short-Term Versus Long-Term Storage

The concept of memory stores that differ in duration has a relatively long history, and it continues to stimulate investigation in both cognitive psychology (see Chapter 3) and biological psychology, although there has often been a lack of communication between researchers in these two fields. Although short-term memory was first named by Broadbent in 1958, as noted in Chapter 3, the concept had already been proposed by James in 1890, as mentioned earlier, and it was espoused by other psychologists in the 19th century. Separate mechanisms for short- and long-term stores were proposed by Mueller and Pilzecker (1900) in their perseveration–consolidation hypothesis. They suggested that the neural activity engendered during learning perseverates and that this leads to the establishment of a long-lasting memory trace. McDougall, in a 1901 review of Mueller and Pilzecker's monograph, noted that their hypothesis could account for retrograde amnesia caused by a blow to the head: The interruption of perseverating neural activity could prevent consolidation of recently acquired information. After a period of popularity, the concept of the consolidation of memory as an explanation for changes in memory strength over time was largely replaced by the concept of interference by interpolated learning (see, for example, the historical review by Keppel, 1984).

The consolidation hypothesis surged back into popularity in the 1940s, at least among biological psychologists, as the result of both experimental and theoretical developments. The experimental work was stimulated by the introduction of electroshock therapy in 1937, because many practitioners observed that electroconvulsive shock led to amnesia for events immediately preceding the treatment and sometimes for even longer periods. Psychologist Carl Duncan (1949) then found that he could impair the formation of memory in laboratory rats by giving them cerebral electroshocks following learning trials; the impairment was more severe the closer the shock followed the learning trial. Duncan suggested that his results could be explained better by consolidation theory than by the interference of interpolated learning. The theoretical contributions were made by psychologist Donald O. Hebb (1949) and neurophysiologist Ralph W. Gerard (1949). Independently of each other, both proposed "dual trace" hypotheses that essentially restated the perseveration–consolidation hypothesis in neural terms, although neither mentioned Mueller and Pilzecker. The following is Hebb's statement, the better known of the two: "To account for the permanence [of some memories], a structural change is necessary, but a structural change would require an appreciable time. ... A reverberatory trace might ... carry the memory until the growth change is made ..." (Hebb, 1949, p. 62). In the same passage, Hebb contrasted "a transient, unstable reverberatory trace" with a "more permanent structural change."

Hebb hypothesized a kind of modifiable synapse that could underlie long-lasting memory, and research on the "Hebbian synapse" continues in neuroscience to this day: "When an axon of cell A is near enough to excite cell B and repeatedly or persistently takes part in firing it, some growth process or metabolic change takes place in one or both cells such that A's efficiency, as one of the cells firing B, is increased" (Hebb, 1949, p. 62).

Much research has been done to try to find the neural processes that underlie transient, unstable short-term memory (STM) and those that underlie long-term memory (LTM). This is a large field of research, so only a few points can be reviewed here. As early as 1950, Katz and Halstead suggested that the formation of LTM required the synthesis of proteins. Support for this hypothesis came in the 1960s both from experiments showing that learning leads to the synthesis of protein in the brain and from experiments showing that inhibition of protein synthesis in the nervous system prevents formation of long-term memory. The discovery that differential learning leads to differences in protein synthesis in the cerebral cortex came from experiments in which rats were housed in enriched standard colonies or impoverished laboratory environments (Bennett, Diamond, Krech, & Rosenzweig, 1964; Rosenzweig, Krech, Bennett, & Diamond, 1962). These experiments, in turn, came from the unexpected finding that rats tested with more or less difficult problem-solving tests developed significant differences in the enzyme cholinesterase in the cerebral cortex (Rosenzweig, Krech, & Bennett, 1961). Control experiments showed that the cerebral differences were induced by differential experience and did not reflect other factors such as differences in nutrition, handling, or rate of maturation. Further analyses revealed that the cortical effects caused by differential experience included not only regional differences in protein and in the thickness of the cortex, but also differences in the anatomy of neurons—size of the cell body and nucleus, branching patterns of dendrites, the numbers of dendritic spines and synapses—and in the numbers of glial cells (e.g., Bennett et al., 1964; Rosenzweig, 1984). Experiments with formal training in rats also produced such cerebral effects (Bennett, Rosenzweig, Morimoto, & Hebert, 1979; Chang & Greenough, 1982). More generally, enriched experience was found to promote full development of brain and of behavior; conversely, impoverished experience stunted development of both brain and behavior. Much of the research on the effects of differential experience on the brain and behavior is reviewed and summarized in Renner and Rosenzweig (1987).

In the 1960s, research with animal subjects using inhibitors of protein synthesis gave some support to the hypothesis of Katz and Halstead, but toxicity of the inhibitors complicated interpretation of the results. These problems were largely overcome when Bennett, Orme, & Hebert (1972) introduced the use of anisomycin, a relatively nontoxic agent, as the protein synthesis inhibitor in this research. (It is true that in the previous year Schwartz, Castelluci, & Kandel, 1971, had shown that anisomycin did not prevent an electrophysiological correlate of short-term habituation or sensitization in an isolated ganglion of *Aplysia*, but they did not show that anisomycin can prevent a correlate of formation of LTM, nor did they deal with associative memory.) Using anisomycin in behavioral–pharmacological experiments with mice, Flood, Bennett, Rosenzweig, and their collaborators (e.g., Flood, Bennett, Orme, & Rosenzweig, 1975; Flood, Bennett, Rosenzweig, & Orme, 1972, 1973; Rosenzweig & Bennett, 1984a, 1984b) provided evidence that protein synthesis must occur in a narrow time window following training if LTM is to be formed. They suggested (Rosenzweig & Bennett, 1984a, 1984b) that proteins might be required, at least in part, for the changes seen in synaptic number and structure as a result of differential experience (Diamond, Lindner, Johnson, Bennett, & Rosenzweig, 1975) or of formal training (Chang & Greenough, 1982). Control experiments showed that protein synthesis inhibition affected formation of LTM as such and that the effects could not be attributed to influences on such factors as perception, motivation, learning, and motor performance.

Meanwhile, attention was also being given to the neurochemical bases of the earlier stage or stages of memory formation. Some investigators have used the term *short-term memory* to designate all of the storage that precedes LTM, and thus they have used "short-term" for phenomena that last much longer than the STM found in cognitive experiments with human subjects. In a review, Rigter and van Riezen (1978) noted, "Whereas estimates of human STM rarely go beyond 60 sec, animal data have been interpreted to reflect durations of STM in the order of minutes or even hours" (p. 677). This continues to be the case; for example, Kandel, Schacher, Castellucci, and Goelet (1987) wrote that in *Aplysia*, "A single training trial produces short-term sensitization that lasts from minutes to hours" (p. 17) and that long-term memory is "memory that lasts more than one day" (p. 35). Squire (1987) admits that most biological psychologists and other neuroscientists use "short-term" in a different way from cognitive psychologists, but this does not trouble him: "Their apparent contradiction arises because in each case a different level of analysis is used to explain memory" (p. 148). However, some other investigators hope to find a closer correspondence between cognitive phenomena and their biological correlates. This is one of the reasons that some investigators consider the possibility that one or more intermediate stages occur between STM and LTM; in that case, STM would not have to last until LTM appears, because the intermediate stage(s) could hold the memory during this period. The model of McGaugh (1968), for example, includes a brief sensory buffer, then short-term, intermediate-term, and long-term stages (see Figure 3). Gibbs and Ng (e.g., Gibbs & Ng, 1977; Ng & Gibbs, 1991) and Rosenzweig, Bennett, and their collaborators (e.g., Rosenzweig et al., 1991) are among those who have proposed

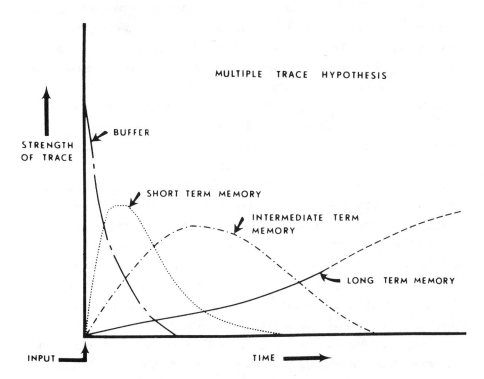

**FIGURE 3** Diagram of a multiple-trace hypothesis of memory formation. (Reproduced by permission from McGaugh, 1968, p. 23.)

different neurochemical mechanisms for short-term and intermediate-term stages of memory formation. So far, the proposal by biological psychologists of an intermediate-term memory (ITM) store has not aroused any response from investigators of human memory.

## What Behavioral Evidence Exists for Intermediate-Term Memory?

Gibbs and Ng (1984), using one-trial peck-avoidance learning in the chick, reported that measures of recall at various time intervals after training showed sharp dips at 15 min and 60 min. They suggested that the first of these may represent the cross-over point between STM and ITM processes, as in Figure 3; the second dip would represent the cross-over between ITM and LTM processes. Other laboratories have not reported these sharp dips in response, and doubts have been raised about them (Roberts, 1987; see also the rejoinder by Ng and Gibbs, 1987).

We have recently obtained information pertaining to the possibility that more than one stage of memory formation precedes LTM (Lee, Murphy, Bennett, & Rosenzweig, 1990; Rosenzweig, 1990; Rosenzweig et al., 1991; Rosenzweig, Lee, Means, Bennett, & Martinez, 1989). These results came from experiments in which we wanted to give chicks weaker training than usual in order to measure the enhancement of learning by various agents. With weaker training, the curve of the strength of memory versus time after training (see Figure 4) shows several components and resembles to some extent McGaugh's (1968) hypothetical curves of memory traces that we saw in Figure 3. Our data show cusps at about 1 min, 15 min, and 60 min, the last two being close to the times of the dips reported by Gibbs and Ng (1984). It seems possible that the weaker training allows the components and the transitions between stages to appear more clearly than with stronger training, where behavior is pushed toward the ceiling at all time points. It should be pointed out that these stages may take more time to occur in chicks than in mammals; in earlier work (Mizumori, Rosenzweig, & Bennett, 1985), we found that the agents that had been found to affect the strength of memory formation in the chick were also effective in laboratory rats. However, using agents that impair the formation of LTM in the chick caused an earlier decline in memory in the rat than in the chick, and the agents that impair formation of STM and ITM in the chick caused such rapid decline of memory in the rat that STM and ITM functions could not be separated.

Many of the processes that lead up to stimulus-induced protein synthesis in neurons appear to be involved in the formation of STM or ITM. Interfering with these processes causes amnesia to begin at precise times, whereas promoting them can enhance memory formation. Experiments in our laboratory with chicks indicate that the following

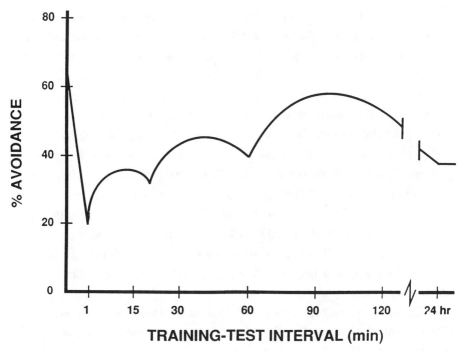

**FIGURE 4**  Smoothed curve of strength of memory versus time after relatively weak peck-avoidance training in the chick. There are dips in memory strength at about the following times: (a) 30 sec – 1 min, (b) 15–20 min, and (c) 60 min.

processes are among those involved in the formation of STM: the stimulation of receptors for neurotransmitters, including the NMDA receptor, and receptors for acetylcholine, glutamate, and opioids; and the influx of calcium ions into the neuron. Among the processes involved in the formation of ITM is the activation of calcium-modulated kinase (calmodulin, or CAM) and of second messengers including adenylate cyclase and diacylglycerol. Protein kinase C (PKC) is involved in the formation of LTM. The kinases phosphorylate and thereby activate transcription factors that bind to specific sequences of DNA in the nucleus. RNA polymerase can then bind to a promotor site and begin to transcribe some early-immediate genes such as c-fos and c-jun. Anokhin and Rose (1991) have recently reported that peck-avoidance training in the chick leads to a significant increase in the concentration of c-fos and c-jun in the chick forebrain. Thus, experiments not only are tracing the neurochemical processes that lead to memory formation but can assign them to successive stages of memory formation.

Some investigators have proposed temporal stages in the formation of long-term potentiation (LTP). (LTP is a phenomenon in which the magnitude of the neural response to a stimulus is significantly increased after the neural tissue has been subjected to one or more brief strains of relatively high-frequency stimulation; the potentiation can last for hours or days. LTP is considered by many neuroscientists as a model system for investigation of the neural mechanisms of learning and memory; see, for example, the review of LTP by Teyler and DiScenna, 1987.) In a recent review of neurochemical mechanisms of LTP, psychologists Colley and Routtenberg (in press) located on a time scale a number of presynaptic and postsynaptic neural processes that appear to be important in the initiation and maintenance of LTP. Many processes are shown by Colley and Routtenberg as occurring within the first minute or so after the stimulation that induces LTP; other processes, within the first 5 minutes; and still others, within the first 30 minutes or so. It is noteworthy that several of these processes are ones that have been found to be important in stages of memory formation in the chick, and their locations on the time scale are similar in both cases.

Knowledge of both behavioral and neurochemical evidence for ITM, as well as for STM and LTM, may lead cognitive psychologists and clinical neuropsychologists to look for evidence of an ITM stage in their experiments and observations.

## Tests of Ribot's Law

On the basis of his penetrating analysis of published cases of amnesia, French psychologist Théodule Ribot (1881) concluded that the loss of memory caused by disease or injury to the brain follows a law that he called the law of regression or dissolution of memory: "The amnesia, at first limited to recent facts, spreads to ideas, then to sentiments and affections, and finally to motor acts" (p. 92). This could be taken as a description of the course of destruction of memory in progressive dementia, such as Alzheimer's disease. Ribot further stated the law in the following way:

> The progressive destruction of memory follows a logical course, a law. *It advances progressively from the unstable to the stable.* It begins with recent recollections which, poorly established in the neural elements, and consequently only weakly associated with others, represent organization in the weakest degree. It finishes with sensory, instinctive memory which, established in the organism, having become part of the organism or rather the organism itself, represents organization at its highest degree. From the first

term in the series to the last, the progression of amnesia, governed by natural forces, follows the path of least resistance. (pp. 94–95)

Ribot pointed out that this law is contraintuitive:

It would be natural to believe *a priori* that more recent facts, closer to the present, are clearer and more stable, and that is true in the normal case. But in the case of dementia … nerve cells that are atrophying … can no longer store new impressions. In more precise terms, neither a change in nerve cells nor the formation of new dynamic associations is possible. … But modifications established in the nerve cells years ago … persist. … This explains the paradox of memory that the new dies before the old. (pp. 92–93)

In a review of what has come to be called Ribot's Law, Rozin (1976) cited several kinds of evidence that appear to support Ribot's position. For example, a major survey of cases of head trauma (Russell, 1959) concluded that, in general, the vulnerability of memories depends directly on their nearness to the time of injury; also, recovery proceeds from the past toward the present, as Ribot had claimed. However, Rozin also noted that most of the cases had not been described with precision. Furthermore, "a number of investigators who have spent much time studying amnesic patients are not convinced of the truth of Ribot's law" (Rozin, 1976, p. 21). Rozin also cited an experiment with patients with epilepsy was done by neurosurgeons to find which ones might benefit from excision of an epileptogenic focus (Bickford, Mulder, Dodger, Svien, & Rome, 1958). The physicians stimulated the midtemporal gyrus electrically, 1.5 to 2.0 cm below the surface. In 2 of the 33 patients tested, this treatment caused retrograde amnesia. The extent of the amnesia was measured by the patient's estimate of the time of day and date, knowledge of the name of the president, and so forth. The extent of the retrograde amnesia varied with the duration of the stimulation, beginning with the recent past and extending back in time the longer the stimulation.

The 1970s saw a renewal of work on the problem, using questionnaires to measure recall or recognition of events or faces from different decades of the past (e.g., Warrington & Sanders, 1971; Warrington & Silberstein, 1970). Squire and Slater (1975) designed a questionnaire with multiple-choice questions about American television shows that were shown weekly but that were aired for only one season at different times in the past. Normal subjects showed a gradual decline of memory as the material extended 5 to 10 years in the past, with stable memory performance for items older than this. Most such studies of amnesic patients showed—as predicted by Ribot's Law—that they had significant impairments of recent materials, whereas their earlier memories were similar to those of control subjects.

The questionnaire technique has been used with patients given electroconvulsive shock therapy (ECT; Squire & Cohen, 1979). This experimental approach permitted before-and-after tests and comparable conditions for a number of subjects. After treatment, the ECT patients showed impaired memory for material dating back about three years, but their performance was equal to that of control subjects for earlier material. So here again, the more recent material was more subject to impairment than the material learned earlier. It is worth noting that within "six months after [ECT] treatment, [the patients] perform as well on new learning tests as they performed before treatment and as well as other patients who had not received ECT. However, information acquired during the days and weeks prior to and following ECT may be permanently lost" (Squire, 1986, pp. 311–312).

## Animal Experiments for Direct Tests of Ribot's Law

A problem with all of this research is that one cannot be certain that the materials learned at different times were equivalent in difficulty. To overcome this problem, some investigators have done animal experiments in which they could use equivalent materials learned at different times before the animals sustained brain lesions. The animal experiments also permitted the investigators to be certain that brain damage was comparable from subject to subject. One such experiment was performed recently by Canadian psychologist Gordon Winocur (1990). Winocur had rats acquire a preference for food with one of two flavors (cinnamon or cocoa) by seeing another rat consume it. The rats were then subjected to one of three surgical procedures under anesthesia: electrolytic lesions of the dorsal hippocampus or the dorsomedial thalamus, or a control operation in which holes were drilled into the skull but no electrode was lowered into the brain. The surgery was performed either immediately after the training session or 2, 5, or 10 days later. Ten days postsurgery, the rats were tested by allowing them to eat from containers of cinnamon-flavored and cocoa-flavored food, and the amounts eaten from each container were measured. The control rats showed 83% consumption of the trained flavor if the operation was done immediately following training; this measure of recall fell to 81%, 78%, and 66%, respectively, if the operation followed training by 2, 5, or 10 days. Rats with dorsal hippocampal lesions showed only chance performance—52% and 56% preferences, respectively—if they had been operated on immediately or 2 days posttraining, but their performance did not differ significantly from that of the control animals if the operations followed training by 5 or 10 days. Rats with dorsomedial thalamic lesions showed only chance performance if they had been operated on immediately after training, but performance like that of the controls if the operation had been done at any later interval. It is possible that the trauma associated with the brain operation obliterated representation of very recent experiences in both the hippocampal and thalamic animals operated on immediately after training, but the hippocampal animals clearly showed a temporally graded retrograde amnesia that lasted between 2 and 5 days.

Psychologists Stuart Zola-Morgan and Larry Squire (1990), who have also studied amnesia in human patients, conducted a similar but more extensive experiment with monkeys in which each animal learned equivalent sets of materials at five different periods before surgery. Each monkey learned five sets of 20 object pairs, approximately 16, 12, 8, 4, or 2 weeks before surgery. Then 11 of the monkeys sustained bilateral ablation of the hippocampal formation, including the subicular complex and the entorhinal cortex; there were 7 unoperated controls. Two weeks after surgery, the animals were tested by presentation of a single trial of each of the 100 pairs in a mixed order. The unoperated monkeys exhibited forgetting that increased over time since learning; this was shown by a trend analysis over the five time points. The operated monkeys performed significantly worse than the controls on the object pairs learned either 2 or 4 weeks before surgery (Figure 5); the groups did not differ significantly for objects learned at the other time points. Also, the operated monkeys performed worse on items that had been learned 2 and 4 weeks before operation than on the older items, whereas the control monkeys performed best on the most recent materials.

Thus, at least in the case of destruction of the hippocampus, both animal experiments show that recently learned materials are more impaired by brain lesions than are older materials, although the difference from the forgetting curve of control subjects does not extend back very far in time.

### Reformulation of Ribot's Law

Although the results of the recent animal experiments support Ribot's Law, they indicate that the greater vulnerability is limited to relatively recently learned materials. The gradient may extend farther back for human subjects—a year or two, and even more in severe cases—as is indicated by the results of the ECT experiment and other work with patients. But even so, there is no evidence that of two relatively old memories, the more recent is necessarily the more vulnerable to impairment.

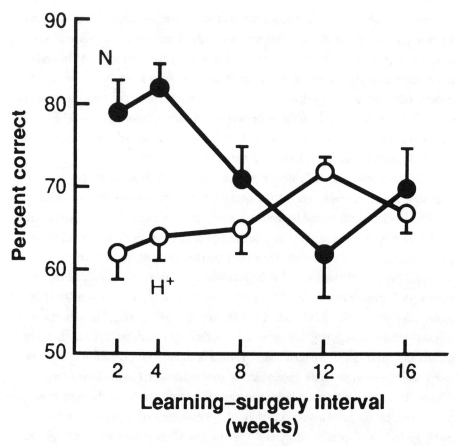

**FIGURE 5** Retention by monkeys of 100 object discrimination problems learned approximately 2, 4, 8, 12, or 16 weeks before hippocampal surgery (20 pairs of objects per time period). Retention was assessed 2 weeks after surgery in animals with hippocampal lesions (H+; open circles) and in unoperated normal controls (N; filled circles). Brackets show standard error of the mean. Differences between H+ and N values are significant only at the 2- and 4-week intervals. (Reproduced by permission from Zola-Morgan & Squire, 1990.)

It is also possible that Ribot's Law applies only to certain sites of damage in the brain. As I noted earlier, the hippocampus is important in aiding the storage of certain kinds of material, but it is not the locus of storage. There is evidence that the dorsomedial thalamus is involved in the processing of information during learning, but perhaps not in the storage of memory (Winocur, 1990). Presumably, much of the storage occurs in the cerebral cortex. In that case, one could hypothesize that destruction of appropriate regions of the cortex would impair more recent and older memories to the same degree; the case of K. C., mentioned earlier, may be an example of this. I do not know of any research that tests whether Ribot's Law is limited to impairments of memory caused by damage to only certain brain structures, and I look forward to tests of this possibility.

In view of the qualifications in the last two paragraphs, perhaps Ribot's Law should be reformulated along the following lines: In cases in which damage to the hippocampal region, and perhaps certain other brain regions, impairs memory for past events, more recently formed memories are more seriously impaired than older memories, at least if both memories were acquired while prolonged consolidation of memory was still in progress.

## Applications of Research on Neural Bases of Learning and Memory

Investigators are not only trying to understand better the neural bases of learning and memory, but they are also attempting in a number of ways to apply this research, and I will mention a few applications briefly here. One is to improve tests, or batteries of tests, in order to diagnose problems of learning and memory and to distinguish better among types of deficits of learning and memory. The recent review of "Measures of Memory" by Richardson-Klavehn and Bjork (1988), mentioned earlier, provides much basic information and theory about testing memory.

Another area of application is the attempt to rehabilitate patients who suffer from various kinds of memory defect, taking into consideration the different types of deficit and the remaining abilities of the patients. An English psychologist who specializes in this area, Barbara Wilson, has written a valuable book, *Rehabilitation of Memory* (1987), that shows the current state of practice and research.

The pharmacological treatment of memory disorders is the goal of much research by psychologists and others in universities, research institutes, and laboratories of pharmacological firms. Basic research on neurochemical mechanisms of memory formation is providing clues for such treatments, and so are clinical findings. One example of this is research with adrenergic drugs used to treat age-related loss of norepinephrine in the cerebral cortex. Psychologist–neuroscientist Patricia Goldman-Rakic found that there is a loss of the neurotransmitter noradrenaline in the cerebral cortex of monkeys with advancing age, and a similar loss has been found in many patients with Alzheimer's disease.

Arnsten and Goldman-Rakic (1985) then found that clonidine, an adrenergic receptor agonist, could improve memory performance in aged monkeys with naturally occurring memory impairment. (Clonidine is best known as a drug used therapeutically to counteract
high blood pressure.) Clonidine has also shown some beneficial effects in patients who
have impairments of memory, but it has drawbacks because the doses that aid memory
also cause sedation and lower blood pressure. Arnsten, Jing, and Goldman-Rakic (1988)
therefore tried a related drug, guanfacine, and found it to improve memory at low doses,
where it does not cause sedation or affect blood pressure. Clinical trials with this drug
are now under way. This is an example of ongoing research in which drugs are screened
with animal subjects to test both main and side effects and to select the most promising
ones for clinical trials.

Research in this field is also being used in various ways to prevent damage to the
nervous system that could impair learning and memory. One obvious way to do this is to
find the brain regions that are important for learning and memory so that they will be
spared in neurosurgical interventions: Once the cause of H. M.'s impairment was found,
no more bilateral operations on the hippocampal region were attempted. Other conditions
can affect the hippocampus; I noted earlier that anoxia can impair the hippocampus,
which is more susceptible to damage from this cause than are other regions of the brain.
Investigators are studying the ways in which anoxia attacks neural tissue and are finding
pharmacological treatments that can prevent this damage if administered promptly
enough.

A kind of prevention that applies to far more people concerns protection from neurotoxins in the environment, such as lead in paints or gasoline. Effects of neurotoxins on
behavior, including effects on learning and memory, provide more sensitive indicators
than do such effects as carcinogenesis and mutagenesis. For that reason, procedures have
been developed to use behavioral tests for the presence of neurotoxins. A recent international psychological symposium on this topic has been published by the U.S. National
Academy of Sciences (*Behavioral Measures of Neurotoxicity;* Russell, Flattau, & Pope,
1990).

A very different kind of treatment to prevent damage to the developing nervous
system is to provide sufficient environmental and social stimulation because, as noted
earlier, insufficient stimulation stunts the development of the brain and of behavior. The
importance of adequate stimulation for child development has been demonstrated by research in several countries, as discussed in Chapter 5, pp. 139–141. Environmental enrichment can also be used to counteract, in part at least, effects of damage to the neocortex

and perhaps to some other parts of the nervous system (Will, Rosenzweig, Bennett, Hebert, & Morimoto, 1977).

At least part of the developmental problems of children born to mothers who abuse drugs is not an inevitable sequel to prenatal exposure to drugs but rather is caused or compounded by inadequate postnatal stimulation and care. A study of such children during their first three years showed that those who received adequate stimulation and good care were able to surmount their early handicap and develop well, as measured by neurological and cognitive tests (Johnson, Glassman, Fiks, & Rosen, 1990). A more direct type of experimental therapy for various kinds of brain disorders consists of grafting nerve cells into the brain. Both successes and failures have been reported with brain grafts. A recent study from the University of Strasbourg reports that neither a brain graft alone nor enriched experience alone was able to improve learning performance in rats with hippocampal lesions, but the combination of a graft and enriched experience proved beneficial (Kelche, Dalrymple-Alford, & Will, 1988). Further unpublished work from the same laboratory indicates that training in various behavioral tests can also modulate positively the effect of a brain graft on learning ability (B. Will, personal communication, February 17, 1992). In other studies of brain grafts, the environment and training have perhaps been uncontrolled variables that have modulated the success or failure of the neural intervention. Both behavioral and somatic interventions affect learning and memory and their neural substrates, and neither the behavioral nor the somatic aspects can be neglected in adequate research and in attempts to apply knowledge about the mechanisms of learning and memory.

# References

Anokhin, K. V., & Rose, S. P. R. (1991). Learning induced increase of immediate early gene messenger RNA in the chick forebrain. *European Journal of Neuroscience, 3*, 162–167.

Arnsten, A. F. T., & Goldman-Rakic, P. S. (1985). Alpha-2 adrenergic mechanisms in prefrontal cortex associated with cognitive decline in aged nonhuman primates. *Science, 230*, 1273–1276.

Arnsten, A. F. T., Jing, X. C., & Goldman-Rakic, P. S. (1988). The alpha-2 adrenergic agonist guanfacine improves memory in aged monkeys without sedative or hypotensive side effects: Evidence for alpha-2 receptor subtypes. *Journal of Neuroscience, 8*, 4287–4298.

Bennett, E. L., Diamond, M. C., Krech, D., & Rosenzweig, M. R. (1964). Chemical and anatomical plasticity in brain. *Science, 146*, 610–619.

Bennett, E. L., Orme, A. E., & Hebert, M. (1972). Cerebral protein synthesis inhibition and amnesia produced by scopolamine, cycloheximide, streptovitacin A, anisomycin and emetine in rat. *Federation Proceedings, 31,* 838.

Bennett, E. L., Rosenzweig, M. R., Morimoto, H., & Hebert, M. (1979). Maze training alters brain weights and cortical RNA/DNA ratios. *Behavioral and Neural Biology, 26,* 1–22.

Bickford, R., Mulder, D. W., Dodge, H. W., Svien, H. J., & Rome, H. P. (1958). Change in memory function produced by electrical stimulation of the temporal lobe in man. *Research Publications of the Association for Research in Nervous and Mental Diseases, 36,* 227–243.

Chang, F.-L., & Greenough, W. T. (1982). Lateralized effects of monocular training on dendritic branching in adult split-brain rats. *Brain Research, 232,* 283–292.

Cohen, N. J., & Squire, L. R. (1980). Preserved learning and retention of pattern analyzing skill in amnesia: Dissociation of knowing how and knowing that. *Science, 210,* 207–209.

Colley, P. A., & Routtenberg, A. (in press). A synaptic dialog model of LTP: Role of pre- and postsynaptic protein kinase C. *Trends in Neuroscience.*

Corkin, S. (1984). Lasting consequences of bilateral medial temporal lobectomy: Clinical course and experimental findings in H. M. *Seminars in Neurology, 4,* 249–259.

Diamond, M. C., Lindner, B., Johnson, R., Bennett, E. L., & Rosenzweig, M. R. (1975). Differences in occipital cortex synapses from environmentally enriched, impoverished, and standard colony rats. *Journal of Neuroscience Research, 1,* 109–119.

Duncan, C. P. (1949). The retroactive effect of electroshock on learning. *Journal of Comparative and Physiological Psychology, 42,* 32–44.

Flood, J. F., Bennett, E. L., Orme, A. E., & Rosenzweig, M. R. (1975). Relation of memory formation to controlled amounts of brain protein synthesis. *Physiology and Behavior, 15,* 97–102.

Flood, J. F., Bennett, E. L., Rosenzweig, M. R., & Orme, A. E. (1972). Influence of training strength on amnesia induced by pretraining injections of cycloheximide. *Physiology and Behavior, 9,* 589–600.

Flood, J. F., Bennett, E. L., Rosenzweig, M. R., & Orme, A. E. (1973). The influence of duration of protein synthesis on memory. *Physiology and Behavior, 10,* 555–562.

Gantt, W. H. (1959). Pavlov. In M. A. B. Brazier (Ed.), *The central nervous system and behavior: Transactions of the first conference* (pp. 163–186). New York: Josiah Macy, Jr. Foundation.

Gerard, R. W. (1949). Physiology and psychiatry. *American Journal of Psychiatry, 105,* 161–173.

Gerstein, D. R., Luce, R. D., Smelser, N. J., & Sperlich, S. (1988). *The behavioral and social sciences: Achievements and opportunities.* Washington, DC: National Academy Press.

Gibbs, M. E., & Ng, K. T. (1977). Psychobiology of memory: Towards a model of memory formation. *Biobehavioral Reviews, 1,* 113–136.

Gibbs, M. E., & Ng, K. T. (1984). Hormonal influence on the duration of short-term and intermediate stages of memory. *Behavioral Brain Research, 11,* 109–116.

Graf, P., Squire, L. R., & Mandler, G. (1984). The information that amnesic patients do not forget. *Journal of Experimental Psychology: Learning, Memory, and Cognition, 11,* 386–396.

Hebb, D. O. (1949). *The organization of behavior.* New York: Wiley.

Hirsh, R. (1974). The hippocampus and contextual retrieval of memory: A theory. *Behavioral Biology, 12,* 421–444.

Hirsh, R. (1980). The hippocampus, conditional operations, and cognition. *Physiological Psychology, 8,* 175–182.

Horel, J. A. (1978). The neuroanatomy of amnesia: A critique of the hippocampal memory hypothesis. *Brain, 101,* 403–445.

Isaacson, R. L. (1972). Hippocampal destruction in man and other animals. *Neuropsychologia, 10,* 47–64.

Johnson, H. L., Glassman, M. B., Fiks, K. B., & Rosen, T. S. (1990). Resilient children: Individual differences in developmental outcome of children born to drug abusers. *Journal of Genetic Psychology, 151,* 523–539.

Kandel, E. R., Schacher, S., Castellucci, V. F., & Goelet, P. (1987). The long and short of memory in *Aplysia:* A molecular perspective. In *Fidia Research Foundation Neuroscience Award lectures: 1986* (pp. 7–47). Padova, Italy: Liviana Press.

Katz, J. J., & Halstead, W. G. (1950). Protein organization and mental function. *Comparative Psychology Monographs, 20,* 1–38.

Kelche, C., Dalrymple-Alford, J. C., & Will, B. (1988). Housing conditions modulate the effects of intracerebral grafts in rats with brain lesions. *Behavioural Brain Research, 28,* 287–295.

Keppel, G. (1984). Consolidation and forgetting theory. In H. Weingartner & E. S. Parker (Eds.), *Memory consolidation: Psychology of cognition.* Hillsdale, NJ: Erlbaum.

Lee, D. W., Murphy, G. G., Bennett, E. L., & Rosenzweig, M. R. (1990). Effects of glutamate, ouabain & anisomycin on memory for weak training in chicks. *Society for Neuroscience Abstracts, 16,* 769.

McGaugh, J. L. (1968). A multi-trace view of memory storage processes. In D. Bovet (Ed.), *Attuali orientamenti della riccerca sull' apprendimento e la memoria* (pp. 13–24). Rome: Academia Nazionale dei Lincei, Quaderno N. 109.

Milner, B. (1965). Memory disturbance after bilateral hippocampal lesions. In P. M. Milner & S. E. Glickman (Eds.), *Cognitive processes and the brain.* Princeton, NJ: Van Nostrand.

Milner, B. (1970). Memory and the medial temporal regions of the brain. In K. H. Pribram & D. E. Broadbent (Eds.), *Biology of memory.* New York: Academic Press.

Mishkin, M. (1978). Memory in monkeys severely impaired by combined but not by separate removal of amygdala and hippocampus. *Nature, 273,* 297–298.

Mishkin, M., Malamut, B., & Bachevalier, J. (1984). Memories and habits: Two neural systems. In G. Lynch, J. L. McGaugh, & N. M. Weinberger (Eds.), *The neurobiology of learning and memory* (pp. 65–77). New York: Guilford Press.

Mizumori, S. J. Y., Rosenzweig, M. R., & Bennett, E. L. (1985). Long-term working memory in the rat: Effects of hippocampally applied anisomycin. *Behavioral Neuroscience, 99,* 220–232.

Mueller, G. E., & Pilzecker, A. (1900). Experimentelle Beiträge zur Lehre vom Gedächtnis. *Zeitschrift für Psychologie und Physiologie des Sinnesorgane, 1,* 1–300.

Ng, K. T., & Gibbs, M. E. (1987). Less-than-expected variability in evidence for three stages in memory formation: A reply. *Behavioral Neuroscience, 101,* 126–130.

Ng, K. T., & Gibbs, M. E. (1991). Stages in memory formation: A review. In R. J. Andrew (Ed.), *Neural and behavioural plasticity: The use of the domestic chick as a model* (pp. 351–369). Oxford, England: Oxford University Press.

Packard, M. G., Hirsh, R., & White, N. M. (1989). Differential effects of fornix and caudate nucleus lesions on two radial maze tasks: Evidence for multiple memory systems. *Journal of Neuroscience, 9,* 1465–1472.

Renner, M. J., & Rosenzweig, M. R. (1987). *Enriched and impoverished environments: Effects on brain and behavior.* New York: Springer-Verlag.

Ribot, T. (1881). *Les maladies de la mémoire.* Paris: F. Alcan.

Ribot, T. (1882). *Diseases of memory.* New York: Appleton. (Reprinted in D. N. Robinson, Ed., 1977, *Significant contributions to the history of psychology, 1750–1920: Series C. Medical psychology, Vol. 1*)

Richardson-Klavehn, A., & Bjork, R. A. (1988). Measures of memory. *Annual Review of Psychology, 30,* 475–543.

Rigter, H., & van Riezen, H. (1978). Hormones and memory. In M. A. Lipton, A. DiMascio, & K. F. Killam (Eds.), *Psychopharmacology: A generation of progress* (pp. 677–689). New York: Raven Press.

Roberts, S. (1987). Less-than-expected variability in evidence for three stages in memory formation. *Behavioral Neuroscience, 101,* 120–125.

Rosenzweig, M. R. (1984). Experience, memory, and the brain. *American Psychologist, 39,* 365–376.

Rosenzweig, M. R. (1990). The chick as a model system for studying neural processes in learning and memory. In L. Erinoff (Ed.), *Neurobiology of drug abuse: Learning and memory* (NIDA Research Monograph No. 97, pp. 1–21). Rockville, MD: National Institute of Drug Abuse.

Rosenzweig, M. R., & Bennett, E. L. (1984a). Basic processes and modulatory infuences in the stages of memory formation. In G. Lynch, J. L. McGaugh, & N. M. Weinberger (Eds.), *Neurobiology of learning and memory* (pp. 263–288). New York: Guilford Press.

Rosenzweig, M. R., & Bennett, E. L. (1984b). Studying stages of memory formation with chicks and rodents. In L. R. Squire & N. Butters (Eds.), *Neuropsychology of memory* (pp. 555–565). New York: Guilford Press.

Rosenzweig, M. R., Bennett, E. L., Martinez, J. L., Jr., Beniston, D., Colombo, P. J., Lee, D. W., Patterson, T. A., Schulteis, G., & Serrano, P. A. (1991). Stages of memory formation in the chick: Findings and problems. In R. J. Andrew (Ed.) *Neural and behavioural plasticity: The use of the domestic chick as a model* (pp. 394–418). Oxford, England: Oxford University Press.

Rosenzweig, M. R., Krech, D., & Bennett, E. L. (1961). Heredity, environment, brain biochemistry, and learning. *Current trends in psychological theory* (pp. 87–110). Pittsburgh, PA: University of Pittsburgh Press.

Rosenzweig, M. R., Krech, D., Bennett, E. L., & Diamond, M. C. (1962). Effects of environmental complexity and training on brain chemistry and anatomy. *Journal of Comparative and Physiological Psychology, 55,* 429–437.

Rosenzweig, M. R., Lee, D. W., Means, M. K., Bennett, E. L., & Martinez, J. L., Jr. (1989). Effects of varying training strength on short-, intermediate-, and long-term formation of memory (STM, ITM, LTM) for a one-trial passive avoidance task in chicks. *Society for Neuroscience Abstracts, 15,* 1171.

Rosenzweig, M. R., & Leiman, A. L. (1989). *Physiological psychology* (2nd ed.). New York: Random House/McGraw-Hill.

Rozin, P. (1976). The psychobiological approach to human memory. In M. R. Rosenzweig & E. L. Bennett (Eds.), *Neural mechanisms of learning and memory* (pp. 3–46). Cambridge, MA: MIT Press.

Russell, W. R. (1959). *Brain, memory, learning. A neurologist's view.* Oxford, England: Oxford University Press.

Russell, R. W., Flattau, P. E., & Pope, A. M. (Eds.). (1990). *Behavioral measures of neurotoxicity.* Washington, DC: National Academy Press.

Schwartz, J. H., Castelluci, V. F., & Kandel, E. R. (1971). Functioning of identified neurons and synapses in abdominal ganglion of *Aplysia* in absence of protein synthesis. *Journal of Neurophysiology, 34,* 939–963.

Scoville, W. B., & Milner, B. (1957). Loss of recent memory after bilateral hippocampal lesions. *Journal of Neurology, Neurosurgery and Psychiatry, 20,* 11–21.

Squire, L. R. (1986). Memory functions as affected by electroconvulsive therapy. In S. Malitz & H. Sackheim (Eds.), *Electroconvulsive therapy: Clinical and basic issues* (pp. 307–314). New York: New York Academy of Sciences.

Squire, L. R. (1987). *Memory and brain.* New York: Oxford University Press.

Squire, L. R., Amaral, D. G., & Press, G. A. (1990). Magnetic resonance imaging of the hippocampal formation and mammillary nuclei distinguish medial temporal lobe and diencephalic amnesia. *Journal of Neuroscience, 10,* 3106–3117.

Squire, L. R., & Cohen, N. (1979). Memory and amnesia: Resistance to disruption develops for years after learning. *Behavioral and Neural Biology, 25,* 115–125.

Squire, L. R., & Slater, P. C. (1975). Forgetting in very long-term memory as assessed by an improved questionnaire technique. *Journal of Experimental Psychology: Human Learning, 104,* 50–55.

Teyler, T. J., & DiScenna, P. (1987). Long-term potentiation. *Annual Review of Neuroscience, 10,* 131–161.

Thorndike, E. L. (1898). Animal intelligence: An experimental study of the associative processes in animals. *Psychological Review Monograph Supplements, 2*(4, Whole No. 8).

Tulving, E. (1989). Remembering and knowing the past. *American Scientist, 277,* 361–367.

Tulving, E. (1992). Concepts of human memory. In L. Squire, G. Lynch, N. M. Weinberger, & J. L. McGaugh (Eds.), *Memory: Organization and locus of change* (pp. 3–32). New York: Oxford University Press.

Tulving, E., Hayman, G., & Macdonald, C. A. (1991). Long-lasting perceptual priming and semantic learning in amnesia: A case experiment. *Journal of Experimental Psychology: Learning, Memory, and Cognition, 17,* 595–617.

Tulving, E., Schacter, D. L., McLachlan, D. R., & Moscovitch, M. (1988). Priming of semantic autobiographical knowledge: A case of retrograde amnesia. *Brain and Cognition, 8,* 3–20.

Wang, J., Aigner, T., & Mishkin, M. (1990). Effects of neostriatal lesions on visual habit formation in rhesus monkeys. *Society for Neuroscience Abstracts, 16,* 617.

Warrington, E. K., & Sanders, H. I. (1971). The fate of old memories. *Quarterly Journal of Experimental Psychology, 23,* 432–442.

Warrington, E. K., & Silberstein, M. (1970). A questionnaire technique for investigating very long-term memory. *Quarterly Journal of Experimental Psychology, 22,* 508–512.

Warrington, E. K., & Weiskrantz, L. (1968). New method of testing long-term retention with special reference to amnesia patients. *Nature, 217,* 972–974.

Weiskrantz, L., & Warrington, E. K. (1975). The problem of the amnesic syndrome in man and animals. In R. L. Isaacson & K. H. Pribram (Eds.), *The hippocampus* (Vol. 2). New York: Plenum Press.

Will, B. E., Rosenzweig, M. R., Bennett, E. L., Hebert, M., & Morimoto, H. (1977). Relatively brief environmental enrichment aids recovery of learning capacity and alters brain measures after postweaning brain lesions in rats. *Journal of Comparative and Physiological Psychology, 91,* 33–50.

Wilson, B. (1987). *Rehabilitation of memory.* New York: Guilford Press.

Winocur, G. (1990). Anterograde and retrograde amnesia in rats with dorsal hippocampal or dorsomedial thalamic lesions. *Behavioural Brain Research, 38,* 145–154.

Zola-Morgan, S. M., & Squire, L. R. (1990). The primate hippocampal formation: Evidence for a time-limited role in memory storage. *Science, 250,* 288–290.

Zola-Morgan, S. M., Squire, L. R., & Amaral, D. G. (1989). Lesions of the hippocampal formation but not lesions of the fornix or the mammillary nuclei produce long-lasting memory impairment in monkeys. *Journal of Neuroscience, 9,* 898–913.

Zola-Morgan, S. M., Squire, L. R., & Mishkin, M. (1982). The neuroanatomy of amnesia: Amygdala–hippocampus versus temporal stem. *Science, 218,* 1337–1339.

# CHAPTER 5

# Research in Child Development, Parenting, and the Family in a Cross-Cultural Perspective

Çiğdem Kağıtçıbaşı

T wo main themes are pursued in this chapter, demonstrating the actual and potential contribution of psychological research to the understanding and support of children's well-being. One of these themes is the rather straightforward contribution of psychology to conceptualizations and applications of health and child development. The other theme has to do with the context of development, mainly the family. An understanding of parental values and behaviors, family systems, and changes in these, is crucial for cross-cultural psychological conceptualization of human development. Furthermore, applications, such as educational intervention programs, parental education and other family–community support programs informed by such cross-cultural research and conceptualization, have a good chance of success. Thus, cultural context needs to be studied and taken into consideration in understanding child development and in applications designed to support it.

In a widely read book published in 1979, Emmy Werner wrote that only 80 out of every 100 children born in developing countries survived. Today, that number of survivors has reached 92, and by the year 2000 the infant survival rate will reach 95%. This is a remarkable improvement that has been achieved through wide-scale concerted health efforts such as immunizations. Considered from this perspective, the picture looks promising, but other perspectives provide sobering facts. The state of the world's children leaves much to be desired and has been called "the quiet catastrophe": "the 40,000 child deaths each day from ordinary malnutrition and disease, the 150 million children who live on with ill health and poor growth, the 100 million 6 to 11-year-olds who are not in school" (United Nations Children's Fund, 1991, p. 3). Even though with better health measures infant survival has increased, the same conditions that used to put infants at risk of death still persist to put the survivors at risk for arrested or delayed development.

In the last decade, a great deal has been done, especially by the United Nations Children's Fund (UNICEF) and the World Health Organization, and large-scale collaborative efforts are currently being made. Several international organizations, states, and governments are taking action, the most important of which has been the World Summit for Children in September of 1990, where 71 presidents and prime ministers met. The participants in this summit stated in their final declaration that they were prepared to make available the resources to meet their commitments.

How does all this have relevance for psychology and psychological research? When the main problem was that of survival, the work of psychologists was not considered of much relevance, and psychologists were not called upon to find solutions to the pressing problems. However, with increasing rates of survival among children throughout the world, the question of what happens to those who survive has finally come to the fore, bringing with it the relevance of psychology.

Recent shifts in the conceptualization of health have contributed to the increasing relevance of psychology in this area. Specifically, a more comprehensive social science model of health has replaced a rather narrow medical model. With this shift has come a corresponding shift in focus from the (sick) individual to the totality of individual-in-context and from the treatment of disease to its prevention, again with a stress on the environmental conditions that bring about morbidity. Thus, the realization that health is as much a social–behavioral issue as a medical issue has provided researchers and practitioners with a new perspective on health. This perspective includes the family and the community as well as the ecological and socioeconomic–cultural context in which the individual is embedded.

# A Holistic View of Human Development

This new perspective requires a more holistic psychological conceptualization of human development and the environmental influences contributing to it. It also calls for psychological methodology to assess this development and to devise indicators of the environmental conditions contributing to it. What is needed are psychological "developmental norms" to parallel the "growth norms" used in growth monitoring by health workers. Furthermore, it is important that these norms be established in such a way that both commonalities and cultural differences are taken into consideration.

Psychologists, however, are newcomers to the field, and they have not yet been able to meet the challenge. There is a long-standing assumption that measuring psychosocial development is too difficult or complex to be of any practical use. This assumption contributed to the tendency to ignore this important sphere of human development and to focus solely on physical growth, which, in turn, reinforced the biological (medical) model of health and human development. With the recent growth of interest in overall child development and of the more comprehensive social–behavioral conceptualization of health, however, psychological development has come to the fore, and it behooves the psychologist to meet the new challenge.

## Nutrition, Health, and Psychosocial Development

The relationship among nutrition, health, and psychosocial development has often been conceptualized in a linear fashion such that nutrition is seen as affecting health and, in turn, health is seen as contributing to psychosocial well-being. In such a linear causal conceptualization, feedback and mutual interactions are ignored. In contrast, a synergistic relationship among nutrition, health, and psychosocial development has been proposed (for example, for infancy) involving a transactional or interactive system of relationships (Brazelton, 1982; Brazelton, Tronick, Lechtig, Lasley, & Klein, 1977; Myers, 1992).

Research has supported the synergistic model. For example, Brazelton and his colleagues (1977), working with infants in Guatemala, showed that subsequent malnutrition could be predicted with 70%–80% accuracy for those infants who demonstrated low interactive ability. In other words, it was found that less active babies get fed less. Because malnourished babies are in fact less active, they get fed less, so that malnourishment breeds more malnourishment in a vicious cycle. In contrast, healthy babies who actively demand to be fed do in fact get fed more, thus activating a benign cycle of further health and development.

The immediate social environment is also a part of this synergism. For example, reluctant babies can get fed more if mothers stimulate them during breast feeding. Such stimulation is a psychosocial factor contributing to better nutrition, which, in turn, contributes to better health. In general, a stimulating psychosocial environment is conducive to good nutrition and health as well as to better psychosocial development, and vice versa. For example, research in Mexico (Carvioto, 1981) showed that mothers of malnourished children were less exposed to the radio, provided lower quality home stimulation to their children, and were less responsive to them than were mothers of normal children living in the same village conditions.

An applied research project in Thailand (Kotchabhakdi, Winichagoon, Smitasiri, Dhanamitta, & Valyasevi, 1987) demonstrated how an intervention project informed by the synergistic model of nutrition–health–psychosocial development can make a positive impact on overall infant development. As part of a large-scale health and nutrition intervention program in 48 northeastern Thai villages, interactive video education was used. This education constituted the independent variable whose effects were afterward assessed in comparison with the situation in villages treated as controls, where no educational intervention was applied. The videotapes were shown in 24 of the 48 villages, to a total of 930 women, 478 men, and 3,225 children several times each during 4 months in 1982. Young mothers with children under 2 years of age in 12 villages receiving video treatment were compared in three different posttests ($N = 322$, 279, and 237, respectively) with those in villages not receiving this treatment.

The nutritional status of the infants and young children was initially assessed, and malnutrition was found to be prevalent. Interviews with mothers and home observations showed serious inadequacies in mothers' knowledge of early infant development and problems in their child rearing attitudes and behavior. Mothers were provided information and feedback through video and discussion sessions at home and in groups. The intervention focused on the psychological aspects of mother–infant interaction and early development. Among the topics covered were information about the infant's capacity to see, hear, and interact in the first few weeks of life (not originally known by the mothers); the importance of early stimulation of and interaction with the infant for better nourishment and health; and techniques of continuing feeding in spite of the infant's tongue-thrusting reflex or turning away.

As a result of the intervention program, the trained mothers, compared with those in the control villages, demonstrated significantly more effective feeding and better interaction with their babies. For example, they stimulated the infants and kept trying to feed them in spite of the infants' tongue-thrusting reflex or turning away significantly more than did the control group (53% and 27% respectively). Also, compared to those in the control villages, significantly more mothers in the treatment villages gave colostrum to newborn babies (73% and 43% respectively) and allowed them to suckle immediately after delivery (60.4% and 44.5%, respectively). They also allowed the babies more direct visual stimulation, by opening up the top of their cribs, because they developed significantly greater awareness of infants' early visual and auditory perceptual ability. Furthermore, the trained mothers provided their children with play materials that they made from materials available at home, as suggested in the education program. In effect, the training program empowered the mothers to realize "their capacity to make a difference in their children's growth and development and to make the most use of their potential and existing resources in creating a more nurturing environment for their children" (Kotchabhakdi et al., 1987, p. 24).

This research provides us with an example of the synergy that exists among health, nutrition, psychological aspects of human development, and the environment in which that development takes place. It also shows the importance of examining that environment to ascertain which elements in it are particularly favorable or unfavorable for human development.

Recent reviews (Jolly, 1988; Zeitlin & Mansour, 1986) have stressed the key roles of the family ties and environmental support systems in so-called "positive deviance." This concept refers to those children who thrive in adverse conditions while others fail. Caretaker (mother)–child interaction, an environmental psychosocial factor, appears to be a key element in promoting resilience in the child, and thus positive deviance. The Mexican and especially Thai research discussed earlier provide support for this conclusion.

Accordingly, a new approach to tackling deprivation is to focus on the existing elements of strength and to capitalize on them. Such an approach of "empowerment," rather than one of compensation for deficiency, is the more positive approach to supporting human development in adverse conditions. The strength may often be inherent in the closely knit human bonds and the indigenous family culture (IDRC, UNICEF, UNESCO, 1988; Jolly, 1988; Kağıtçıbaşı, 1990).

To look for these strengths and especially to understand and use the environmental support systems, the collaboration of social scientists and especially psychologists with health professionals is needed. Such collaboration was not very common until recently. However, with the recent shift in focus to child development beyond survival, this collaboration is becoming inevitable, and psychology is now enjoying increased relevance.

## What Can Psychology Offer?

Psychology, especially developmental psychology, can make an important contribution to understanding and dealing with the issue of worldwide child development. Such a contribution would be especially notable in two realms: first, in the culturally sensitive conceptualization of healthy human development and its corollary environmental conditions, and, second, in their culturally appropriate and valid operationalization and measurement.

## The Conceptualization of Child Development

A conceptualization of child development that is informed by sound psychological theory and research is the first and perhaps the most important step in dealing with everyday issues of child development. The synergistic model used in the Thai project represents an interactional or transactional perspective because it stresses the mutual interaction of nutrition, health, and psychosocial development, as well as the interaction of the infant and its environment.

The interactional model is quite different from some other psychological conceptualizations of human development. It contrasts mainly with the organismic and the mechanistic models. The organismic model focuses on the maturational causes of behavior at the expense of environmental causes. From a biological–genetic–maturational perspective, this model postulates sequential stages of development that lead toward a well-defined optimal stage of growth. Psychoanalysis and the Piagetian theory of cognitive development both adhere to the organismic model.

How human development is conceptualized determines how it is operationalized and assessed. If constitutional or genetic factors are stressed in human development, the implication of such an approach is a focus on the developing child as such, to the exclusion of the environment. Accordingly, the assessment technique used reflects a normative orientation to maturation, as for example that seen in Gesell's approach (Gesell & Ilg, 1943).

The mechanistic model of human development, espoused by behaviorism, has a contrasting approach in stressing environmental factors to the exclusion of the maturational variables. Typically, a unidirectional causal influence is conceptualized in which the environment is defined as the proximal surround that acts on the rather passive individual. Human development is thus conceived as the sum of responses to environmental stimuli. Today, this conceptualization of the passive individual is modified with the recognition that through cognitive structuring the individual processes and interprets the environmental information and stimuli. For example, in social learning theory, a more active role is accorded the individual, but the emphasis remains on the environment.

The interactional orientation mentioned above deals with the complex interactions between the individual and its total environment, going beyond the organismic and the mechanistic models. It has a systemic perspective in which human development is seen to be the result of the interpenetration of the psychological (individual) and the social (environmental) systems. For example, ecological theory, which utilizes this general model, looks into the "dynamic interplay between the developing person and the environment" (Bronfenbrenner, 1979). The interactional orientation has also a contextual perspective in which a lifelong process of interaction is postulated. Thus, the individual is "in a permanent process of acquisition from and confrontation with the social environment" (Hurrelmann, 1988, p. 7), a dynamic process in which one is active in choosing contexts, which in turn shape one's behavior.

Especially with the impetus provided by Bronfenbrenner's (1979) ecological theory and the life-span approaches to human development (e.g., Baltes, Reese, & Lipsitt, 1980), psychological theories of human development have tended to move toward more systemic–contextual models with an interactional perspective. Such a perspective contributes to a better and more holistic conceptualization of child development in context. Indeed, any culturally sensitive conceptualization of human development has to have a contextual approach and to study development within its familial–communal environment.

Nevertheless, such a holistic approach has not been prevalent in mainstream developmental psychology, given the tradition of organismic and mechanistic models (see Dasen & Jahoda, 1986; Kağıtçıbaşı, 1990, for reviews). Also, the complexity of the family as an intergenerational system moving through time has made it difficult to treat it in its totality. Developmental psychology has typically focused on the individual as its unit of analysis and has not ventured into the larger environment. A shift in focus is thus needed, and is apparently coming about.

## The Assessment of Child Development

The operationalization of an interactional (contextual) model of human development requires not only child development measures but also environmental measures to assess the context in which development takes place. Thus, in addition to assessing physical growth and sensorimotor, language, cognitive, and socioemotional development, one needs to assess the physical environment, environmental stimulation, caretaker attitudes and behavior, and the child–caretaker interactions. The demands coming from health workers, policymakers, and others in "the field" also converge with this need because work in real-life contexts often involves community-based interventions, such as parent education, designed to act on the environment to make it more conducive to optimal child development. Especially in "high-risk" environments, where children survive in ever increasing numbers but where their development is often arrested, it is of crucial importance to determine and assess the environmental variables that make a difference for healthy child development.

The very concept of environmental risk needs to be better operationalized. General indicators such as socioeconomic status are not adequate because there is variation in child development within the same socioeconomic conditions. As demonstrated by Carvioto's (1981) research in Mexico, discussed earlier, such factors as exposure to the radio, quality home stimulation, and responsiveness of the caretaker can make the difference between good and bad environments within the same village. An unraveling of the environment is needed to determine the mediating factors that predict healthy child development and to measure them. This is a challenging task, given the cross-cultural variability in "family culture," including such basic variables as parental attitudes, beliefs, and behaviors.

The assessment of child development itself should also be culturally appropriate. Given the great variability in the conditions of development (e.g., nutrition, ecology, socio-economic and cultural differences), context-specific norms of child development need to be developed, paralleling physical growth norms. Similarly, simple measures of psychological development are needed to parallel growth monitoring techniques used by health workers. The greatest need arises for the detection and screening of developmental problems and risks, and for the periodic monitoring of development in different socioeconomic and cultural contexts.

## Culture as Context
Up to now, I have discussed a contextual approach to child development, especially in the area of health and development, and have stressed the potential contribution of psychology to such an approach. A contextual approach is also necessary to understand person–environment relations, which are of crucial importance in psychosocial development across cultures because culture often constitutes the context of meaning attached to human affairs. In other words, the meaning attributed to some behavior, or how that behavior is understood, is often culturally constructed and therefore may vary from culture to culture. Cultural meaning systems may affect even such basic concepts as the self and normality–abnormality. Ethnopsychology and ethnomedicine are based on this contextual hermeneutic (interpretive) premise.

An insightful study of person descriptions (Shweder & Bourne, 1984), for example, showed that the Oriyas of India described a person in terms of his or her *relations* with others rather than in terms of his or her enduring abstract traits, whereas Americans showed the opposite tendency. Similar relational conceptualizations of the person have also been widely reported in other communities where closely knit human relations are prevalent. The particular situations involving relations with others constitute the context or the reality in which the self is defined.

Given such a powerful sociocultural influence on the definition of "reality," cultural and cross-cultural analysis assumes great importance for the study of psychological phenomena. This is particularly the case for child development and socialization, which take place within the family. The family itself is both the context of child socialization and a part of the larger sociocultural context. Basic family processes acquire meaning in the particular sociocultural context in which the family is imbedded. Therefore, there is much diversity in family processes, paralleling the diversity of the larger context. This calls for cross-cultural research to discover how the meaning of familial processes varies.

A series of studies based on Rohner's (1984) parental acceptance–rejection theory have dealt with the concept of perceived parental control and acceptance. They provide a good example of culturally determined shifts in the meaning of family processes. Research carried out with children and adolescents in the United States (cited in Pettengill & Rohner, 1985) and in Germany (Trommsdorf, 1985) showed that parental control was perceived as parental rejection. In other words, children and adolescents who thought that their parents used restrictive discipline (a high level of control) perceived them as hostile and rejecting. This is because in cultural contexts in which permissive, nonrestrictive discipline is the norm, children perceive restrictive discipline as a lack of love. However, in a different cultural context the same restrictive discipline may be interpreted differently. For example, in Korea (Rohner & Pettengill, 1985) and in Japan (Trommsdorf, 1985), the same parental control was found to be associated with perceived parental acceptance and warmth. In other words, in these East Asian societies, parental strictness was perceived by adolescents as a sign of care, not neglect. Thus, Trommsdorf (1985) wrote, "Japanese adolescents even feel *rejected* by their parents when they experience only little parental control and a broader range of autonomy" (p. 238).

Clearly, the common pattern in a society is perceived by the members of that society as "normal," and what deviates from that pattern is seen as "abnormal." With shifts in the common patterns, as in culture contact situations of migration, adjustment problems can arise. For example, Pettengill and Rohner (1985) studied Korean–American adolescents' perceptions and found them to be similar to those of American adolescents, rather than to those of Korean adolescents. That is, the Korean–American adolescents also interpreted parental control as rejection. This is because the relevant environment has an influence on the individual's perceptions of what is normal or abnormal. Because the Korean–American adolescents compare their own experiences with those of the American adolescents, rather than with those of Korean adolescents in Korea, and because they adopt the majority culture's values, they use the same interpretations as the American adolescents do. This is often a source of conflict between generations of immigrants because the older generation's meaning systems persist, whereas that of the younger generation changes.

# Parental Orientations

The above research examples demonstrate how family processes assume culturally determined meaning and how therefore the meaning of the same process or behavior pattern can change across cultures. Often, family processes themselves vary cross-culturally. Such variation is particularly noticeable in parental beliefs, attitudes, and behaviors.

Parental beliefs about the "nature of the child" constitute the context in which child development takes place. A series of studies carried out by Educational Testing Service researchers with Black, Anglo, and Mexican–American parents in the United States (e.g., Sigel, 1985) showed that parents have rather complex belief systems about how children develop and even some "theories" about how they learn. Ethnic and social class differences in these "parental theories" were also discovered. Such belief systems that parents hold regarding their children have also been found in cross-cultural research.

### Parental Beliefs Regarding Competence

Parents' beliefs about child development directly influence their child rearing behavior and therefore have crucial importance for the development of their children. Super and Harkness (1986) have developed the concept of the "developmental niche," paralleling the biological niche, in studying child development in context. One of the three components of this developmental niche is the "psychology of the caretaker," the others being the physical and social setting, and child care and child rearing. Parents' beliefs form a part of their "psychology" and have variously been called "ethnotheories," "indigenous theories," and "naive theories" affecting children's development. For example, Dasen (1988) has shown that the Baoule of Africa define intelligence primarily in terms of social skills and manual dexterity. They therefore stress these skills in their child rearing orientation rather than cognitive skills such as abstract reasoning, which are commonly associated with intelligence in Western cultures.

Similar "social" definitions of intelligence have been reported for other societies in Africa. Berry (1984) reviewed many studies, mostly conducted in Africa, on folk conceptions of intelligence. The one common finding of all of the African studies is an emphasis on social skills and on characteristics such as cooperation, conformity, obedience, and responsibility as constituting intelligence. Beginning with Irvine's (1966) pioneering work two and a half decades ago, the "socio-affective" aspects of intelligent behavior have been found to be stressed by people in Africa, compared with an emphasis on cognitive aspects in Western technological societies.

A study by Serpell (1977) demonstrated the contrast between the folk conceptions of intelligence and what is measured by intelligence tests. In a Zambian village, 5 adults were asked to rate the village children of about 10 years of age in terms of identifying the ones they would choose to carry out a particular task such as conveying an important message to someone. They were also asked to rank the children in terms of "intelligence," using the local term for it. The 42 children thus rated were then given psychological tests developed mainly in Zambia for use in nonschool contexts. Children's test scores did not correlate well with the ratings they received from the adults. Thus, even though free of educational bias, the tests did not assess the characteristics of the children that the adults considered to reflect intelligence, which had to do with social responsibility and skill.

Such a social/relational conceptualization of intelligence is not unique to Africa. In many traditional societies, similar findings have been reported. Such "folk" conceptualizations reflect the "realities" of these societies, that is, the objective conditions of life and the skills that are functional for the lifestyles framed by those conditions. Thus, for example, under conditions in which there is much continuity and little change in work conditions, as in subsistence farming, where there are limited resources and there is much at stake in risk taking, and where the well-being of the individual is dependent on the well-being and support of the larger group, children are rewarded for compliant and cooperative behavior, upholding group interests, and are discouraged from being independent and adventurous.

However, today both socioeconomic conditions and life-styles are changing, more in some places than in others. Conflicts occur in the process of change. A dilemma sometimes faced by policy-oriented researchers is the clash between traditional values and conceptualizations and the requirements of "modern" institutions such as schools. The skills that are valuable for rural traditional life-styles may not be adaptive for modern urban living conditions. In the context of change, "Western" standards, for example, schooling and skills gained in school rather than traditional indigenous skills, often become more instrumental in obtaining high-paying, high-prestige positions in society. On the one hand, researchers are concerned about biases in judging performance with "Western" standards; on the other hand, however, those may be the very standards against which "success" will be judged in the changing society.

### Diversity in Parental Expectations

Social change notwithstanding, there is much diversity in parenting along social class and cultural differences. A great deal of cross-cultural research has pointed to higher parental expectations of conformity from children among lower social classes in Western countries and in traditional societies with tight, closely-knit family and human relations. On the one hand, such expectations and values lead to social conceptualizations of competence, as discussed earlier; and on the other hand, they affect familial relationships and the very place of the child in the family.

An early explanation of the social class differences in parental expectations in the United States was provided by Kohn (1969) in terms of the anticipatory socialization of children to develop orientations adaptive to the different future environmental (especially occupational) demands, as perceived by parents. Thus, individual autonomy was encouraged in middle-class contexts, which allow greater freedom of individual decisions and action, whereas working class parents emphasized obedience and conformity to external constraints. These differences were in line with what each group of parents expected their children would have to cope with in their future occupational roles.

Taking this reasoning one step further, LeVine (1974) stated that socialization that produces compliant behavior in children is adaptive for survival, especially in hazardous environments, as he observed in Africa. This conforms to basic parental goals for children. Expectations of dependency and compliance from children can also be important for the livelihood of the family.

A cross-cultural study on the value of children for parents, conducted with nationally representative samples in the United States, Turkey, Korea, Taiwan, Thailand, the Philippines, Singapore, and Indonesia, as well as a smaller sample in Germany, totaling 20,000 respondents, provides further evidence of parental goals and values (see Fawcett,

1983; Kağıtçıbaşı, 1982a). In this study, parental values and expectations regarding their children were studied through in-depth interviews.

"Obedience to parents" was found to be valued the most and "being independent and self-reliant" the least among respondents in less developed countries, as well as in lower socioeconomic strata and especially among traditional rural-agricultural traditional groups with larger, closely knit families, in each country (Kağıtçıbaşı, 1982b).

Further analysis of the findings provided insight into some links between these expectations from young children and those from grown-up adult offspring. The "old-age security value" of children assumed great importance. Among the characteristics people would like to see in their children when they grow up to be adults, "being close and loyal to parents" was highly salient in traditional societies. Old-age security as a reason for having a child or wanting another child was greatly stressed among respondents who also valued obedience in young children. It is expected that a child who is compliant and dependent on parents in young age grows up to be a loyal adult offspring who upholds family well-being rather than looking after his own self-interest. An independent child, however, may separate himself from the family, which is seen as a threat to the very livelihood of the family.

The responses of the American and German respondents clearly contrasted with those from the other countries in this study. Specifically, a question asking about expected financial help from adult offspring in old age was found offensive by the American and German respondents, who denied being dependent on anyone, especially on their children. A common response was, "I don't want anything from my children; if they can take care of themselves, I'll be glad." By contrast, Turkish parents, for example, were offended that their children's loyalty was being questioned; a common response was, "Of course, a loyal child (adult offspring) would never let down his parents."

The variations among the countries roughly paralleled differences in their overall levels of development. For example, the responses from Singapore and Korea, both of which were going through rapid economic growth and decreased fertility, fell halfway between the extremes (Kağıtçıbaşı, 1982b). Thus, objective socioeconomic conditions (lack of widespread social welfare institutions, social security systems, and the like) are also associated with these values and expectations. In the context of material dependence on the family, high values are put on closely knit interpersonal ties and interdependence, rather than on independence. This interdependence first takes the form of the child's dependence on parents and then, in old age, parents' dependence on the grown-up offspring. This is the kind of home environment that is conducive to the socialization of familistic and communal values of mutual support, rather than to individualistic values.

# Dependence–Independence in the Family

A theme underlying the diversity in parental values and expectations discussed up to now is the dependence–independence dimension. How much dependence or independence exists or is valued in family relations is a key to understanding both the child socialization process and family functioning. Research has shown that human relations in general and familial relations in particular vary along this dimension. In general, in sociocultural contexts in which child socialization stresses compliance and obedience and in which the old-age security value of children is important, dependence characterizes intergenerational relations within the family. Where, however, autonomy and self reliance are stressed in child socialization, independence is the result.

## Relatedness-Separation

Much psychological thinking puts a high value on individual independence and autonomy. From a psychoanalytic perspective, object relations theory (Mahler, Pine, & Bergman, 1975) considers "individuation/separation" as the basic issue of human development. According to this view, it is through separation and individuation that healthy personality development is possible.

From a rather different perspective, family systems theory (Minuchin, 1974) proposes a similar model of healthy family interactions, emphasizing the importance of the boundaries separating the subsystems (selves) within the family system. "Enmeshed" families with unclear and overlapping boundaries among persons are considered pathological.

Such thinking reflects Western individualism. Individual autonomy is a cherished value, integrated into both psychological theory and practice. Applications can be seen, for example, in parent education courses in the United States in which mothers are taught to "let go" of their young children. The related concepts of self-reliance, self-sufficiency, privacy, individual achievement and freedom are also valued. Kagan (1984) has observed, for example, that "in American families, the primary loyalty is to self—its values, autonomy, pleasure, virtue, and actualization"(p. 245).

Clearly, some early selfhood differentiation has to occur for the identity formation of an individual, and this is doubtless true universally. At this absolute, existential level, separation/individuation is a given. Beyond this level, however, cultural differences emerge, and psychological interpretations of what is healthy or unhealthy reflect these differences.

In different cultural contexts, different conceptions of healthy human development and human interaction may be seen. For example, a contrasting portrait is drawn by Azuma in describing the Japanese mother's message to the child: "I am one with you; we can be and will be of the same mind" (reported in Kornadt, 1987, p. 133). This would be interpreted by Western psychology as the expression of a pathological "symbiotic" relationship and "enmeshment." Thus, the separation of the child from the mother may not be considered essential for or even conducive to healthy child development in cultural contexts in which relatedness rather than independence is valued.

An insightful study by Choi (in press) throws some light on the possible antecedents in early mother–child interaction of the two contrasting orientations of relatedness–separation or dependence–independence. This was an in-depth psycholinguistic study of middle-class mother–child dyads from Canada and Korea, based on transcribed videotaped interactions. Specific communicative patterns were analyzed, and some substantial differences were found in the interaction of the two groups of mothers with their young children.

Generally, the Korean mothers were observed to make an enthusiastic effort to insure the children's reciprocity, whereas the Canadian mothers readily assumed it. The Korean mothers tended to "insert" themselves into their children's reality, having "difficulty maintaining the children's psychosocial reality as being independent. The children are viewed as having to be specifically guided and stimulated . . . the mothers come to be psychosocially present in the children's reality and create a 'relationally attuned' psychosocial dynamic." In contrast, the realities of the Canadian mothers and children were "individually attuned": "The mothers allow the children to be psychosocially differentiated." They are "distinguished by their effort to detach themselves from the children . . . withdrawing themselves from the children's reality, so that the children's reality can remain autonomous." Thus, whereas the Korean mothers made an effort to "fuse" their reality with that of their children, the Canadian mothers made an effort to "detach" themselves from their children.

These contrasting communicative patterns point to some basic differences in early child rearing that may underlie the diversity along the dependence–independence dimension. More research into such early interaction patterns can provide the clues to understanding how and when this diversity comes about. Other research (Keller, Schölmerich,

& Eibl-Eibesfeldt, 1988) has provided evidence for universally invariant adult–infant communication patterns. Thus, variation apparently arises after infancy and develops through verbal interactions with the young child.

## Two Basic Needs

The dependence–independence dimension has to do with basic human merging and separation, respectively. These orientations, in turn, reflect two fundamental albeit conflicting human needs for relatedness and autonomy, and have been well recognized in the conflict theories of personality, especially those of Rank, Angyal, and Bakan. For example, in *The Duality of Human Existence*, Bakan (1966) refers to "communion" and "agency" as basic needs that have to be recognized and fulfilled. He further stresses the danger of denying communion (merging with another), possibly reacting to the dominant individualistic ethos of the Western world. These conflict theories of personality recognize the simultaneous process of differentiation from and integration with others toward a compromise resolution or dialectic synthesis of these opposing forces.

Other theoretical approaches in social psychology and in gender relations have also differentiated between these two basic needs (see Kağıtçıbaşı, 1990, p. 158–159). Nevertheless, the need for dependence or relatedness is rarely deemed to be as important as the need for independence and autonomy, reflecting again the individualistic bias in psychology. It would appear that individualistic sociocultural contexts satisfy the need for independence while undermining the need for dependence, whereas collectivistic contexts curb the need for independence by promoting dependence and loyalty to the group.

## Assumption of Change

Despite the above shortcoming of both of the two sociocultural contexts, there is a general assumption that societies and families are in a process of change from a collectivistic to an individualistic culture, rather than to a third sociocultural context that may integrate some elements of the two. This assumption is based on the modernization theory and is widely held. It predicts a decrease in the diversity of family patterns with socioeconomic change and a convergence toward the Western middle-class family pattern of individuation and separation.

As discussed in detail elsewhere (Kağıtçıbaşı, 1990), this expectation of unidirectional change is based on two further assumptions: first, that the individualistic family–human relations pattern is compatible with economic development, but that collectivistic close-knit relations are not, and, second, that the Western family–human relations pattern itself has changed from a collectivistic to an individualistic one as a necessary outcome of industrialization, and that the same change is thus inevitable in all industrializing societies.

Both of these assumptions are now being questioned by contrary historical evidence and current research (see Kağıtçıbaşı, 1990, for a review). On the one hand, the notable economic growth in Japan and the Pacific basin provides important evidence against the first assumption. On the other hand, historical evidence points to the existence of individualistic cultural/familial themes prior to industrialization in northern Europe and the United States, showing that it was not industrialization that produced individualism. This finding questions the second assumption and has the implication that industrialization need not produce individualism in other sociocultural contexts.

Considering the evidence above and the two basic human needs for autonomy–independence and relatedness–dependence, the unidirectional convergence of family patterns toward the Western model of separation and individuation appears doubtful. If such convergence does take place, it is probably due more to cultural diffusion through the mass media, which are dominated by Western sources, than to the "inevitable" social structural changes accompanying industrialization and socioeconomic development.

What appears to happen with economic development, including urbanization and industrialization, is a decline in material dependencies within the family, but no significant change in emotional dependencies. For example, the cross-cultural *Value of Children* study (Fawcett, 1983; Kağıtçıbaşı, 1982a) discussed earlier showed that children's old-age security value and economic value decrease with economic development, and less financial help is expected of them. In the context of material dependence on the family, the child's dependence on the parents, and in time, the elderly parents' dependence on the grown-up offspring are the rule. This pattern weakens with economic development. However, emotional dependencies, in the form of the continuing, even increasing, psychological value of the child and closely knit family interactions, were found to persist, even though not necessitated by material needs (Kağıtçıbaşı, 1982a, 1982b; 1990).

For example, Yang (1988) reported the continuing importance of "familism" in China despite government policies during the Cultural Revolution undermining its role (p. 94), and of close networks among the elderly and their offspring, as shown by recent surveys. This interdependence was reported to continue even though the elderly do not have to depend on their grown-up children financially, thus without material dependencies. Yang described this as a situation "indicative of the traditional parental protection of children until [parents'] death" (p. 109).

Further evidence for decreasing material dependencies and continuing emotional dependencies comes from a study conducted in Turkey (Erelcin, 1988) using an instrument developed by Fijneman, Willemsen, and Poortinga (in press). This questionnaire assesses the readiness to give and the expectation to receive material and emotional resources with regard to different target persons. Individuals are assessed as to the amount of resources that they are willing to give to others and that they expect to receive from them. An example of an emotional resource question is "How often would you visit your son/daughter (cousin/acquaintance/a sick person/ . . .) who is in the hospital for a long period?" An example of a material resource question is "How much money which you are not using would you give to your son/daughter (cousin/ . . .)?"

The Turkish study was conducted with university students and older subjects (above age 40). Most had an urban background, but some had rural origins. Previous research in Turkey (Kağıtçıbaşı, 1982a) had shown urban–rural variation to be an important factor in modernity and socioeconomic development. A main finding of the Erelcin (1988) study was the greater tendency to give, and greater expectation to receive, psychological resources than material ones, which was also found in the other four countries where the instrument was used (Fijneman et al., in press).

For the rural-origin subjects and the older group in the Turkish study (Erelcin, 1988), however, there was no difference between the readiness to give psychological and material resources. This corresponds to decreasing material, but not emotional, interdependencies with socioeconomic development and modernization. Because rural standing indicates lower socioeconomic development in Turkey, the lack of a difference between giving material and emotional resources indicates the importance of material dependencies in less developed contexts. Thus, rural-origin subjects were found to be more ready than urban-origin subjects ($t = 2.03$, $p = .05$) to give material resources as much as emotional ones. Similarly, the older subjects, reflecting old ways, were more ready to give material resources than were the younger (and more modern) subjects ($t = 2.67$, $p = .01$), although there was no difference between them in the readiness to give emotional resources.

## A Model of Family Change

It thus appears that in sociocultural contexts characterized by relational family patterns and collectivistic culture, economic development is associated not with complete separation and independence, but rather with independence mainly in the material realm. A model of family change has been proposed (Kağıtçıbaşı, 1990) that differentiates three

ideal–typical patterns of family interactions: X, the collectivistic model based on communion (interdependence in both the material and emotional realms); Z, the individualistic
model based on agency (independence in both realms); and Y, a dialectical synthesis of
the two (independence in the material realm and interdependence in the emotional
realm).

The last model (Y) has the potential to fulfill the two basic needs of autonomy
and relatedness better than the other two models. Therefore, it may be expected that
there is a general shift toward this model in human–family relations. There is accumulating evidence for such a shift, especially in the urbanized developed areas of developing
countries, beginning with a collectivistic culture base, and even in some Western post-
technological societies, with the emergence of postmodern values and the search for relatedness (see Kağıtçıbaşı, 1990, for a review).

In pattern X, parent–child interactions are oriented toward obedience; in pattern Z,
autonomy and self-reliance are stressed. However, in pattern Y, both control–dependence
and autonomy orientations are seen in child rearing. The latter change occurs because
total dependence (full obedience orientation) of the child on the parent is no longer
needed to ensure the complete loyalty of the grown-up offspring, whose subsequent financial contribution is no longer crucial for the livelihood of the economically better-off
elderly parents. Thus, autonomy can be integrated into child rearing. Some recent research has provided evidence for the coexistence of control and autonomy or of dependence and independence orientations in the family and particularly in child rearing,
supporting Model Y. For example, Lin and Fu (1990), in a comparison of Chinese,
Chinese–American, and Caucasian American parents, found the two Chinese groups to be
higher in parental control, encouragement of independence, and emphasis on achievement than the Caucasian group. Furthermore, ongoing cross-cultural research by Phalet
and Claeys (1991) has found combined preferences among modern urban Turkish youth
for both loyalty (to the family and society) and "self-realization," compared with self-realization alone among Belgian youth.

An applied study in the low-income areas of Istanbul (Kağıtçıbaşı, 1991) provides
further evidence for the coexistence of dependency and autonomy orientations in mothers' child-rearing values. In this study, 250 families were examined for 4 years, during
which an intervention was carried out. Initial assessments of mothers revealed strong
needs for close ties with their children and a high value put on dependence and obedience. A randomly selected group of mothers then participated in a 2-year parent education program involving both cognitive enrichment (which they gave to their own children)

and sensitization to the needs of the children. In the training, existing closely knit emotional ties were reinforced, but new values were also introduced supporting children's autonomy.

In the reassessments after the intervention, it was found that the experimental group that participated in the training valued autonomous behavior in their children more than did the control group. However, there was no difference between these groups in the encouragement of relational dependent behavior in their children and in close-knit ties. A coexistence (perhaps a synthesis) of individualistic and relational values was thus made possible through an applied research program.

# Conclusions

The research findings and theoretical orientations discussed above throw light on some important issues regarding child development in a cross-cultural context, with a focus on the family and parenting behaviors. The current problems of child development in the world require urgent solutions. Given the synergistic relationship among child health, nutrition, and psychological development, the latter assumes great importance, and psychological expertise is required for the solution of these problems.

The great diversity in the patterns of family interaction across cultures points to the need to develop culturally relevant psychological conceptualizations of human development. Such psychological conceptualizations are necessary for the establishment of culturally valid developmental and environmental norms/indicators, which are badly needed.

To develop such norms, psychologists need to be sensitive to culture because such work requires an understanding of diversity and change and therefore can best be accomplished with an interactional/contextual perspective. Future research thus has to go beyond transferring theoretical models and assessment techniques developed in a Western, middle-class setting to other sociocultural contexts; it has to be research in context.

Good conceptualization in a cross-cultural context is needed for policies not to be expensive trial-and-error endeavors or shots in the dark. Applications informed by sound and culturally valid theoretical models have a much higher chance of succeeding in solving problems than those that merely transfer Western experiences or blind empiricism. Of particular importance is a good understanding of the family culture, based on solid research rather than on stereotypic assumptions. In the context of socioeconomic development, knowledge about what in the family culture is changing and how it is changing is a requisite for developing policies that promote the well-being of children.

It is important to recognize that in the context of wide-scale urbanization and modernization in the developing countries with a collectivistic culture base, human–family relations may be shifting toward pattern Y. This means a rather different picture of family values and child rearing than is characteristic of the individualistic Western middle-class family or the traditional family in rural contexts. In this pattern, both individual and group loyalties are stressed in child socialization, which combines both control and autonomy orientations. Applications (e.g., parent education, etc.) thus need to be based on this apparently conflicting pattern rather than on assumptions derived from Western research on the family.

Informed with this knowledge, psychological research has a higher chance of achieving "ecological validity" (Bronfenbrenner, 1979) and cultural relevance. Applied research, in particular, is more likely to achieve its goals if its assumptions fit the local "reality." For example, if in an attempt to promote individual autonomy, an effort is made to separate the child from the family and to inculcate competitive individualistic achievement, such an intervention would not be successful because of the resistance of the indigenous culture. To have an impact, applied research has to be cognizant of the cultural values and to work with them.

Future research in family and child development needs to have a thorough understanding of culture and cultural change. It needs to be theoretically sophisticated while sensitive to the applied and policy-relevant issues requiring solutions. It needs to be truly international, with a cross-cultural orientation. It needs to take a holistic approach to child development, with an interactional–contextual orientation to person-environment relations. And finally, it needs to face the challenge posed by the pressing problems of children in the world and to share in multidisciplinary efforts to understand and solve those problems.

# References

Bakan, D. (1966). *The duality of human existence.* Chicago: Rand McNally.

Baltes, P. B., Reese, H. W., & Lipsitt, L. P. (1980). Life-span developmental psychology. *Annual Review of Psychology, 31,* 65–110.

Berry, J. W. (1984). Towards a universal psychology of cognitive competence. *International Journal of Psychology, 19,* 335–361.

Brazelton, B. T. (1982). Early intervention: What does it mean? In H. E. Fitzgerald (Ed.), *Theory and research in behavioral pediatrics* (Vol. 1, pp. 1–34). New York: Plenum Press.

Brazelton, B. T., Tronick, E., Lechtig, A., Lasley, R., & Klein, R. (1977). The behavior of nutritionally-deprived Guatemalan neonates. *Developmental Medicine and Child Neurology, 19,* 364.

Bronfenbrenner, V. (1979). *The ecology of human development: experiments by nature and design.* Cambridge, MA: Harvard University Press.

Carvioto, J. (1981). *Nutrition, stimulation, mental development and learning.* W. O. Atwater Memorial Lecture presented at the 12th International Congress of Nutrition, San Diego, CA.

Choi, S. H. (in press). Communicative socialization processes: Korea and Canada. In S. Iwawaki, Y. Kashima, & K. Leung (Eds.), *Innovations in cross-cultural psychology.* Lisse, The Netherlands: Swets & Zeitlinger.

Dasen, P. R. (1988). Développement psychologique et activités quotidiennes chez des enfants Africains [Psychological development and daily activities of African children]. *Enfance, 41*(3–4), 3–24.

Dasen, P. R., & Jahoda, G. (1986). Cross-cultural human development. *International Journal of Behavioral Development, 9,* 413–416.

Erelcin, F. G. (1988). *Collectivistic norms in Turkey: Tendency to give and receive support.* Unpublished master's thesis, Bogazici University, Istanbul, Turkey.

Fawcett, J. T. (1983). Perceptions of the value of children: Satisfaction and costs. In R. Bulatao, R. D. Lee, P. E. Hollerbach, & J. Boongaarts (Eds.), *Determinants of fertility in developing countries* (Vol. 1, pp. 347–369). Washington, DC: National Academy Press.

Fijneman, Y. A., Willemsen, M. E., & Poortinga, H. (in press). Individualism–collectivism: An empirical study of a conceptual issue. In U. Kim & H. Triandis (Eds.), *Theoretical and methodological issues in individualism–collectivism.* London: Sage.

Gesell, A., & Ilg, F. L. (1943). *Infant and child in the culture of today.* New York: Harper.

Hurrelmann, K. (1988). *Social structure and personality development.* Cambridge, England: Cambridge University Press.

IDRC, UNICEF, & UNESCO. (1988). *The learning environments of early childhood in Asia: Research perspectives and changing programmes.* Bangkok: UNESCO.

Irvine, S. H. (1966). Towards a rationale for testing abilities and attainments in Africa. *British Journal of Educational Psychology, 36,* 24–32.

Jolly, R. (1988). Deprivation in the child's environment: seeking advantage in adversity. *Canadian Journal of Public Health Supplement, 20.*

Kagan, J. (1984). *Nature of the child.* New York: Basic Books.

Kağıtçıbaşı, C. (1982a). *The changing value of children in Turkey.* Honolulu, HI: East-West Center.

Kağıtçıbaşı, C. (1982b). Sex roles, value of children and fertility in Turkey. In C. Kağıtçıbaşı (Ed.), *Sex roles, family and community in Turkey* (pp. 151–180). Bloomington: Indiana University Press.

Kağıtçıbaşı, C. (1990). Family and socialization in cross-cultural perspective: A model of change. In J. Berman (Ed.), *Nebraska symposium on motivation: 1989* (pp. 135–200). Lincoln, NE: Nebraska University Press.

Kağıtçıbaşı, C. (1991). The early enrichment project in Turkey. In *Notes, Comments . . . No.193.* Paris: UNESCO–UNICEF–WFP.

Keller, H., Schölmerich, A., & Eibl-Eibesfeldt, I. (1988). Communication patterns in adult-infant interactions in Western and non-Western cultures. *Journal of Cross-Cultural Psychology, 19(4),* 427–445.

Kohn, M. L. (1969). *Class and conformity: A study in values.* New York: Dorsey.

Kornadt, H. J. (1987). The aggression motive and personality development: Japan and Germany. In F. Halisch & J. Kuhl (Eds.), *Motivation, intention and volition.* Berlin: Springer-Verlag.

Kotchabhakdi, N. J., Winichagoon, P., Smitasiri, S., Dhanamitta, S., & Valyasevi, A. (1987). The integration of psychosocial components in nutrition education in northeastern Thai villages. *Asia Pacific Journal of Public Health, 1*(2), 16–25.

LeVine, R. A. (1974). Parental goals: A cross-cultural view. *Teachers College Record, 76,* 226–239.

Lin, C. Y., & Fu, V. R. (1990). A comparison of child rearing practices among Chinese, immigrant Chinese, and Caucasian–American parents. *Child Development, 61,* 429–433.

Mahler, M., Pine, F., & Bergman, A. (1975). *The psychological birth of the human infant.* New York: Basic Books.

Minuchin, S. (1974). *Families and family therapy.* Cambridge, MA: Harvard University Press.

Myers, R. (1992). *The twelve who survive.* London: Routledge.

Pettengill, S. M., & Rohner, R. P. (1985). Korean–American adolescents' perceptions of parental control, parental acceptance–rejection and parent–adolescent conflict. In I. R. Lagunes & Y. H. Poortinga (Eds.), *From a different perspective: Studies of behavior across cultures* (pp. 241–259). Lisse, The Netherlands: Swets & Zeitlinger.

Phalet, K., & Claeys, W. (1991). *Toward a collectivistic work ethic? A comparative study of achievement motivation in Turkish and Belgian youth.* Unpublished monograph, University of Leuven.

Rohner, R. P. (1984). *Handbook for the study of parental acceptance and rejection.* Center for the Study of Parental Acceptance and Rejection, University of Connecticut.

Rohner, R. P., & Pettengill, S. M. (1985). Perceived parental acceptance–rejection and parental control among Korean adolescents. *Child Development, 56,* 524–528.

Serpell, R. (1977). Strategies for investigating intelligence in its cultural context. *Quarterly Newsletter, Institute for Comparative Human Development, 1*(3), 11–15.

Shweder, R. A., & Bourne, E. J. (1984). Does the concept of the person vary cross-culturally? In A. J. Marsella & G. M. White (Eds.), *Cultural conceptions of mental health and therapy* (pp. 97–137). London: D. Reidel.

Sigel, I. (1985). A conceptual analysis of beliefs. In I. E. Sigel (Ed.), *Parental belief system* (pp. 345–371). Hillsdale, NJ: Erlbaum.

Super, C. M., & Harkness, S. (1986). The developmental niche: A conceptualization at the interface of child and culture. *International Journal of Behavioral Development, 9,* 545–570.

Trommsdorf, G. (1985). Some comparative aspects of socialization in Japan and Germany. In I. R. Lagunes & Y. H. Poortinga (Eds.), *From a different perspective: studies of behavior across cultures* (pp. 231–240). Lisse, The Netherlands: Swets & Zeitlinger.

United Nations Children's Fund. (1991). *The state of the world's children.* New York: Author.

Werner, E. (1979). *Cross-cultural child development: A view from the planet earth.* Monterey, CA: Brooks/ Cole.

Yang, C. (1988). Familism and development: An examination of the role of family in contemporary China Mainland, Hong Kong, and Taiwan. In D. Sinha & H. S. R. Kao (Eds.), *Social values and development: Asian perspectives* (pp. 93–124). New Delhi: Sage India.

Zeitlin, M., & Mansour, M. (1986). *Positive deviance in child nutrition with emphasis on psychosocial and behavioral aspects and implications for development, a state-of-the-art-paper, including research guidelines, prepared for the WHO/UNICEF Joint Nutrition Support Programme.* New York: UNICEF.

# CHAPTER 6

# Visual Perception

Qicheng Jing

T he world in which we live is ever changing, of enormous complexity, consisting of a variety of objects, and rich in colors. For the human race to survive, to work, to create material and spiritual civilizations, we have to make use of our senses to perceive objects and their changes in the surrounding world. It is estimated that about 80% of the information we acquire from the environment comes through vision. It is difficult to overstate the importance of visual perception in our lives. We use visual perception to organize our daily living, to observe the facial expressions of friends, and to appreciate the beauty of natural scenes or pieces of art. Visual perception guides us in our interactions with the environment and provides much of our knowledge about the world.

It is important to study visual perception if we are to understand the nature of the mind. The study of visual perception has a long history. Throughout the ages, philosophers have argued about how human beings are able to know about the external world. We rely on our senses to learn things about our surroundings, and from that information we build a concept of the world. The problem for perceptual psychologists is how information is processed by the eye and the brain and to what extent our perception is a true reflection of the objective world. To answer these questions, one has to study cognitive psychology and the philosophy of knowledge—epistemology.

There are also practical reasons for the study of perception: Studying perception enables one to design devices that ensure optimal perceptual performance. Traffic lights, video displays, and instruments on the dashboard of an airplane all have to be tailored to the human perceptual system. Furthermore, if we knew more about how human visual perception works, we would be in a position to endow machines with similar capabilities. Researchers are developing reading machines for pattern recognition, and a new field has emerged called *computer vision*. Thus, visual perception is an important part of cognitive science and, especially, of artificial intelligence.

The three sections of this chapter outline the highlights of the field of visual perception: the perception of objects, color perception, and the perception of space.

# The Perception of Objects

We perceive the surrounding environment as a layout of objects. The perception of objects seems to be simple and effortless and to need no explanation. On second thought, however, this achievement is puzzling because visual information for objects is incomplete and may be different from what we perceive. Objects cast images on our eyes in which they lie on top of and next to each other. Some objects are not shown to the eyes in full because they are partially hidden by other objects, and the back of an object is not seen. When we move our eyes or head, the images we see continuously undergo transformations relative to our eyes. Despite these complexities, we perceive objects as individual, complete bodies with meaningful relations in space, and they seem to exist independently of the eyes of the beholder.

## The Origins of Visual Knowledge
### Object Perception in Infancy
Two kinds of theories have dominated the speculation and research on the origins of perception in the young child. One is called the empiricist theory, or the perceptual–motor theory, which holds that newborns can only perceive fragmentary patches of light and dark from outside stimuli, and through a process of learning, especially through the coordination of the visual sense and the sense of touch, they gradually learn to distinguish objects from their background and to infer complete and bounded objects from the partial visual information provided to the eyes. The long-standing opponent of empiricist theory is nativist theory. Among the nativists of the early 20th century, the Gestalt psychologist tried to explain perception in terms of intrinsic organizational properties of the brain by which stimuli from the outside world are organized into bounded unities governed by some simple principles of organization. This allows the perceiver to see stimuli as individual objects or figures standing out from their backgrounds. Because this theory

claims that the perception of objects follows from the innate properties of the nervous system, the ability to perceive objects was thought to be present at birth, with learning playing only a minimal role in the development of object perception.

The rivalry between the empiricist and nativist theories has remained alive and in recent years has stimulated much research in the developmental study of perception in infancy. Some of the noteworthy studies of infant object perception were done by E. S. Spelke (1990) and her colleagues with partly occluded objects. They used the so-called habituation method, an experimental technique widely used in the study of infant perception. When young infants are presented repeatedly with the same visual display, they tend to get habituated to this display and are no longer interested in it. Thus, after repeated presentations, the infants tend to look at this display less and less. When a novel display is presented to the infant, it pays attention to or looks longer at the new display. The number of looks and length of time an infant devotes to visual displays can be used as a measure to assess the preference for looking at familiar and novel displays. With this habituation method, one can find out whether an infant discriminates between two visual displays and which is familiar and which is novel. This method has been used to study a variety of infant perceptions including the ability to perceive shapes and objects.

In one such experiment, Kellman and Spelke (1983) presented to 4-month-old infants an object with its center part occluded by a nearer object. This presentation was repeated until the infants became habituated to the object (i.e., they were no longer interested in this object and their looking time declined). The infants were then presented with two stimuli: the same complete object without occlusion, and two object fragments that corresponded to the two visible parts of the partially occluded object. Infants were expected to look longer at whichever display appeared more novel to them. If the original display had appeared to them as fragmented pieces, then, after habituation, they should have looked longer at the second complete object; if they saw the original display as a single object, they should have looked longer at the second object fragments. It was discovered that the infants were unable to perceive a center-occluded object as a complete and continuous unit. However, if the visible areas of the object moved in unison, then infants perceived a center-occluded object as a complete object. This study provides evidence that motion specifies object unity, whereas fragments of an object do not carry information of a complete object to the infant. Work with older infants revealed that sensitivity to stationary configurational properties of object unity appears to emerge gradually and becomes fully developed only after 1 year of age (Spelke, 1990).

## Depth Perception in Infancy

Another question to be answered in the study of the origins of visual knowledge is whether the perception of depth is innate or acquired through learning. Walk and Gibson (1961) first introduced an interesting technique to study this problem. They designed a "visual cliff," shown in Figure 1. The child is placed on a narrow central board, on both sides of which are glass surfaces. One glass surface (the near side in the figure) is covered with a checkered design. The other glass surface (the far side in the figure) is not covered with a checkered design, but a checkered surface is placed at a distance below the glass, creating a visual cliff effect. When an infant of 7 to 8 months was placed on the central board, if the mother called from the side that had the cliff (with checkered surface beneath the glass), the infant was tense and reluctant to crawl onto the glass surface to the side of the mother; apparently, it feared falling from the cliff. However, if the mother called from the checkered side of the table, the infant readily crawled to her. This experiment demonstrated that infants at 7 months perceive depth. It also showed that

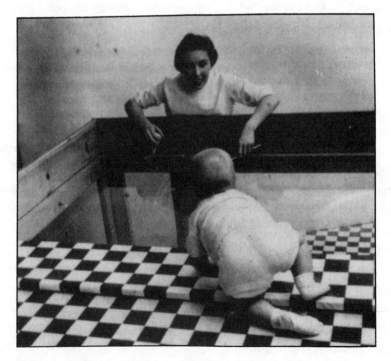

**FIGURE 1**    The visual cliff. Reprinted from E. J. Gibson and Walk, 1960.

infants, without using the sense of touch, can visually sense affordance, the quality of surfaces capable of supporting the body. It seems that infants at an early stage are capable of perceiving situations that are of biological significance to them. Critics of Walk and Gibson's studies of human infants asked whether infants perceive depth at an even earlier age, because the experiment required the infant subjects to crawl to test their depth perception, and humans do not begin to locomote independently until about 7 months of age.

As is often the case, research with other animals helped to solve a question raised by observations of human behavior. E. J. Gibson and Walk (1960) found cliff avoidance in almost every terrestrial animal they tested. Avoidance was observed as soon as an animal was capable of independent locomotion. For example, goats can walk at birth, and they demonstrate cliff avoidance on the first day after birth. Rats begin to see and to locomote by sight at 2 weeks; when tested at this age, they show cliff avoidance. Dark-reared rats, tested on first exposure to light at 3 months, are sensitive to the visual cliff. Depth perception appears to develop without visual experience in many species. These studies provided evidence that the capacity to perceive depth emerges very early and spontaneously in terrestrial animals, including humans.

Thus, the visual capacity to perceive depth appears to form part of our innate endowments, whereas object perception seems to depend more on experience and learning. It is therefore difficult to take a stand as either an empiricist or a nativist. How much is given and how much is learned depend on what kind of capability is in question.

## Pattern Recognition

One of the most striking abilities of visual perception is the sorting out of familiar patterns or objects from the enormous quantity of information received through the eyes. All activities of our daily life, from looking at pictures to reading a book, have to do with pattern recognition, which has become the subject of study for both psychologists and computer scientists. Many theories have been put forth, but only recently has the scientific approach to pattern recognition made much progress.

### Detection of Edge and Texture

Current theory suggests that visual perception is a complex process that cannot be performed at a single stage; rather, it can be broken down into a number of subprocesses. According to Marr (1982), the first stage of pattern recognition involves the perception of edges and textures. The most basic problem underlying visual perception is the detection of edges. Stimulations from the outside world form an image in the eye that is the input for visual processing, and the visual field can be thought of as made up of points of different light intensities. The edge of an object is a set of contours where the image intensity changes significantly. Intensity changes in the image usually correspond to features in the scene such as boundaries of objects and surface changes. A type of boundary which cannot be detected by a difference in light intensity is texture boundary: When two pieces of differently designed cloth are laid side by side, their average intensity may be similar, yet the observer easily distinguishes between the two different pieces of cloth. The human visual system is capable of making basic information processing of edge detection and texture segmentation at the first stage of vision. It describes significant features in the image, and it also involves more global processes that group these features to make up meaningful patterns.

Thus, when an observer sees a group of complex stimuli and is able to discern it to be something that he or she has experienced before, this group of stimuli can be called a pattern and is being recognized; when a group of stimuli can repeatedly elicit a certain kind of behavior, it is said to have been recognized. For a very simple stimulus to be sensed, it needs to be of a certain form and intensity to act on the sense organ; pattern recognition requires a much higher level of information processing. In pattern recognition, a group of stimuli must stimulate the sense organ, information stored in memory is retrieved, and, finally, the brain performs a comparison of the current stimuli and the information in memory. Sometimes, the observer needs to formulate a concept from the stimuli in order to identify the object perceived. For example, when something moves in a dark night, we have to judge from its movements that it is a person and not a tree. Thus, pattern recognition involves a series of psychological processes and their interactions, which include perception, memory search, concept formation, and, finally, the recognition of the object.

An astonishing aspect of human pattern recognition is its flexibility. We can read the letter A easily, be it a printed A, an upper- or lowercase A, a handwritten A, a bigger or smaller A, an inclined or inverted A, or even an A written on your back. We can easily recognize the face of a friend, either shaved or with a moustache, in different hair styles, even after years of separation. What kind of traces have to be stored in memory, and how are they stored, to permit comparison with the ongoing stimulus to achieve recognition? One explanation is that for every letter or object known by the perceiver there is a template stored in long-term memory. Incoming patterns would be matched against their templates. However, such a template-matching scheme would not work because there are so many patterns we have experienced that it would be almost impossible to store all of them in memory and because there are so many patterns that are alike, which may result in confusion in the process of recognition.

### Feature Analysis

A far better model of pattern recognition is a process called *feature analysis*. Feature analysis models of recognition were popular with psychologists and computer scientists in the 1960s, when neurophysiologists discovered feature detectors in the brain for the sensing of shapes and orientations of stimuli. According to the feature analysis model, objects are characterized by the set of perceptual features of which they are composed. Selfridge (1959) designed the Pandemonium system for the discrimination of English alphabets. This system has several levels, each of which has its own feature mechanisms, and they work in sequence, which results in pattern recognition. Selfridge calls each level of analysis the work of a kind of demon; hence, the various levels of demons together form a pandemonium, a place where all kinds of demons reside.

The first level of the Pandemonium system is an image demon, which performs the simple task of registering the original form of the incoming pattern; it performs a function like the retina of the eye. At the next level are the feature demons, whose tasks are to further analyze this image, each finding the number of features in the pattern that corresponds to its own feature. For the letter R to be recognized, the feature demons report one vertical line, two horizontal lines, one oblique line, three right angles, and one closed curve, respectively. The cognitive demons at the third level of the system receive the reports from the feature demons, and each cognitive demon is responsible for the recognition of one letter: One demon is responsible for A, another for B, and so on. Cognitive demon A tries to look for the features reported by the feature demons that correspond to A. When it discovers these features it shouts out; the more features it discovers to be its own, the louder its shouts. At the final level, the decision demon picks out the cognitive demon that makes the loudest shout to determine the letter to be recognized.

The above example demonstrates that for the recognition of a letter not all seven feature demons are necessary. In the recognition of the letter R, only the responses of one acute angle and one closed curve are enough. If the information for the angles of R is extracted, three right angles and one acute angle would also suffice to perform the recognition. Thus, to recognize any one of the 26 letters of the Roman alphabet, the information from the seven feature demons is more than necessary. In recognizing a letter, even if some feature demons are not working, the recognition can still be well performed. However, all of the letters together consist of seven features, so seven feature demons are required to recognize the alphabet. For a pattern recognition system to recognize more patterns, more feature demons have to be added according to features present in these patterns.

The Pandemonium system may be useful for the recognition of simple letters or codes; however, as a general model for human pattern and object recognition, it is unsatisfactory. Confusions in the discrimination between F and ⌐ or between T and ⊥ may occur, but these are mistakes that humans typically do not make. In addition, the system discards all information that distinguishes different characteristics of the same pattern. The output of the decision demon would be the same irrespective of the particular type of letter A shown. We recognize someone's handwriting by the particular shape of the letters he or she writes down, and a bank clerk must identify customers' signatures in making financial transactions. One difficulty with the feature analysis approach to pattern recognition is that the necessary features that underlie some patterns cannot be specified. Thus, we need a representational format that allows us to describe the differences between patterns that are important for their discrimination, and at the same time preserve important structural differences between different instances of the same pattern. Psychologists and computer scientists are working at other approaches to pattern recognition that may be more effective and more comparable to human recognition.

### Spatial Frequency Model

Another approach to the study of pattern recognition has been to use very simple parameters capable of describing visual patterns in quantitative terms. Based on the 19th-century mathematician Jean Baptiste Joseph Fourier's wave form analysis, a technique of spatial frequency analysis was developed to study pattern perception. Any repeatedly occurring wave form can be described in terms of frequency, amplitude, and phase. The left panel of Figure 2 is a grating with a brightness distribution of light–dark cycles whose wave form is a square wave. This is called a *square-wave grating*. The brightness distribution of the grating in the right panel of Figure 2 is also in light–dark cycles, but with a gradual change in brightness and a sine-wave wave form. This is called a *sine-wave grating*. By spatial frequency we mean the number of light–dark cycles per degree of visual angle from the eye of the observer. The gratings in Figure 2 have light and dark cycles, and the cycles per degree of visual angle increase with observation distance. Thus, once the distance between the two peaks of the waves and the distance from the observer are known, the visual angle of each cycle can be defined by

$$\frac{\text{distance between wave peaks}}{\text{observation distance}} = \tan \text{visual angle},$$

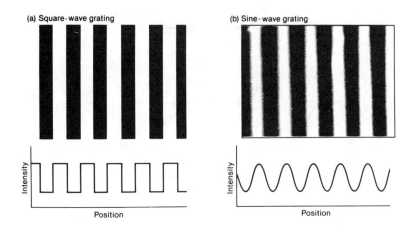

**FIGURE 2** Square and sine-wave gratings with the same spatial frequency.

and from this the spatial frequency of a grating in terms of cycles per degree of visual angle can be calculated.

As Fourier pointed out, any kind of wave form can ultimately be analyzed into the sum of a fundamental sine wave and its odd harmonics. The fundamental frequency of a square wave is the sine wave of the same frequency, which has the highest amplitude, 1.273 (4/π) times the square wave. This is the first harmonic of the compound wave. The frequency of the second sine wave component is three times the fundamental frequency, and its amplitude is ⅓ of the first harmonic; this is the third harmonic. Then come the fifth and seventh harmonics, whose amplitudes are ⅕ and ⅐ the fundamental frequency, respectively. When all of these sine waves are added together, a wave form very similar to that of a square wave will result (see Figure 3). A complex visual pattern or scene can also be similarly analyzed by the Fourier technique into its sine-wave components. To perceive the complex pattern or scene accurately, the visual system has to handle all of the spatial frequencies that are present. If high frequencies are filtered out, the small details and sharp contrasts are lost; if low frequencies are filtered out, the large uniform areas and gradual transitions are lost (see Rosenzweig & Leiman, 1989, p. 341).

In 1968, Campbell and Robson suggested that the visual system has several channels that are tuned to different spatial frequencies, such that one channel is most sensitive to a low frequency of 1 cycle/degree; a second channel to a frequency of 3 cycles/

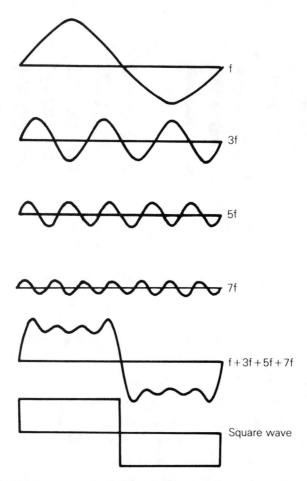

**FIGURE 3**  Fourier components of square wave-grating.

degree; and a third channel to a frequency of 12 cycles/degree. The overall sensitivity of
the visual system is composed of many selective channels for a wide range of fine discriminations. Campbell and Robson's hypothesis of multiple spatial frequency channels
was confirmed by experiments by other investigators. This approach breaks down complex stimuli into their individual spatial frequency components. The model of multiple
spatial frequency channels had great impact on visual science because it led to entirely
different conceptions of the way in which the visual system might operate in processing
spatial information, and it has proved useful in explaining various aspects of human pattern vision.

# Color Perception

We live in a world in which objects have light and color. Color provides an important dimension in acquiring knowledge of the environment, and it also stimulates the feelings of pleasure and beauty of scenes that attract the eyes. Color vision originates when electromagnetic waves of certain wavelengths stimulate the eye and are processed by the brain. Studies of color are increasing and form a new discipline called " color science." Color is also a main area of study in visual perception, dealing with various color phenomena, the laws that govern these phenomena, and the theories that try to explain various color phenomena.

## Color Phenomena

### Attributes of Color Vision

Color vision has three attributes: brightness, hue, and saturation. A color may be designated by these three attributes to distinguish it from other colors. The brightness of a color denotes what we usually call a light color or dark color; it varies from white to black. One red color may be brighter or darker than another red color. The physical stimulus for brightness is the reflectance of a colored surface. Hue is an attribute that distinguishes one color from another color: Yellow is different from red, and red is different from blue; so yellow, red and blue are different hues. Hue is related to the wavelength of the color stimulus. For example, if a light of 700 nm is sufficiently intense, it is seen as red; 579 nm is yellow, and 510 nm is green. The human eye can distinguish about 100 different hues on the spectrum. Saturation designates the purity of a color: A color is said to be more saturated when it deviates from gray. The colors of the spectrum are the most saturated colors. When grey, black, or white is added to a color, it is desaturated. A color of 680 nm on the spectrum is a saturated red; when a white light is mixed with this red color, it becomes pinkish, which is a desaturated red. The more white light is added, the more desaturated it becomes until it looks white.

When differently colored lights from the spectrum are mixed in certain proportions, an achromatic color, or white, may result. When two colors mix so as to produce white, these two colors are called complementary colors. Thus, when red and bluish-green lights are mixed, one sees white. Blue and yellow lights, when mixed together, also produce white. (Mixing lights follows a different principle from mixing pigments, as will be explained later.)

## Interaction of Color

The color we perceive on the surface of objects is determined not only by the physical stimulus itself, but also by the colors surrounding it. The surrounding colors may affect both the perceived brightness and hue of a color. When a color changes in the direction opposite to that of the surrounding color (i.e., to the complementary color of the surrounding color), the phenomenon is called simultaneous interaction or color contrast. A grey square on a red background may appear greenish, and a grey square on a green background may appear reddish. A colored surface usually has its appearance shifted toward the complementary color of the surrounding color. When a color is presented on a surround of higher or lower brightness, it changes in the direction opposite the surrounding brightness level; this is called brightness contrast. A grey square on a white surround appears darker, and the same grey square on a black surrounding appears whiter than before.

How black or white an object appears does not completely depend on how much of the surrounding light it reflects; it also depends on the relative quantity of light reflected in relation to its background and surrounding objects. A piece of coal under the sun reflects a thousandfold more light than a piece of white paper in the dark, yet the coal is perceived as black and the paper is perceived as white. Whether we see things as black, white, or gray is determined by the relative brightness of an object in relation to its surrounding objects. A piece of coal under the sun is darker than a piece of stone, or the pavement, and therefore the coal is perceived as black. The color or brightness of an object is also determined by the usual color of the object in our memory. A banana is yellow and a cherry is red. Our previous experience helps us to perceive the color of objects.

When the spectral components of a light source change, the light reflected from an object into our eyes should also change. But in our daily experience the color of familiar objects under changing illumination may not change. When a friend is under the shade of a tree, some parts of the face are covered by shadows of leaves; however, we still see the same face and do not note the patches of light and dark on the face. But when we look at the same face on a flat color photograph, the patches are clearly seen. This phenomenon of the unchanging color appearance of familiar objects is called color constancy.

The color and brightness of an object do not completely depend on the stimulus, but are also influenced by the after-effects of previous stimulation. This is called successive interaction or successive contrast. When you look at a red square for several minutes then fixate on a grey surface, a green square will eventually appear; it fluctuates in vivid-ness, lasts for a while, and then fades and disappears. This color is the complementary color of the inducing color. This phenomenon is called a negative after-image. A yellow stimulus induces a blue after-image, a white stimulus induces black, and black induces white. When a colored after-image is projected on a colored surface, (i.e., when we look at a colored surface after fixating another colored object), the color we see is usually a mixture of the negative after-image and the color of the second surface. For example, when we project the after-image of a red color on a yellow wall, we see a yellowish-green-colored wall. When we project the negative after-image of a red color on a bluish-green wall, we perceive a more saturated bluish-green wall surface.

An after-image may also take the same color as the original stimulus. This is called positive after-image, and it lasts a very short time. When we move a lighted cigarette quickly in the dark, we see a streak of light rather than a moving point of light. This streak is caused by the positive after-image of the cigarette light. Thus, after a light is extinguished or taken away, there first appears a very short duration of a positive after-image of the same color as the original stimulus; then comes a longer period of a nega-tive after-image that takes the complementary color of the original stimulus.

## Color Mixture

Research on color mixture can be dated back to Sir Isaac Newton in the late 17th cen-tury. Newton's experimental set-up is shown in Figure 4. He made a hole in an otherwise covered window to let a beam of sunlight pass through; a prism was placed on the path of this beam, and a screen was used to receive the light that passed through the prism. The prism dispersed this beam of white light into various colors of the spectrum. Newton used another piece of paper with a slit to let pass only one hue from the spectrum and to project this color onto a second screen. If this slit is moved sidewise and successively lets other colors pass through, one sees individual colors on the screen. These colors are saturated monochromatic lights. If another prism is placed in the path of one monochro-matic light, then this monochromatic light cannot be dispersed further, and it still remains its original color. Newton also discovered that if he used a lens to focus all of the colored lights of the spectrum onto one spot on a screen, so that this spot was a mixture of the spectral lights, they formed the same white light as the beam of sunlight. From these ex-periments, Newton concluded that white light is a mixture of different colored monochro-matic lights. Monochromatic lights of the spectrum, being the components of white light, cannot be broken down any further because they are the basic colors of the spectrum.

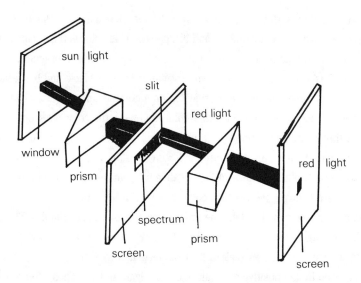

**FIGURE 4**   Newton's experiment on the spectrum. Reprinted by permission from Kaufman (1979).

Newton's experiments laid the foundation for color mixture. We now know that when two monochromatic lights of the spectrum are projected onto the same spot on a screen, one is able to see the mixture of these two colored lights. This mixture is caused by the simultaneous stimulation of the eyes by two different colors, and is therefore called an additive mixture. The mixture of two different colors of the spectrum produces a new color such that when green and red are mixed one sees yellow and when red and yellow are mixed one sees orange. The resulting color can be found on the spectrum: Yellow lies between red and green, and orange lies between red and yellow. Generally, the new color produced by mixing two nearby colors of the spectrum occupies an intermediate place between the two colors being mixed; the resulting color is called an intermediary color. However, when the two colors being mixed are colors that lie far apart on the spectrum, they may produce white. Thus, when red and bluish green are mixed, white may result; when blue and yellow are mixed, we may also see white. This occurs when the colors that are mixed are complementary colors and the resulting color is a neutral color. When the two colors on the extreme ends of the spectrum (i.e., red and blue), are mixed, we see purple, which is not found on the spectrum. This principle of color mixing is used in modern color research: Two projectors, each with a color filter placed over its lens system, are focused on the same spot on a screen, and the mixed color is either an intermediary color or a neutral color. It has been discovered that three colors from the spectrum, when mixed, are enough to produce white. The best three colors for producing white are red, green, and blue.

Another way of mixing colors is by using a color disk whose different sectors are of different colors; when the disc is turned at a fast speed, we see a mixed color. If the sectors are the colors on the spectrum, we see a white disc. This is because when we look at the disc, different colors successively stimulate the eye. The image of the first color mixes with the second incoming color, and this mixes with the third and other color stimuli until we see a mixed color, which is produced by neural mechanisms in the eye and brain.

Another way of mixing different colors is to arrange different tiny color spots next to one another on a surface. When this surface is far enough from the eyes as to not be perceived as individual spots, we see a mixed color. This principle is used in color printing, color television, and some schools of painting. If we look at a color television screen through a magnifying glass, we see little red, green, and blue phosphor spots. The colored spots on the screen are so near to each other and far enough from the viewer that they cannot be detected as individual spots. Each small patch of red, green, and blue spots forms a group; the different brightness of these three spots stimulate a very small area of the fovea in the eye, are mixed together by a psychophysical process, and produce a particular color for the observer.

The mixing of color pigments, such as water colors and paints, is different in principle from mixing colored lights. The mixing of colored lights is *additive* color mixture, whereas the mixing of color pigments is *subtractive* color mixture. As we mentioned before, yellow light mixed with blue light produces white light, but when yellow and blue paint mix, they do not produce white, but result in green. The mixing of two lights is the simultaneous stimulation of lights of two wavelengths on the retina, which is an additive process. On the other hand, although color pigments on a surface reflect some wavelengths of light, they absorb some other wavelengths. The color resulting from the mixture of pigments depends on the wavelengths of the reflected light. A yellow pigment reflects yellow and the neighboring green color of the spectrum, but absorbs blue and all other colors of the spectrum. A blue pigment reflects the blue color and its neighboring green color of the spectrum and absorbs yellow and all colors. When yellow and blue pigments are mixed, they both reflect the green color of the spectrum, but all other colors of the spectrum are absorbed either by the yellow pigment or by the blue pigment, so the resulting mixture is a green color. Hence, the mixture of color pigments is a subtraction process, each pigment subtracting some portion of the colors from the spectrum.

## The Measurement of Color

Physical objects can be measured in terms of size, weight, volume, and other standard units of metrology. Color is a subjective visual phenomenon elicited by the physical stimuli of the outside world. Can color be measured? What are its units of measurement? If color can be measured in terms of standard units, it would be very convenient in science and business for people to convey a specific color without producing the colored object itself. For example, when wool yarn is exported to another country, it is agreed upon that this batch of wool yarn is to be of a certain color. It is difficult to check whether the wool received is of the right color unless a sample is provided. However, the sample may fade in color, or people may disagree as to whether the exported yarn matches the sample. Because of the necessity of measuring colors, various systems of color representations have been developed. To develop a color representation system we have to study the relationships among different colors, discover laws governing the changes of colors, and describe these relationships in quantitative terms. The measurement of color is a subject of study in psychology, particularly in psychophysics. Even not knowing the physical properties of a color stimulus, we can describe colors according to their visual characteristics and classify them according to their appearances. Eventually, we can design a representation system to describe all of the colors that we see.

### The Color Diagram

Suppose that there are many pieces of differently colored chips placed on a grey surface and someone is asked to arrange these chips in a straight line by their similarity to each other, for example, by placing orange near red, yellow near orange, and so on (i.e., by placing colors very similar to each other at short distances, and colors not very similar at a farther distance). The person will eventually find out that no matter how he or she arranges these hues, the colors at the two ends are always similar, for example, red may be at one end and blue may be at the other end; but red and blue both resemble purple and therefore should be near each other. So it is not possible to arrange hues by similarity in a straight line. But if the observer is asked to arrange these colors in a two-dimensional space, he or she may easily succeed in arranging all of the colors in an orderly system by placing them in a circle. In this circle (Figure 5), colors similar to one another are neighboring colors.

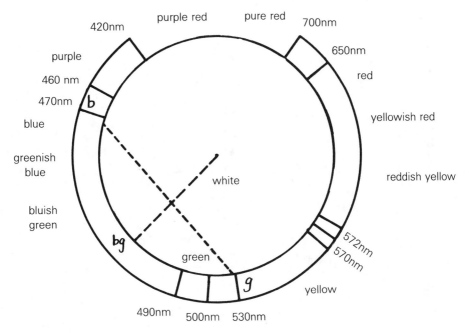

**FIGURE 5**   Color circle.

We can use a color circle to describe all of the phenomena of color mixture. On the circumference of the circle in Figure 5 are the basic hues of the spectrum (i.e., red, orange, yellow, green, blue, and purple). The center of the circle is white. This diagram can predict the results of mixtures of colors of the spectrum. For example, b on the circle represents a blue light of 470 nm, and g represents a 530-nm green light. If these two lights are mixed in equal amounts of intensity (luminosity), a line is drawn between b and g, and another line is drawn from the center of the circle through the center of the first line to a point bg on the circle. This point is the result of the color mixture that is bluish green.

If another dimension, brightness, is added to this color diagram, we have a color solid, as in Figure 6. The vertical axis represents brightness. The top end of this axis is white, the bottom end is black, all along the axis are different shades of grey, the upper parts are light greys, and the lower parts are dark greys. The midpoint of this vertical axis represents medium grey. This color solid can represent all colors. Saturated colors are on different points of the largest circumference of the solid; a change in saturation of a color is represented along the line between medium grey and a point on the circumference.

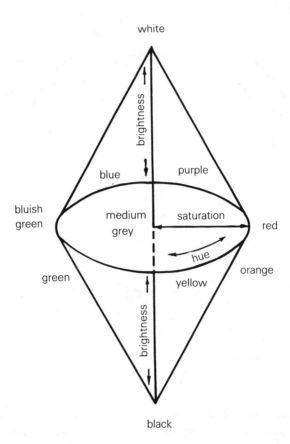

**FIGURE 6** The color solid.

When the brightness of a color is increased or decreased it moves upward or downward in the color solid. When a color is brighter or darker than medium grey, it becomes less saturated and must lie somewhere at a level higher or lower than the largest circumference of the color circle.

## The CIE Color System

It is known that almost all colors can be produced by the mixture of three colored lights, with the restriction that any one of these three colored lights cannot be produced by the mixture of the other two colored lights. The best set of three colors are red, green, and blue. These are called primary colors. Any color can be denoted by the relative amount of these three primaries (see Jing, Jiao, Yu, & Hu, 1979). For example, an orange can be mixed by a large amount of red, some green, and very little blue. This is done by a color matching experiment that uses three projectors, each with a filter: red, green, and blue, respectively. These three lights are projected on the same spot on a screen, and the amount of each color (i.e., the luminosity of the color) is controlled by the intensity of the light emitted from each projector. To the left of this spot is a colored light from a projector to be matched. In our case the color to be measured is an orange light. The observer looks at both sides of the partition. When an appropriate proportion of the three primaries is being mixed, the resulting color on the right will appear as the same color as on the left side. In this way, the orange color can be measured by the amount (intensity) of the three primaries.

The result of this color matching experiment can be represented by a color equation as follows:

$$(C) \equiv R(R) + G(G) + B(B),$$

where (R), (G), and (B) represent the three primary colors red, green, and blue, and $R$, $G$, and $B$ denote the respective amounts of the three primary colors. (C) is the color to be matched by the three primary colors. The symbol $\equiv$ means "matches" or "looks the same as."

The Commission Internationale de l'Eclairage (CIE) has standardized the three primaries so that any color can be designated by a common measure that is understood by all color workers in science, business, and industry. The red primary is a spectral light of 700 nm, the green primary is a spectral light of 546.1 nm, and blue a spectral light of 435.8 nm. The CIE has designed a color diagram in which any color can be plotted. This diagram is called the CIE 1931 Color Diagram, which is internationally adopted for the specification of colors. Figure 7 shows the CIE 1931 Color Diagram. The abscissa x represents the amount of red, and the ordinate y represents the amount of green. Blue is not designated on this diagram because blue $= 1 - (x + y)$. The horseshoe-shaped curve is called the *spectrum locus*, and on it are the hues of the spectrum. The line connecting the 700-nm red and 400-nm blue is purple, a mixture of red and blue that is not on the spectrum. The center of the diagram, x $= 0.33$, y $= 0.33$, is white.

A color located near the center is an unsaturated color, and a color on the spectrum locus is a saturated color. All colors on a line connecting the center and a certain wavelength on the spectrum locus have the hue of this specific wavelength but vary in saturation. When a line is drawn between two points of the spectrum locus, the colors on this line denote the resulting colors of the mixture of these two spectral colors, such as the line between 510-nm green and 590-nm orange. Any two colors connected by a

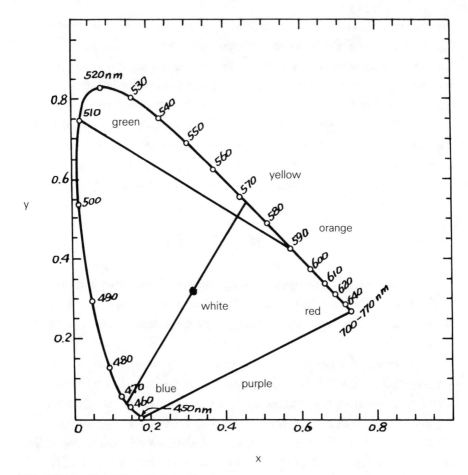

**FIGURE 7**   The CIE 1931 Color Diagram.

straight line passing through the center are complementary colors, such as 465-nm blue and 572-nm yellow. Hence, once the chromaticity coordinates x and y of any color are known, one can locate it on the CIE 1931 Color Diagram.

### Measurement of Skin Color

An illustration of the use of color measurement is the measurement of skin color. When we see colored scenes on TV or on color prints, the colors are usually approximate reproductions of natural colors. If a colored object on a color print deviates too much from the natural colors of objects, the picture does not look nice. Allowances may be relatively great for objects, but not for the human face. A small deviation from the natural facial color is detected by the eyes and may look bad. Thus, in the television industry, in photography, and in the design of lighting systems, it is essential to know the colors of the human face, especially that of the cheek, for purposes of color reproductions. Such measurements are made in the United States, Japan, China, and other countries. The American white has higher reflectance than the Asian and American black on all wavelengths of the spectrum. These three facial colors, when calculated for their x and y coordinates and plotted on the CIE 1931 Color Diagram, show that the Asian facial colors are more yellowish and more saturated than the American white and black complexions. When these color specifications are known, they are used by international satellite television transmissions to reproduce the correct facial colors of different ethnic groups, and are also used by the photographic industry to reproduce better pictures.

In industry, color measurements are widely used to check the quality of commercial products. In some instances, exaggerations are made to improve the visual effects of color reproductions. In television and photographic reproductions, colors are often transformed into preferred colors that are more pleasing to the eyes. In grocery stores, lighting systems are used to make vegetables and fruits look fresher and better. The preferred, more pleasing colors of certain objects are a subject of study in visual perception in psychology. In China, a book by psychologists who are experts in color perception (Jing et al., 1979) is used by color scientists in many industries including textiles, paper manufacture, painting, photography, and television.

## The Perception of Space

The retina of the human eye is essentially a flat surface, but we perceive the environment as a three-dimensional space that extends in depth. How is this achieved? This has been a puzzling question to philosophers. It has long been known that vision with two eyes, binocular vision, has the unique function of providing information of visual direction and depth. Recent studies have also shown that light distribution itself from the environment can provide us with information of space.

### Binocular Vision

In most species of the animal kingdom, the sense organs and organs of locomotion are arranged in pairs. One point of biological significance of this pairing is that one organ of the pair serves as a supplement or reserve of the other, taking over its function in the case of the latter's impairment. But the pair of organs also has a unique function of its own that cannot be performed by either member of the pair alone. Let us take the example of the human hands. Each of the hands is capable of feeling the size, texture, form, or weight of an object that is in its grasp. But with a larger object—say a football—holding it with both hands gives us fuller information as to its size, form, and weight. Note that we still have the impression of only one football and not of two footballs, even though the left hand is touching a ball and the right hand is also touching a ball. This means that when used together, the two hands have a unique function besides their individual functions for processing information on the qualities of external objects. The two hands together function as a third hand, so to speak, that has better capability. If the question is pressed further as to how the two hands process information as a single organ, and how the brain is involved in this processing of information, then complications arise. It is for psychologists and physiologists to solve the mystery.

## Cyclopean Eye

In the case of vision, the modality that has been most thoroughly studied, it has long been known that binocular vision has a special function for processing information of direction and depth. Although we have two eyes, we do not see things as double. In ordinary circumstances, when we fixate a distant object in space, the axes of the two eyes must converge to point at the object; in this way, the images of this object in the two eyes fall on identical positions, the foveas, of the two retinas. Nevertheless, we are not conscious that we are using two eyes; objects in space seem to be perceived by a single eye, and we have a single impression of the object. The singleness of binocular vision makes it appropriate to assume that the two eyes when used together are but a single organ, better represented by an imaginary eye called the Cyclopean eye (see Figure 8). This "eye" is situated midway between the two real eyes, just above the bridge of the nose. If the two retinas are superimposed, making the foveas and spatial relations congruent, this superimposed retina represents the retina of the imaginary Cyclopean eye.

The Cyclopean eye is the anchorage with which we make our orientations in space. Our visual direction is not determined by either the left or the right eye. The straight line projected forward from the Cyclopean eye is the basis by which we judge directions in space. In Figure 8, an object F in a frontal position from the observer stimulates $f_1$ and $f_2$ on the foveas of the two eyes. Assuming that the two foveas are congruent, overlapping each other, they form a fovea of the Cyclopean eye, and f is the stimulated point on this fovea. From the Cyclopean eye a line is extended forward that is the frontal direction, and F falls on this line. Every two corresponding points on the two retinas have a common visual direction that lies on either the right or the left of the visual direction of the

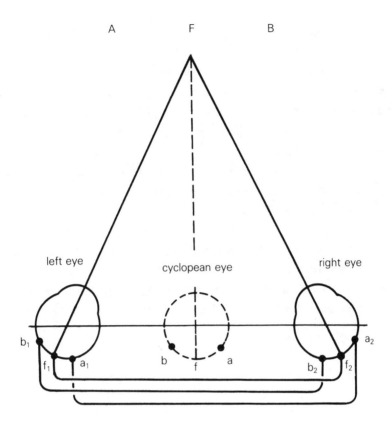

**FIGURE 8**   The Cyclopean eye, in an observer looking straight ahead.

Cyclopean eye. Take the corresponding retinal points $a_1$ and $a_2$: They can be represented by a in the Cyclopean eye and have the visual direction of A, which is projected to the left of the Cyclopean eye. Note that the fovea of the Cyclopean eye points to the basic visual direction of straight ahead if the observer is facing object F. All other pairs of corresponding points on the two retinas each have a common visual direction in reference to the direction line of the Cyclopean eye. In this way, we know the whereabouts of objects in space in relation to our body.

### Convergence

The convergence of the two eyes plays an important role in the perception of distance. As mentioned above, when we observe an object in space we converge our two eyes to fixate this object so that the image of this object falls on the foveas of the two eyes to obtain clearest vision. When we see a near object, the axes of the two eyes have to converge to a greater extent to form a greater convergence angle. When we look at a faraway object, the eyes do not converge as much, hence decreasing the convergence angle. When we look at a very distant object, the axes of the two eyes are nearly parallel. The convergence angle $\alpha$ of the axes of the two eyes is determined by the interocular distance a of the two eyes and the distance c of the object P from the eyes (i.e., $\alpha$ = a/c; $\alpha$ is in radians). When an object is at a very far distance, where c almost equals $\infty$, the change in distance of P causes very little change in the convergence angle. In this case, the mechanism of convergence no longer plays a role in distance perception.

In order to test how well human observers can use convergence to judge distance, Fang and Jing (see Jing, Jiao, & Ji, 1987) asked each of their subjects to wear a pair of eyeglasses with Polaroid lenses; two light stimuli at a distance were also fitted with Polaroid lenses. The Polaroid lenses were rotated in such a manner that each eye could only see one stimulus (see Figure 9). By making small changes in the distance between the two stimuli, the angle of convergence of the eyes of the observer could be altered. By

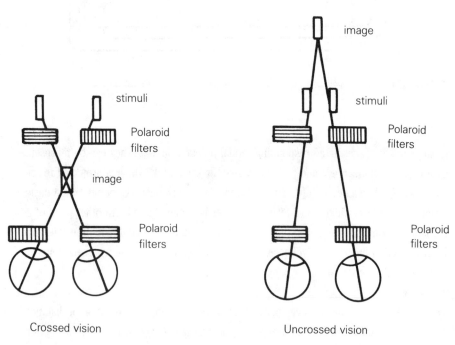

Crossed vision          Uncrossed vision

**FIGURE 9**   Experimental setup for studying convergence of the eyes.

arranging the different rotating angles of the Polaroid lenses, the experimenter could make the observer's eyes see the stimulus with crossed or uncrossed vision. With this experimental setup, the observer saw not two images, but only one virtual image, which appeared to lie at a certain distance away from the observer. When the distance between the stimuli was changed, the convergence angle was forced to change. When the convergence angle was large, the image seemed to be near; when the convergence angle was small, the image seemed to be far. During the experiment, a distance marker was used for comparison so that the observer could make quantitative judgments of the apparent distance of the light.

Figure 10 shows the results of this experiment, in which the perceived distances changed with changes in the convergence angle: With a greater convergence angle, the object image was perceived as nearer, and vice versa. The judged distances fell very near the calculated distance predicted by trigonometry. If convergence were of no effect to perceive distance, the results would fall on the constant line. It was suggested that we can rely on the mechanism of convergence to provide information for distance fairly accurately within a distance of 45 meters. In this respect, the visual system acts like the mechanism of a viewfinder in a camera system.

### Binocular Disparity

When we fixate a flat surface in front of us, the image of this surface falls on the corresponding foveas of the two eyes. But when we observe a solid object, such as a triangular solid, because our two eyes are about 63 mm apart, we see this object from different directions: The left eye sees more of the left side of the object, and the right eye sees more of the right side. The fact that the two eyes receive slightly different stimulations from the object is called *visual disparity* of the two eyes, or *binocular disparity*. This stimulation of binocular disparity, when transmitted to and processed by the brain, produces stereoscopic vision, which is the perception of three-dimensional objects.

When we observe with two eyes objects at various distances from us, binocular disparity occurs on our retinas, and we see objects in depth. In Figure 11, P is a fixated object, its images fall on the two foveas $p_1$ and $p_2$ of the eyes. Another object B, which is nearer to us than P, has its images fall on $b_1$ and $b_2$, which are noncorresponding points of the retinas. This causes visual disparity, and we perceive B as nearer than P. Another object R, which is farther away than P, has its images fall on $r_1$ and $r_2$, which are also noncorresponding points on the retinas. This visual disparity makes us perceive R as farther away than P. We can see from this figure that objects farther or nearer than the object of fixation all stimulate noncorresponding points on the two retinas (i.e., one point

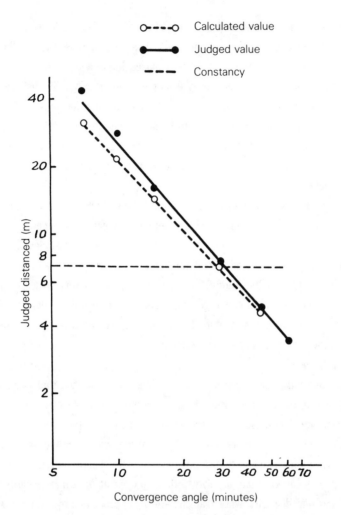

**FIGURE 10**   Effect of convergence on distance judgment.

nearer to the fovea on one eye, and the other point farther from the fovea on the other eye). If the stimulation point farther from the fovea lies on the nasal side of the eye ($r_2$), we perceive this object as more distant than the object of fixation (R). If the stimulation point farther away from the fovea lies on the temporal side of the eye ($b_2$), the perceived object is seen as nearer than the object of fixation (B).

The binocularity of the human visual system was further demonstrated by Julesz (1971) with random-dot stereograms. When the stereograms are viewed by the two eyes

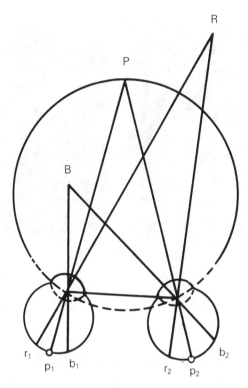

**FIGURE 11**    Binocular disparity of objects at different distances.

through a stereoscope, because some parts of the random-dot pairs are displaced laterally to one eye relative to the other, the observer sees the stereograms as a figure standing out or receding in depth from its background. Figure 12 is a pair of black and white stereograms. Stereodeficient or stereoblind people are unable to detect this depth effect, presumably because they have a history of strabismus or amblyopia, in which the joined activity of the two eyes is impaired, resulting in the loss of binocularity. This is further evidence that the visual system is able to make a point-by-point comparison of the retinal images of the two eyes and that the coordinated activity of the two eyes acts as a Cyclopean eye in stereoscopic vision.

To make a pair of random-dot stereograms, one has to first generate two identical random-dot pictures by a computer, and these two random-dot pictures will serve as backgrounds in the left and right figures. Then two smaller, identical random-dot squares (or some other shape) are placed on top of the two larger random-dot pictures, but the

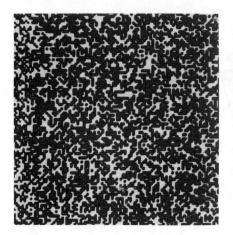 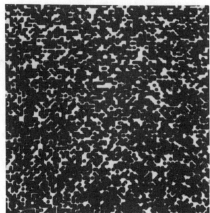

**FIGURE 12**    Random-dot stereograms.

two smaller squares are a little displaced in their relative positions on the backgrounds. They can be displaced either toward each other or apart from each other. When this pair of random-dot stereograms is viewed through a stereoscope, one sees an inner square either coming out from its background (if the smaller shapes were displaced toward each other) or receding into a distance from its background (if the smaller shapes were displaced away from each other). With a larger displacement of the two smaller squares, a greater depth effect is perceived. But the displacement can only be made within a certain limit; when the displacement is too large, the stereoscopic effect breaks down. When the observer views a pair of random-dot stereograms, the larger backgrounds are the fixated surfaces, and the displaced smaller squares stimulate noncorresponding points on the two retinas, producing disparity in the two eyes and resulting in the perception of depth. The random-dot stereograms experiment demonstrates that with a group of meaningless visual stimuli, without any cue for depth, once the condition of disparity stimulations on the retinas is fulfilled, one is able to perceive things in three-dimensional space. This direct perception of depth contradicts an older view that the perception of depth is derived from the perception of objects distributed in space.

Hubel and Wiesel (1962), working with microelectrodes to record the activity of single nerve cells in the visual cortex of the cat, discovered that there are binocular cells in the visual cortex to process information fed from the two eyes. These cells respond selectively to pairs of optically fused stimuli with binocular disparity, which code depth in space. However, recent discoveries have indicated that most visual cortical cells are not tuned to differences in binocular disparity and that those that are sensitive to disparity are not tuned selectively to a variety of depths. Rather, there are two types of cells that respond to binocular disparity, and they are both tuned to a wide range of disparities: One type is excited by stimuli in front of the fixation plane and inhibited by stimuli beyond the fixation plane, and the other type has the opposite pattern (see Poggio & Poggio, 1984). Psychophysical results with human observers have given independent evidence that there are only a few pathways or channels for depth perception. Investigators found that some "normal" viewers are actually partially stereoblind. Some are unable to localize, by stereo clues alone, the depth of an object that lies beyond the fixation plane; others are unable to localize, using such clues, the depth of an object in front of the fixation plane. These results point to the existence of two broadly tuned depth channels; either one may be missing or functioning poorly in a small number of individuals (see Jones, 1977).

## Spatial Information From the Environment
### Ambient Light

Gibson (1966, 1979) developed a theory of perception on the assumption that light stimulation from the environment is enough to produce the perception of space. Radiation energy from light sources (the sun or other light-emitting bodies) radiates in all directions. When light rays encounter opaque surfaces, some are reflected and some are absorbed. When light rays encounter transparent or translucent objects, some are reflected and some are transmitted through or into the objects. Low-reflectance (black) surfaces reflect little of the light rays and absorb most of the rays. High-reflectance (white) surfaces reflect most of the light rays and absorb only a small portion of them. Light is transmitted through the air in straight lines; however, some light rays meet particles in the air and are dispersed in different directions.

The reflection from a surface may be either specular or diffuse. When a surface is very smooth, incident light rays are reflected in a fixed direction; this is mirror-like specular reflection. When a surface is very rough, incident light rays strike on the numerous tiny deformations of the surface and are reflected in all directions; this is diffuse reflection. Not all objects in our environment receive direct illumination from light sources, but because of the diffuse reflection of objects, they are still illuminated by light reflected from other objects. Objects under a shade, or in secluded parts of a room, are illuminated by light reflected from other parts of the environment, often after many times of reflection. We have in our environment surfaces of objects that are different in size, in their distances from us, in coarseness, in reflection, and in their selectivity of absorption of different wavelengths of light. They receive light from different directions and reflect light at different angles. Therefore, our environment is, so to speak, "filled" with light; it comes from all directions and is distributed differently at each point in space. This distribution of light in the environment is called *ambient light*. Ambient light has important biological significance because it provides human beings with spatial information of our environment. As the observer moves around and takes up any point in space for observation, he sees around him different patterns of light distribution. The different patterns or structures of ambient light make up the optic array that contains special information about space.

### Visual Stimulation and Stimulus Information

If someone stands in a dense fog, the receptors on the retina of his or her eyes receive visual stimulation, and the optic nerve transmits nervous impulses to the brain. But under this circumstance there is no object for observation because light that enters the eyes is the same in all directions. This is diffused light, which cannot form an image on the retina. If the observer moves or turns his or her eyes, there is no change in the visual field; the only change possible is to open or close the eyes, and the observer sees only light or dark (i.e., with or without visual stimulation). Even if there is light in the eyes, the observer sees no objects, just like a patient suffering from severe cataract. This example demonstrates that visual stimulation is different from visual information. Light may be visual stimulation to the eye, but it may contain no information. Only when light in the environment exhibits differences is there visual information that tells us about objects in the outside world. A person in the dark receives no visual stimulation and cannot have vision. In diffuse ambient light there is visual stimulation, but because it does not contain visual information, it gives rise only to the sensation of light but cannot produce visual perception. Thus, visual stimulation of the visual receptors is a necessary, but not a sufficient, condition for visual perception.

### Ecological Information of Space

When an observer looks around in space, the ambient light at any point of observation has a unique array of light distribution. If we stand in an open field and observe the terrain, the earth's crust, grass, and hollow places on the ground near us appear large and clear, but they appear small and hazy in the far away part of the terrain. The pattern of optic array shows that near objects are spaced apart and far objects are densely spaced. This gradient of texture in the optic array contains information for distance perception.

Figure 13A has a greater density on optic array and smaller objects at the top of the picture; it is perceived as a surface extending into the distance or inclining backwards. If we turn the picture upside down, we see it as a ceiling extending into the distance or as a surface inclining forward. Figure 13B has no such difference in the layout of the optic array, so it is seen as a surface in the frontal parallel position. If an object is placed on a ground surface with differences in optic array density, the object takes the distance of the surface on which it is placed, and a perspective effect of distance perception can be obtained. In Figure 14, the square A on the ground is nearer to the observer and occupies one unit of patterned structure, but the more distant a, although smaller than A, also occupies one unit of patterned structure; it is perceived as similar in size as A but lying at a farther distance. The region b, although smaller than A, occupies more structural units and is seen as larger than A. The region c is of the same area as A on the page but is seen as much bigger than A lying at a distance. An observer can perceive

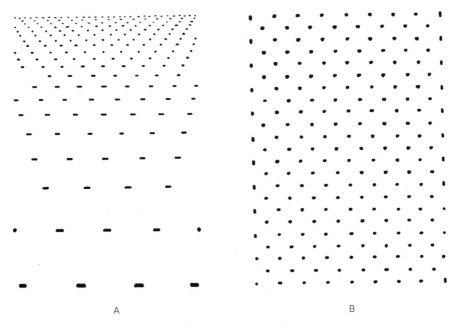

A                                                B

**FIGURE 13**    Optical array of different surfaces. Reprinted by permission from J. J. Gibson (1950).

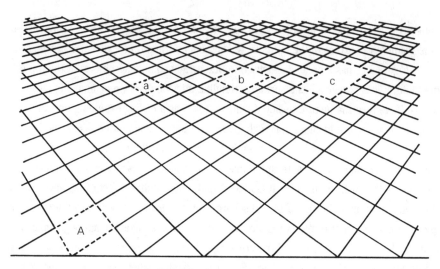

**FIGURE 14**    Perspective produced by differences in optical array density. Reprinted by permission from Hake (1979).

directly the relation of size and distance according to the size of the retinal images of objects and the patterned structural density of the ground.

When a person moves, the surrounding pattern of the optic array constantly changes, which provides information about orientation in the larger spatial environment. If an observer moves forward in a car, only the point toward which the car moves is relatively stationary; the near and far landscape array on both sides moves backward at different speeds. When an airplane flies towards the horizon, only one point on the horizon ahead is stationary, and the optic array of the ground and the clouds overhead all undergo continuous transformations. The speed of transformation is different at different places from the observer: Near distances undergo faster transformations, and farther distances undergo slower transformations (see Figure 15, left panel). When an airplane pilot makes an approach when landing, the point of approach forms the center of an optic array distribution that radiates away in all directions. The ground seems to expand from this point of observation, and the speed of expansion increases from the center toward the periphery (see Figure 15, right panel).

## Postural Changes and Perception of Space
The world of objects that we see is normally described with reference to our body—whether they are near or far, to the left or right—even the size of objects is judged in

**FIGURE 15**    Optical flow viewed by an airplane pilot during flight and landing. Reprinted by permission from J. J. Gibson (1950).

relation to other objects as we normally see them. In normal conditions, the perceived size of objects at different distances from us remains relatively unchanged. This is called *size constancy*. Human beings usually perceive the outside world in an upright position. What happens to the perception of space if things are observed with an unusual posture, such as what airplane pilots experience during maneuvers? The normal relation between body posture and the environment is an important condition for size constancy. When the posture of an observer changes, the constancy of size perception is also affected. To measure these effects, Jing and his colleagues (see Jing et al., 1987) used balloons as visual stimuli and asked observers to make size judgments on a sports field of 250 meters. The observers took different postures in making judgments of size at various distances. The standard stimulus was a balloon of fixed size (32 cm) placed alternatively at various distances from the observer: 50, 100, 150, 200, or 250 meters. The comparison stimulus was another balloon placed at 1 meter distance by the side of the observer. The observer was asked to adjust a valve to regulate the amount of air injected into the comparison balloon to make it of the same perceived size as the balloons at various distances. Figure 16 shows the results. When the observer sat erect (shown at the midline of the graph), size constancy was maintained quite well for distances of 50 to 150 meters but broke down at 200 and 250 meters. When the observer was in a prone position (raising his head and eyes), shown on the left, and in a supine position (lowering his head and eyes), shown on the right, the perceptual size shrank in comparison with the results obtained in the erect observations. The prone positions caused a more marked decrease in perceptual size, and observations made in a fully prone position yielded smaller perceptual sizes than those

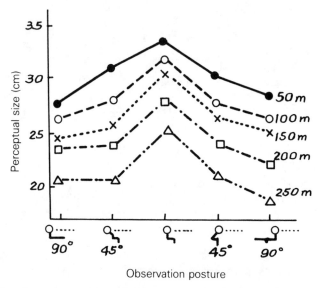

**FIGURE 16** Size judgments at different body postures.

made in semiprone positions. Interestingly enough, when a supine observer was asked to bend his head backward to see the stimulus in an inverse visual field, the perceptual size decreased to a minimum (the size change was as large as 1:0.53) and the observer reported an increase in perceptual distance. In another experiment, the subject was asked to sit on a tilting chair that could be turned laterally from an upright position to an upside-down position, and make distance judgments of an object as far as 120 meters. It was found that underestimation increased as body posture deviated from normal.

Jing and his colleagues (see Jing et al., 1987) sent a large hydrogen-filled balloon up into the air to as far as 250 meters; the subject was asked to make size judgments when the balloon was raised to various angles of elevation in relation to the subject's horizontal line of vision. The subject perceived the stimulus in two postures: (a) sitting erect on a chair and viewing the elevated stimulus by raising his or her head and eyes, and (b) sitting with his or her back and head against the pivoted and adjustable rear of the chair, which was then continually adjusted to remain at a right angle to the elevated stimulus, so that the subject always saw the stimulus straight ahead. When the subject sat in the erect position, the apparent size diminished gradually as the angle of elevation of the stimulus increased, and reached a minimum near the zenith (Figure 17, solid lines).

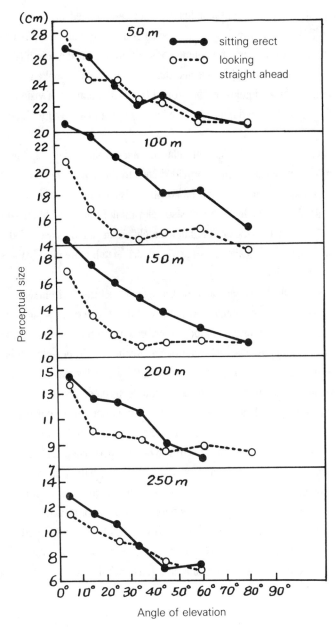

**FIGURE 17**   Visual size of an object in elevation under two modes of observation.

However, when the subject sat in the adjustable chair and looked straight ahead, the apparent size diminished abruptly: It was much smaller at 20° elevation and reached a minimum at about 40° elevation, then remaining constant up to near the zenith (Figure 17, broken lines). The same study also revealed that when the subject looked downward from a high building at a stimulus on the ground (i.e., with an angle of vision below the horizontal), the apparent size diminished to a lesser degree than it did with a raised angle of vision.

The above results suggest that muscular feedback from the neck and eyes, when looking upward at an elevated object, provided cues to the angular relation between the stimulus and ground that tended to yield a constant visual size, and that the effect of these cues diminished gradually with increased elevation. In the straight-ahead posture, the subject lost reference to the ground immediately as the stimulus ascended 20° to 40° above the horizontal, which made apparent visual size match more closely the size of the visual image on the retina.

Jing and his colleagues concluded that a regular posture–environment relation is important for maintaining perceptual constancy and that the nervous system makes use of proximal stimulus and information about body posture in relation to the ground to interpret the distal stimulus. The distortion of the posture–environment relation causes a breakdown of perceptual constancy. The results of these studies may have implications for visual problems encountered by astronauts and deep-sea divers.

The human body's relation to the ground is very important for our perception and orientation in space. The perception of any distal stimulus has to be weighed against the perceiver's relation to the gravity of the earth. When we perceive objects as stationary or moving, located far or near, big or small, we have to first ascertain the relation of our own body to the ground. As an analogy, for a theodolite to be accurate, it has to be leveled and aligned properly to the ground, its telescope's angle of elevation has to be calibrated, and so on. Human beings live on the earth, are nurtured by the earth, and make use of the earth as their point of departure in the perception of space. Antaeus lost all of his powers when lifted off the ground, and, in a sense, we do too.

## Summary and Conclusions

Visual perception, as reviewed in this chapter, may be seen as a process of sensing and interpreting the environment. It is a process of the brain in which stimulations of the eyes from the outside world are transformed into meaningful representations. This process not only is related to vision itself but is interpreted on the basis of information from other sense modalities and from one's past experience. Psychologists have often tried to make distinctions between sensation and perception: Sensation is seen as the reflection in the brain of the elementary physical attributes of objects, and perception as the reflection in the brain of meaningful objects. Thus, red color and round shape are sensations, but a red apple is a perception, the latter being the synthesis of various sensations. Perception is related to the perceiver's knowledge and his or her past experience and attitudes. The life experience of an individual enriches the precision and comprehensiveness of his perceptions, and the attitude he takes in perceiving things gives direction to the interpretations of his perceptions. Strictly speaking, it is difficult to distinguish clearly between sensation and perception. One has hardly any pure sensations; most of our visual experience consists of meaningful perceptions.

Visual perception is one of the basic processes of human cognition. Psychologists use modern scientific techniques to analyze the perceptual processes. A psychologist can either study the phenomena and laws of visual perception and make theoretical formulations at an information-processing level, or he or she can inquire into the brain mechanisms underlying the perceptual processes, and modern advances in the neurophysiology of vision have brought much knowledge to the understanding of visual perception. Evidence from both areas of study enables us to arrive at a fuller understanding of visual perception, which is one of the most intriguing areas of study in psychology as well as in the broader discipline of cognitive science.

# References

Campbell, F. W., & Robson, J. G. (1968). Application of Fourier analysis to the visibility of gratings. *Journal of Physiology, 197*, 551–566.

Gibson, E. J., & Walk, R. D. (1960). The "visual cliff." *Scientific American, 202*(4), 64–71.

Gibson, J. J. (1950). *The perception of the visual world.* Boston: Houghton Mifflin.

Gibson, J. J. (1966). *The senses considered as perceptual systems.* Boston: Houghton Mifflin.

Gibson, J. J. (1979). *The ecological approach to visual perception.* Boston: Houghton Mifflin.

Hake, H. (1979). Perception. In M. E. Meyer, *Foundations of contemporary psychology.* New York: Oxford University Press.

Hubel, D. H., & Wiesel, T. N. (1962). Receptive fields, binocular interaction and functional architecture in the cat's visual cortex. *Journal of Physiology, 160*, 106–154.

Jing, Q. C., Jiao, S. L., Yu, B. L., & Hu, W. S. (1979). *Colorimetry.* Bejing: Science Publishers. (In Chinese)

Jing, Q. C., Jiao, S. L., & Ji, G. P. (1987). *Human vision.* Beijing: Science Publishers. (In Chinese)

Jones, R. (1977). Anomalies of disparity in the human visual system. *Journal of Physiology, 264,* 621–640.

Julesz, B. (1971). *Foundations of cyclopean perception.* Chicago: University of Chicago Press.

Kaufman, L. (1979). *Perception: The world transformed.* New York: Oxford University Press.

Kellman, P. J., & Spelke, E. S. (1983). Perception of partly occluded objects in infancy. *Cognitive Psychology, 15,* 483–524.

Marr, D. (1982). *Vision: A computational investigation into the human representation and processing of visual information.* San Francisco: Freeman.

Poggio, G. F., & Poggio, T. (1984). The analysis of stereopsis. *Annual Review of Neuroscience, 7,* 379–412.

Rosenzweig, M. R., & Leiman, A. L. (1989). *Physiological psychology* (2nd ed.). New York: Random House/ McGraw-Hill.

Selfridge, O. (1959). Pandemonium: A paradigm for learning. In *Symposium on the mechanization of thought processes.* London: HM Stationery Office.

Spelke, E. S. (1990). Origins of visual knowledge. In D. N. Osherson, S. M. Kosslyn, & J. M. Hollerbach (Eds.), *Visual cognition and action.* Cambridge, MA: MIT Press.

Walk, R. D., & Gibson, E. J. (1961). A comparative and analytical study of visual depth perception. *Psychological Monographs, 75*(15, Whole No. 519).

# CHAPTER 7

# Health Psychology

Wayne H. Holtzman

H ealth psychology is one of the newest and most vigorous areas in which the science of psychology has found a useful application. The contributions of psychology to the prevention and treatment of illness, as well as to the promotion of health, are being increasingly recognized throughout the world as an essential component of improved health and well-being. In the words of one of its early leaders, Joseph Matarazzo (1980), health psychology has been defined as "the aggregate of the specific educational, scientific, and professional contributions of the discipline of psychology to the promotion and mainte- nance of health, the prevention and treatment of illness, the identification of ideologic and diagnostic correlates of health, illness, and related dysfunction, and to the analysis and im- provement of the health care system and health policy formation" (p. 815).

## Historical Highlights

The modern field of health psychology has historical roots that can be traced to early religious beliefs. Until recent times, there was no clear-cut division between behavior and health because individuals were considered to be ill or "possessed" if they were not act- ing as they should. Much of early treatment, as well as certain forms of folk medicine today in different cultures, was primarily behavioral, consisting of sacrifice, prayer, and the power of suggestion as an integral part of health care. Such mainline "fathers of medicine" as Hippocrates integrated culture and human behavior into the study of health. Only since the late 18th century have there been signs of a separation between medicine and psychology, a separation that accelerated rapidly when the role of microbes in disease, together with the beginnings of modern biology, chemistry, and physics, spurred the development of modern medicine. The two disciplines of medicine and psychology developed more or less independently of each other during the last two centuries.

Philosophical arguments about whether the mind and body are separate entities with little interaction between them or are inextricably tied together, perhaps with the conscious mind being a manifestation of bodily processes, remained unresolved from the days of the early Greek philosopher Plato until the early part of this century. As Heidbreder (1933) pointed out over half a century ago in her review of seven systems of psychology, a growing tendency at that time to disregard the metaphysics of this mind–body problem was one of the surest signs that psychology was finally becoming a true science.

At the same time that psychology was shifting from early structuralism to behaviorism and functionalism early in this century, the field of medicine was going through a similar evolution. Although the term *psychosomatic* was first used by Heinroth in 1818 to denote the effect of mental and emotional activities on the body, it was not until the 1930s that the recognition of psychosomatic medicine as a field was first clearly expressed, most notably in the psychoanalytic essays of Franz Alexander and Flanders Dunbar. It is interesting to note that the first volumes of *Psychosomatic Medicine* were sponsored in 1939 by the Division of Anthropology and Psychology of the U.S. National Research Council, with Dunbar as editor. The extent to which this emerging field was truly interdisciplinary is evident in the composition of the first board of editors of the journal, from the following disciplines: psychoanalysis, internal medicine, neurology, physiology, psychiatry, psychology, comparative physiology, and pediatrics.

One of the first scientific efforts to demonstrate mind–body–environment interactions in the causation of disease was the recording of the effects of psychological stress on gastric secretions as photographed through an opening in the stomach wall of a patient by Stewart Wolf and Harold Wolff (1942). When anger or resentment were induced in the patient by discussing emotionally charged situations in his life, gastric motility and acidity occurred, conditions conducive to the formation of an ulcer. When the patient experienced sadness or fear, the gastric mucosa became pale and acidity dropped.

The early psychoanalytic approaches soon gave way to experimental studies aimed at identifying psychological factors believed to play a major role in the development of specific somatic complaints. These initial attempts to link personality types to specific disease states were generally disappointing but nevertheless established a firm basis for interdisciplinary research in the new field of behavioral medicine.

The emergence of health psychology as a vigorous new discipline is a natural outcome of scientific and technological advances within psychology. Experimental and physiological psychology have contributed greatly to this evolution, beginning with Pavlov's early work with dogs at the turn of the century. His concept of conditioned reflex provided the basis for much of classical learning theory. In the 1920s, Walter Cannon introduced the concepts of homeostasis and fight versus flight. More recently, Neal Miller (1969) applied aspects of these earlier theories to an understanding of the role of conditioning in psychophysiological change and how certain aspects of the autonomic nervous system could be controlled. The modern use of biofeedback treatment to teach an individual how to control muscle tensions, blood pressure, and other physiological processes developed out of these earlier efforts.

Following World War II, the establishment in the United States of the National Institutes of Health and the governmental support of psychologists in the U.S. Veterans Administration Hospitals led to the rapid expansion of clinical psychology. Psychologists serving as professors in medical schools and as members of medical research teams stimulated the development of medical psychology and behavioral medicine, which focuses on the integration of behavioral science methods with biomedical knowledge and techniques. Although most clinical psychologists work primarily in the broad field of mental health, medical psychologists began applying their scientific skills to the problems of physical illness and health. Considerable progress was made in the 1950s and 1960s. For example, Jenkins (1971) cited 162 references from these two decades to studies of psychological and social factors implicated in the etiology of coronary heart disease.

By 1973, these developments had grown to the point where the Board of Scientific Affairs of the American Psychological Association formed a task force on health research to explore ways in which psychology could contribute to a better understanding of health and illness. The task force concluded in 1976 that there was no specialty field within psychology that could not contribute to the discovery of behavioral variables crucial to a full understanding of an individual's susceptibility to physical illness, adaptation to such illness, and ways of preventing or overcoming such illness. This report led in 1978 to the formation of the Division of Health Psychology of the American Psychological Association, a division that has grown rapidly, with over 2,900 members in 1991.

# International Perspectives

Similar explosive growth has taken place among the other highly developed countries of the world, especially those of North America and Western Europe. Not far behind, however, are the psychologists of Japan, Australia, New Zealand, Eastern Europe, South Africa, and, to some extent, the more developed countries of Latin America, such as Mexico, Brazil, Argentina, Chile, Colombia, and Venezuela. Most other regions of the world have also shown great interest in health psychology. For example, since about 1980, medical universities in the People's Republic of China have been adding departments of medical psychology to their faculties. But with some notable exceptions (Hong Kong, India, the Philippines, Singapore, Indonesia, Thailand, South Korea, Taiwan, and perhaps Nigeria), most of these developing countries do not yet have the resources or trained psychologists to undertake advanced research in health psychology.

## North America

Research on health and behavior has grown most vigorously in the United States, where public awareness of behavioral factors in such chronic illnesses as coronary heart disease and cancer has become widespread. An indication of this growth is the increase in annual expenditures on health and behavioral research in the U.S. National Institutes of Health (NIH). Starting in 1983 at the request of Congress, the NIH has prepared annual reports on the status and direction of health and behavioral research supported by its various institutes. Nearly all of the institutes, centers, and divisions of the NIH have research programs relevant to health and behavior. The total of funds for research of this kind in the annual NIH budget has increased from $66 million in 1983 to $309 million in 1990. The NIH anticipates that annual expenditures on health and behavior intramural and extramural research and research training will increase to $359 million by 1992, an increase of 16 percent over 1990. In spite of these marked increases, the proportionate amount of total funds in the NIH research and training budget has increased only a small amount—from 3% ten years ago to 4.4% in 1990.

In response to the U.S. Congress, a 10-year plan for increasing health and behavior research at the NIH has been developed, encompassing four broad categories of research: (a) behavioral epidemiology, dealing with the incidence and prevalence of various unhealthful behaviors, such as smoking; (b) the development, maintenance, and change of certain behaviors and lifestyles that affect health; (c) the scientific study of basic biobehavioral mechanisms underlying the linkage between health and behavior; and (d) behavioral interventions to prevent and treat illness or to promote health.

One of the leading organizations in the NIH dealing with health and behavior is the National Heart, Lung, and Blood Institute. The Institute is a leader in supporting multidisciplinary approaches that include behavioral as well as biomedical sciences and that address a broad spectrum of health and behavior issues. Included in its program are basic research, clinical investigations, and epidemiological studies that address such major problems as the following: (a) the role of stress and personality factors in hypertension and coronary heart disease; (b) the importance of changes in lifestyle for ameliorating coronary heart disease and for preventing chronic obstructive pulmonary disease; (c) the effects of various kinds of treatments on the health quality of life for persons with chronic illness; and (d) the effectiveness of large-scale community interventions in modifying disease risk factors among both children and adults. An example of research in one of the most important of these areas, behavioral factors in the prevention and treatment of cardiovascular diseases, will be given in detail toward the end of this chapter.

The U.S. Office of Disease Prevention and Health Promotion has recently estimated that 45% of the deaths from cardiovascular disease, 23% of the deaths from cancer, and 50% of the deaths from diabetes could be prevented by a combination of changes in behavior, early detection, and intervention. Large-scale research such as the early Framingham study (Dawber, Meadors, & Moore, 1951), and the subsequent massive promotional efforts to change people's behavior, has resulted in a decline of smokers from 40% in 1965 to 28% in 1990. During the 1980s, death rates declined for three of the leading causes of death among American—heart disease, stroke, and motor vehicle crashes—testifying to the value of investment in prevention and health promotion based on sound research in behavioral medicine and health psychology.

The growth of health psychology in Canada parallels closely the developments of the last 15 years in the United States. As full partners in the health care delivery systems for Canada, psychologists have been leaders in conducting research and developing new methods of intervention for many of the problems that physicians and other health care professionals have frequently found to be the most difficult to treat by traditional medical procedures. Like many other countries, including the United States, most of the Canadian psychologists identifying themselves as working within the health care system are involved as professional practitioners offering services to individuals in hospitals, clinics, or private practice rather than as scientists in major research projects. Although not contributing directly to scientific advances in health psychology through research, such professional practitioners usually keep abreast of research pertinent to their practice, leading to improved health for the people they serve. In Canada, as well as elsewhere, the growth of psychological services and of the public recognition of psychologists as vital participants in the health care system has contributed greatly to increased support for research and research training in various areas of health psychology.

## Europe

Health psychology in Europe is developing along similar lines to that in North America, but with a greater diversity from one country to the next because of differences in health care policies, research funding, and university education. There are also important differences across many European countries in terms of the stage and direction of development in health psychology, differences due largely to approaching the subject from different perspectives varying from medical psychology to social psychology and health education (Maes, 1990). Only recently was the European Health Psychology Society established after several regional conferences on health psychology that were held in Bilthoven, the Netherlands; Trier, Germany; and Rome, Italy. Sweden, the Netherlands, Czechoslovakia, Germany, Poland, Italy, Spain, and Great Britain are among the growing number of European countries with recently established societies of behavioral medicine, health psychology, or both. The newly formed International Society of Behavioral Medicine, which comprises mainly health psychologists from Europe and North America, held its first International Congress of Behavioral Medicine in Uppsala, Sweden, in June 1990.

Although the organization of health psychologists into specialized societies has taken place only very recently in Europe, major studies on health and behavior go back many years, as in the case of North American research. For example, the North Karelia project was begun in 1972 after the discovery that death from cardiovascular disease in this small rural province was far more frequent than elsewhere in Finland. Puska (1984), from the National Public Health Institute in Helsinki, designed and carried out a community-based, large-scale, educational intervention program lasting five years that successfully reduced the levels of smoking and other known cardiovascular risk factors among the population of North Karelia.

In Belgium, it was discovered that cardiovascular disease and cancer were responsible for more than two thirds of that country's mortality, leading to some initial worksite studies that showed the need for intervention directed at whole communities. Health psychologists at universities in Brussels, Ghent, Leuven, and Liège designed and carried out a large-scale intervention in the different regions of Belgium (Kittel, 1984). Like the North Karelia project, this Belgium study, designed to decrease the morbidity and mortality associated with cardiovascular disease, was very similar to studies carried out about the same time in the United States.

Evidence for behavioral treatment techniques and for combinations of both pharmacological and behavioral therapies has become sufficiently strong to justify collaborative international studies on a large scale. Several such investigations are currently being conducted under the auspices of the U.S./U.S.S.R. Scientific Exchange Agreement to determine the transferability of U.S. and Russian methods for the treatment of hypertension in each other's cultural milieu (U.S. Department of Health and Human Services, 1984).

## The Pacific Rim and Asia

Health psychology is also expanding rapidly in the more highly developed countries of the Pacific area, most notably Australia and Japan. Only recently have major research funding organizations in Australia made any major commitment to behavioral and psychological research dealing directly with health; the spectrum of activities is similar to that in North America and Europe.

Psychological research on health has grown most rapidly in Japan during the last decade. The establishment of the Japanese Association of Health Psychology and the inauguration of the new *Japanese Journal of Health Psychology* in 1988 stimulated the interests of many psychologists to conduct research in this field. The content of this research is similar to that in Europe and North America.

Elsewhere in Asia, there is growing interest in the ways in which psychology can contribute to better health, but resources for research are severely limited. In China, for example, there is a severe shortage of psychologists, but the potential role of psychology in medicine is now recognized. Unfortunately for scientists elsewhere, most studies and all textbooks have been published only in Chinese where they are generally inaccessible. The prevailing conditions in most of Asia are very different from those of the highly industrialized world, making it likely that the kinds of strategies developed for the prevention of disease, the treatment of illness, and the promotion of health will be quite different. The World Health Organization (WHO), through its Southeast Asia and Western Pacific offices, has done remarkably well in beginning to develop indigenous research activities in spite of these limitations.

## Africa

As pointed out by Peltzer (1990), health psychology in African has had only very limited development. The diseases associated with severe poverty—malnutrition, malaria, and other infectious diseases—are particularly prevalent, although such diseases of affluence as alcoholism, motor accidents, and cardiovascular disorders are on the increase. As in India, the strategies of cross-cultural psychology, transcultural psychiatry, and ethnomedicine are particularly critical if health psychology is to find a place in the national health care programs of most African countries (Dasen, Berry, & Sartorius, 1987). The African nation with the greatest amount of development in health psychology, as well as in other areas of psychology, is the Republic of South Africa. Rigid adherence to apartheid has led to the creation of two quite different, largely segregated, societies: an educated, White European society, consisting of a small minority of the population, within which most of psychology has developed, and a relatively uneducated, ethnically very different society composed largely of Blacks. A recent survey of health psychology in South Africa (Visser, 1990) uncovered an extensive amount of interest and research in the field. Although most of the work to date has focused on the high incidence of health-related problems in the White community, there has been a marked shift in the last several years toward community psychology and primary health care among the Black, Colored, and Indian populations as well. An example of contemporary work in the field is the Birth-to-Ten study started successfully between April 23 and June 8, 1990 (Yach et al., 1991).

All babies born in the Johannesburg and Soweto areas during these six weeks, about 4,000 infants, will be tested and followed up for 10 years by an interdisciplinary team of research scientists. The aim of the study will be to determine the biological, environmental, economic, and psychosocial factors that are associated with the survival and health of children from different ethnic groups living in an urban environment. The health, growth, and well-being of each child will be monitored every six months during the first 2 years, and then again at the ages of 5 and 10 years. The caregivers will also be assessed concerning their access to resources, knowledge and attitudes, family relationships, social support, and ongoing life stresses, as well as physical features of the home environment. This collaborative effort, the largest of its kind attempted anywhere in Africa as a longitudinal study, will set the stage for many additional studies in health psychology well into the next century.

Elsewhere in African and in certain regions of Asia, the problems of war, refugees, and migration have vastly increased human suffering and disease. Rapid urbanization and uncontrolled population growth have added to this migration, causing dramatic changes in lifestyles and family patterns. The emphasis in these lesser-developed countries is more on health promotion and the prevention of illness through improved public health practices and education aimed at changing the ideas, attitudes, and behavior of people than on the treatment of illnesses and their basic biobehavioral mechanisms. Health psychology focusing on community and family-oriented education and lifestyles is quite different from health psychology dealing with cardiovascular diseases or cancer in a modern, highly industrialized society.

## Latin America

During the last several decades, the major migration of the desperately poor from rural to urban areas has produced highly concentrated urban populations, placing a great strain on underdeveloped health facilities. Many communities are completely unprotected from industrial waste, unduly exposing them to chemical toxins. In spite of these problems and a relative lack of resources, research in health psychology has grown rapidly in the leading countries of the region, such as Brazil, Argentina, and Mexico. A survey by Rodriguez, Hernandez-Pozo, and Ramos-Lopez (1990) in 17 Latin American countries revealed a wide variety of areas ranging from basic psychophysiological research and behavioral studies of chronic diseases to public health efforts in community-wide health promotion. Two thirds of the studies were being conducted without external financial support. Rodriguez et al. reported that many of these health psychologists are isolated from their colleagues, who are scattered over a large geographic area, making communication difficult.

The Interamerican Society of Psychology has encouraged special interest groups, such as health psychologists, to organize on a continental rather than a national basis. Recently, the Society joined with the American Psychological Association, the Pan American Health Organization, and the Committee on Psychology and Health within the International Union of Psychological Science to form a new inter-American consortium for psychology and community health care. One purpose of the consortium is to stimulate regional training programs and information exchange on health psychology and community mental health. The University of Buenos Aires, the University of Costa Rica, and the National University of Mexico have been particularly active in these efforts. Central offices for the consortium are provided by the American Psychological Association in Washington, DC.

A successful program has been initiated in Cuba in which psychologists have become an important part of health teams serving local communities in polyclinics (Bernal & Marin, 1985). A psychologist is involved at every level of the health system, doing research and providing care in specialized health centers and participating in the health planning process. There is a strong emphasis on the integration of personal health and community life, a concept that is particularly important among the Latin American countries.

As in most other countries, the involvement of psychologists in the primary health care system of Mexico is highly limited. Of over 10,000 psychologists who graduated from institutions of higher education in the last 10 years, less than 20% are working in the various institutions of the public health care system. In most cases, they are constrained to a minor role as medical assistant or are assigned tasks of an administrative, nonprofessional nature. Recognizing that a major human resource was not being effectively used within the national health care system, the government encouraged the development of a pilot master's-level program in the School of Psychology at the National University in Mexico City.

One of the newest professional programs in Mexico is particularly interesting because it deals effectively with the problem of the unemployment and underemployment of psychologists, who typically complete their studies with no particular job in mind. Under a special agreement between the Health Ministry and the National University, the new six-year program will emphasize health and community psychology to prepare specialists who can work with primary health care centers throughout the country. Each student admitted to the program is guaranteed placement for practicum training in a health care center, with assurance of subsequent professional employment once the advanced training has been completed. As in Cuba, the psychologist then works on an equal footing with medical doctors and other health care specialists as part of the primary health team in a given community.

Begun in the spring of 1988, this new graduate program now has 32 students who are providing services and conducting research at two primary health centers located in low-income towns on the edge of Mexico City. The main objectives of the program are the following:

1. The promotion, care, and maintenance of health among individuals—a family and community approach.
2. The use of psychological principles for behavioral change toward better health care, for the detection of behavioral immunogens and pathogens, and for the increase of immunogens and decrease of behavioral pathogens.
3. Research to generate new knowledge and technological development.
4. The assessment of the impact of health programs.

Much of the training in this program is of a practical nature under difficult field conditions where the students are fully integrated into the primary health team. They conduct epidemiological studies in the center; participate in research aimed at detecting the risk of illness or pathology, with an emphasis on behavioral, community, and environmental factors; and learn to provide direct psychological services where needed. In addition, they assist in monitoring the care of chronically ill patients by conducting home visits and encouraging family support systems.

During the second year of training, the graduate program concentrates on penetration of the community in greater depth and the detection of behavioral risk factors as well as the appraisal of both behavioral pathogens and immunogens. The students also undertake studies in behavioral epidemiology, develop strategies and programs for bringing about behavioral change within the community, and then assess the impact of such interventions.

Because the program is strongly endorsed and funded by the Ministry of Health as well as the National University, there is every expectation that the number of students will grow rapidly, making it possible to deploy health psychologists as members of the primary health care system throughout the country. The right of every citizen to health care is a major national priority in Mexico, as it is becoming in many other countries throughout the world. Efforts are underway in Mexico to strengthen national legislation concerning health care and to increase substantially the public funds available for making the right to health care a reality before the turn of the century.

## Global Programs Under the World Health Organization

WHO is sponsoring the MONICA study, a large-scale investigation of cardiovascular morbidity and mortality that involves over 40 centers around the world. The purpose of this 10-year study is to assess the relationship of trends in cardiovascular disease to changes in known risk factors, lifestyle patterns, socioeconomic status, and health care. In 26 of these centers, data on psychosocial determinants of cardiovascular diseases are being collected that emphasize psychological stress, social support, life events, personality characteristics, and social mobility. Results of this study will not be known for several more years.

During the last decade, the Division of Mental Health of WHO has been giving special attention to the psychosocial aspects of health and illness in less developed nations. The Global Strategy for Health for All by the Year 2000 (WHO, 1987) stresses the close and complex links that exist between health and socioeconomic development. The objective of WHO's Global Strategy is the attainment by all peoples in all countries of the highest possible level of health, by which is meant not merely the absence of disease or infirmity but also a state of physical, mental, and social well-being. As a minimum, all people should have a sufficient level of health to be capable of working productively and participating actively in the social life of their community.

Psychologists can play an important role in these efforts because of their special training in social scientific methods, communications skills, and the technology of behavior change at both the individual and the community levels. For example, studies by Guthrie and his associates in the Philippines (Fernandez & Guthrie, 1984; Guthrie, Fernandez, & Estrera, 1984) illustrate this kind of social psychological research. They found that folk beliefs and practices often lead to unnecessary termination of lactation. Similarly, resistance to reliable methods of contraception reflected fears about side effects such as the disruption of intimacy between husband and wife. When these fears were recognized and dealt with appropriately by trained field workers, breast feeding and the use of contraceptives were commonly practiced.

It is now generally well accepted that programs aimed at the prevention of diseases and the promotion of health must be based on an understanding of the culture, traditions, and beliefs, as well as the patterns of family interaction. Of equal importance is the understanding that the structure and function of health services are significantly influenced by psychosocial factors such as the motivation of health workers and the perceptions of disease.

Earlier in this century, there was a notable shift within the highly industrialized societies from the infectious diseases of poverty to the chronic illnesses arising from affluence, urban stress, and longevity. In North America and Europe, better nutrition, improved sanitary measures, universal immunizations, and the use of antibiotics have changed the nature of morbidity and mortality profoundly in the last two generations, leading to a great increase in life expectancy and the emergence of cardiovascular disease as the leading cause of death in the highly developed countries of the world. However, studies of these "most developed countries" since about 1960 show that it is now the poorer and less educated segment of the population that bears the most severe burden of mortality from all of the modern killers—cardiovascular, and cerebrovascular conditions, the cancers, and external causes.

Recent studies by the Institute of Medicine of the U.S. National Academy of Sciences and the U.S. Centers for Disease Control estimate that nearly one half of current mortality from the 10 leading causes of death in the United States can be traced to such behavioral pathogens as alcohol consumption, overeating, and high risk-taking behavior. When added to lack of exercise, poor diet, and poor hygienic practices, such health-impairing habits and lifestyles provide a major challenge to behavioral medicine and especially to health psychologists.

The less developed countries of the world are also encountering rapid growth in the so-called diseases of affluence, while continuing to suffer from the diseases of poverty arising from malnutrition, infections and communicable diseases, and tropical diseases. The alarming rise in such noncommunicable diseases as cardiovascular illness, cancer, and diabetes, along with regional outbursts of malaria, tuberculosis, cholera, and other infectious diseases, including the dreaded acquired immune deficiency syndrome (AIDS), has been widely publicized in the last decade, creating a strong interest in health psychology and behavioral medicine even in countries where psychologists are not prepared to meet these challenges.

In a major initiative to bring about a better understanding of behavioral and psychosocial factors that surround all forms of disease, the Division of Mental Health of WHO in Geneva has embarked upon a major international project to develop learning modules for integrating psychosocial and behavioral skills into the teaching of clinical and community health care (David Jenkins, personal communications, January 24, 1990, and September 6, 1991). A WHO Collaborating Center for Psychosocial Factors and Health has been established at the University of Texas Medical Branch in Galveston under the leadership of David Jenkins, a health psychologist who is directing the construction, testing, and dissemination of these learning modules. In spite of the fact that this international project is being undertaken primarily by volunteers, scientific background documents have been completed for 15 of the 33 proposed modules. On the basis of contemporary research in behavioral medicine, each document contains five sections as follows:

1. A definition of the condition being dealt with and its limits;
2. a description of what groups might benefit most (or least) from the new approach and what groups need to be referred to more specialized diagnostic or therapeutic approaches;
3. a full description of the procedure (diagnostic or treatment) and exactly how it is performed;
4. a statement of how long the intervention should continue, criteria for success or failure, and indications for referral to a more specialized form of treatment; and
5. evidence for benefits obtained by applying the procedure.

The list of modules covers a wide range of topics, such as obtaining compliance with special diets, increasing adherence to medication schedules, communicating a poor prognosis to patients and families, motivating mothers to use oral rehydration therapy for children with diarrhea, working with schools to prevent or delay tobacco use among children, a program to stop tobacco use among smokers, coping with life-distressing changes, reducing alcohol abuse, maintaining a low-sodium diet, overcoming sleep disturbance problems, promoting five nonpharmacologic interventions to lower elevated blood pressure, helping communities organize themselves to deal with health problems, and coping with community disaster.

The initial modules were ready for preliminary testing late in 1991, with the prospect of further field testing to begin in 1992. The materials are pitched at a level to prepare average health professionals for their daily work with individual patients, families, and communities. These kinds of low-technology approaches are essential in many parts of the world where the only alternative would be no health service at all. In addition to participating as developers of these modules, health psychologists will be deeply involved in conducting research on their dissemination and effectiveness in many different cultures and types of situations, ranging from family practice medicine in the United States to village primary health care work in Asia, Africa, and Latin America.

Resources available to WHO for research on developments in health psychology are severely limited. Only by establishing partnerships with other organizations on an international basis can WHO exert a major influence on trends in the field. Nearly all of the research in the fields of health psychology and behavioral medicine is supported by a variety of public and private sources outside of WHO. Probably as much as 90% of the published health psychology research is conducted by scientists in North America and Europe. Consequently, the topics that receive the most attention are those for which the greatest amount of support is forthcoming in the highly developed nations, particularly the United States. For this reason, Dasen et al. (1987) concluded that although there is much in the western psychological literature that is relevant to issues of health, there is little that is immediately and directly applicable to the promotion of health in other parts of the world. This same point has been made with respect to other areas of psychology, but it applies even more forcefully where the solution of widespread human problems is sought, as in health.

# A Sampling of Research Topics

Because health psychology is still an evolving subdiscipline with a great deal of diversity and ill-defined boundaries, a complete review of all research topics would be nearly impossible to finish. Although there are growing numbers of psychologists who identify themselves as working in the field, there are many others who are engaged in psychological research that relates to the understanding and improvement of health and health care. Moreover, all of the research topics that are recognized within this broad field are interdisciplinary. Consequently, most of the significant scientific work is the result of close collaboration between psychologists and other biomedical, behavioral, and social scientists. Unlike some areas within the discipline of psychology, research dealing with health and illness cannot be conceptualized as psychology alone.

A broad view of health and health psychology must also take into account mental health and illness, areas in which the majority of psychologists have been involved for many decades. Although it is becoming increasingly difficult to draw a clear separation between physical and mental health, for purposes of the present review attention will be focused primarily on illnesses that are generally recognized as predominantly physical. Limiting research to studies that focus primarily on the psychosocial aspects of physical health comes close to what is generally thought of as behavioral medicine or health psychology. Rather than attempting to survey the entire field of health psychology, some selected areas of research in which psychologists have been particularly active internationally will be presented.

### Measuring the Toxic Effects of Environmental Chemicals on Behavior

The adverse effects on health of toxic chemicals in the environment, particularly in our large industrial communities, is now widely recognized. Less well known is the fact that measures of behavior are often particularly sensitive to toxic agents, revealing significant defects even when no overt symptomatology is observable. Although certain heavy metals such as lead or mercury have been known for many years for their irreversible toxic effects on the central nervous system, the explosive development of thousands of new chemicals in the last several decades has created chemical time bombs that may adversely affect the health of many millions of people. Unfortunately, the deleterious effects of such toxic exposure may take many years to show up in gross symptomatology, illness, or death. Can a battery of psychological tests be used to measure a variety of subtle changes in motor functions, vision, hearing, or cognition as early indicators of neurotoxicity? Can some toxic chemicals be identified solely on the basis of their measured effects on behavior? These and many other questions like them have spurred a great deal of scientific interest in the emerging new field of neurobehavioral toxicology.

At a major international symposium to review the scientific evidence for answering such questions, Russell (1990) outlined three major objectives for research on neurobehavioral toxicity testing in both animals and humans: (a) to determine whether exposure to a potentially toxic chemical produces effects on nervous system functioning that exceed the organism's ability to adjust, (b) to assist in identifying the nature of such malfunctions through basic research to ascertain the underlying mechanisms, and (c) to provide information about the effects of extended exposure in both dose and time effects that may be useful in establishing threshold limit values for purposes of human safety.

One of the earliest studies in this field was carried out by Hanninen (1971), who compiled a psychological test battery to study the neurotoxic effects of carbon disulfide at the Institute of Occupational Health in Finland. Tests were borrowed primarily from earlier studies in clinical psychology and neuropsychology to cover a wide range of psychomotor, visual, and mental abilities. Since then, a number of batteries have been developed for use, particularly in occupational studies of workers in Europe and North America who are repeatedly exposed to various industrial chemicals. These studies have proven sufficiently promising, often leading to important settlements in occupational injury cases, that WHO has organized an expert group to develop the Neurobehavioral Core Test Battery (NCTB). This test battery is intended for use in health hazard evaluations in which testing time is limited and the use of sophisticated equipment is not possible. Comprising seven tests, the NCTB includes Pursuit Aiming for motor steadiness. Simple Reaction time for attention and response speed, Digit Symbol for perceptual motor speed, the Santa Ana Finger Dexterity test, the Benton Visual Retention test for visual perception and memory, and the Digit Span test for auditory memory (Johnson, 1987). The idea is to have a test battery that is sufficiently universal in its application that would be translated for use in many different societies and situations.

There are several serious problems with such a short series of tests. First of all, it is difficult to measure reliably some of the functions involved when abbreviated tests are used. Second, many aspects of human behavior must simply be left out because they are not amenable to short testing of this kind, thereby limiting severely the kinds of neurotoxicity that could be measured. Third, the successful measurement of deterioration requires repeated testing, an expensive, often impractical procedure. And fourth, some of the test are not as culture-free as one would like for valid measurement in many different languages and societies. Nevertheless, the NCTB seems sufficiently sensitive to detect neurotoxic effects in the most hazardous exposure situations.

The directions for the future development of neurobehavioral toxicity testing are many. Is it better to use simple or complex tests? Can the reliability of measurement be improved without inordinate increases in expense and time for measuring each function? Can normative data be obtained on large samples of individuals that can then be used as reference groups for determining deficit functioning without repeated testing? Because many behavioral effects of neurotoxic substances include changes in mood, affect reaction, and personality, can such changes be measured precisely and validly enough to be included in standard batteries of tests? Can such psychological tests be further standardized and made more efficient by computer-based testing, where the person responds at a computer terminal to questions and tasks presented by a video screen? All of these questions and the research that they imply are sufficiently promising that they are being diligently pursued by psychologists, toxicologists, biologists, neuroscientists, and computer specialists.

## Psychological Stress and the Immune System

It has been believed for some time that prolonged psychological stress can have a significant adverse impact on an individual's health, but only recently has there been an accumulation of scientific evidence in support of this idea. An impressive array of research has now been accumulated indicating that stress is a complex individual experience with both objective and subjective features that are revealed in a nonspecific bodily response to a threatening or noxious situation that, if prolonged, can lead to exhaustion or illness. Much of the early work in this field was summarized by Lazarus and Folkman (1984). Typical of many studies in this field is the work of Shigehisa and his colleagues in Tokyo (Shigehisa, Fukui, & Motoaki, 1989). In this study, four types of disease-prone behavior patterns were measured by a questionnaire designed by Grossarth-Maticek, Eysenck, Vetter, & Schmidt (1988), and two coping strategies and four modes of coping were assessed by a checklist designed by Lazarus and Folkman (1984). A special Japanese translation of both the checklist and the questionnaire were given to 70 adolescents who responded for themselves and for their mothers and fathers. Shigehisa and colleagues found that a cardiovascular-disease-prone behavior pattern on the Grossarth-Maticek questionnaire was positively correlated with a cognitive strategy of coping and a preferred mode of coping by searching for information, whereas the cancer-prone behavior pattern was uncorrelated with either component. Although of some interest in its own right, the main difficulty with this kind of finding is that it is based solely on correlations among scales derived from paper-and-pencil questionnaires completed by school children, rather than on comparisons of psychological stress measures with actual health or illness.

A much stronger kind of evidence is that obtained from experimental studies such as a recent one examining psychological stress and susceptibility to the common cold. The relation between psychological stress and the frequency of documented, clinically diagnosed colds was studied by American psychologist Sheldon Cohen (1991) and British co-workers David Tyrrel and Andrew Smith. The volunteer British subjects were 154 men and 266 women. They were intentionally exposed to respiratory viruses by nasal drops. An additional 26 subjects received only saline nasal drops, providing a control group. All 416 subjects were then quarantined and monitored for cold symptoms.

Stress was measured by a combination of the List of Recent Experiences (67 items dealing with major stressful life events; Henderson, Byrne, & Duncan-Jones, 1981), a 10-item Perceived Stress Scale (Cohen & Williamson, 1988), and a negative-affect scale containing 15 adjectives (*distressed, sad, angry,* etc.) indicating intensity of feeling during the past week on a 5-point scale. Because the three measures proved to be highly intercorrelated, a more reliable stress index was computed by combining the three scores.

Of the 394 subjects who received virus, 38 percent developed the clinical symptoms of a cold, whereas none of the 26 who were given saline drops has a cold. A direct, positive correlation was found between degree of psychological stress and the appearance of cold symptoms: The higher the stress index, the higher the rate of catching a cold. The relationship between stress and infection was even more dramatic when subclinical infection was measured by refined laboratory methods such as the analysis of virus-specific serum antibodies. These significant effects remained unaltered even when controlled for such variables as age, sex, allergic status, the season, smoking, exercise, white-cell counts, and total immunoglobulin levels, as well as such personality variables as self-esteem, personal control, and introversion–extraversion.

Cohen et al. (1991) concluded that psychological stress alone was responsible for the increased rate of infection. The results strongly suggest either that stress is associated with the suppression of a general resistance process, leaving a person vulnerable to multiple infectious agents, or that stress is linked to the suppression of many different immune processes. The net result in either case would be the same.

## Cancer

Can psychosocial factors influence tumor outcomes? Thought unlikely by many specialists only two decades ago, recent research indicates that the answer to this question is a qualified yes. The central nervous, endocrine, and immune systems form a complex, regulatory, homeostatic network that can at least partially control the growth of tumors. The mental and emotional state of an individual, the amount of psychological stress experienced, and related external behaviors of the individual have at least a potential modifying impact on the immune system through hormonal and central nervous system interactions. The trick is to tease out these complex pathways and to demonstrate convincingly that certain behaviors, emotions, and thought processes can actually modify the direction and extent of tumor growth. To be sure, some behaviors have an obvious effect, such as carcinogens resulting from smoking, excessive alcohol consumption, and other risky behaviors that make up an individual's lifestyle. Even dietary factors enter in by exposing people to a large variety of naturally derived mutagens and carcinogens. For example, dietary fiber appears to speed intestinal transit time and reduce the risk of colon cancer. Although many health psychologists have focused on identifying and altering such unhealthful habits, the possibility of mental and emotional activity directly influencing tumor growth by disrupting the endocrine and immune systems is quite another matter, one that we will now examine.

Animal studies by psychologist Robert Ader and immunologist Nicholas Cohen (1984) provided strong evidence that the brain can influence immune responses. Working with laboratory rats, Ader was studying conditioned taste aversion. As expected, animals who first received saccharin solution (a sweet, pleasant taste designed to become the conditioned stimulus) followed by the immunosuppressive drug cyclophosphamide (the unconditioned stimulus that nauseates the rat) learned to avoid drinking the saccharin even though they formerly liked it. Later on in the experiment, to Ader's surprise, the conditioned rats were dying at an unusually high rate, especially those that drank the most saccharin. A control group of unconditioned animals who also drank the saccharin showed no signs of ill effects. Later studies done with Cohen indicated that the rats had been conditioned to associate the sweet taste of saccharin with suppression of their immune systems because of the linkage of saccharin with the immunosuppressive drug in the earlier conditioning experiment. In other words, the immune system's response had been altered by classical conditioning.

Following up on this earlier work, Levy (1985) conducted clinical studies of breast cancer patients. She and her colleagues found that patients who suppressed their anger, who were apathetic, or who lacked strong social support showed significantly lower natural killer cell activity in their immune systems, which in turn appeared to contribute to the spread of the cancer. Although such a clinical finding is intriguing, the only way to be sure that the psychological factors actually lowered the immunity, thereby playing a major role in the spread of the cancer, would be to do controlled intervention studies. Studies are now under way in several centers to see if cancer patients improve when they are given specialized therapy to modify their behavior and feelings. Although it is clear that interactions between the immune and nervous systems go far beyond the traditional pathways that involve adrenal secretions, much more carefully controlled research with both animals and human patients must be done to clarify the psychological factors that can influence tumor growth by direct interaction of the brain and the immune system. Because the immune system plays a pervasive role in many illnesses, the results of these studies could have farreaching ramifications. An up-to-date review of psychoneuroimmunology will appear in 1993 (Ader, in press).

## Social Support and Coping With Chronic Disease

How individuals adapt to stressful life circumstances associated with chronic, debilitating illness has been studied extensively. Effective coping behavior can play an important role in recovery from illness, as well as reducing the likeliness of illness in the first place. Coping can influence hormone levels, cause direct tissue changes, and even affect the immune system, as noted above in the discussion of cancer. A large number of studies have been done recently examining the relationship among stress, social support, and coping processes as they affect health and illness (Coyne & Downey, 1991).

Typical of work in this area is the Oldenburg longitudinal study in Germany, conducted for a five-year period after heart attacks (Badura et al., 1988). Nearly 1,000 men suffering from their first myocardial infarction were surveyed by written questionnaires at five different times: in the hospital about four weeks after the heart attack, six months later, one year later, and then again three and a half and four and a half years after the onset of illness. Data were collected in 213 hospital from the doctor, the patient, the patient's spouse, and the general practitioner serving the patient in his local community. In addition to obtaining biomedical information about the patient and the medical treatment offered, personality variables, coping with the social security system, the family, and the work situation were all evaluated.

After three and a half years, nearly one third of the sample still reported serious symptoms of anxiety and depression. Indeed, years later, mean levels of anxiety and depression, as measured by the scales in the questionnaire, were higher than they were immediately following onset of the heart attack. Social support by the spouse and a cohesive social group in the work setting were two of the most significant positive indicators of later well-being. Social class and work status also seemed to contribute significantly to the process of recovery. Curiously, there were no differences in objectively measured health between patients who later returned to work and those who did not. However, those who went back to work and were still at it one year after their heart attack were much better off with respect to all of the outcome variables than were patients who were still on sick leave from work or who had accepted early retirement.

### Psychological Aspects of the Work Setting

Most adults spend a major portion of their daily life in an industrial factory, a clerical office, a small shop, or some other kind of productive work setting. One of the major changes in the last several decades has been the introduction of highly mechanized and automated production technologies, many of which are now being exported to developing countries. A second major change, particularly in the highly developed countries, is the introduction of computers and other forms of information technology, which bring some of the adverse factors characteristic of traditional mechanized, industrial production into the white-collar sector.

Time pressures, segmentation into repetitive tasks, social isolation, and the inability to use one's talents effectively constitute some of the adverse factors often encountered in the work setting. When such factors are also accompanied by a lack of autonomy and personal freedom on the job, the incidence of illness may increase still further. Social reorganization of the work setting can be an important way of improving health and reducing periods of sick leave. An example is the attempt in car manufacturing industries to introduce alternatives to the traditional assembly-line production. Some of the research on psychological aspects of work that was conducted in Scandinavian countries resulted in an enlarged work environment concept and influenced recent work environment legislation (Gardell, 1981).

The reported incidence of stress-related illnesses in industry is increasing. How an individual interprets potential stressors in the environment can be just as important as the objective nature of the noxious nonphysical stimuli themselves. All aspects of work can be a source of stress—heat, noise, too much or too little light, too great or too small a workload, or too much or too little responsibility.

Many of these factors apply as much to the larger environment as to the workplace itself. Crowding has been subject to research in both animals and men, leading to new architectural specifications for many settings ranging from prisons to apartment buildings. Noise is another stressor that has become more prominent in the minds of many psychologists concerned with health and the environment.

## Anger, Hostility, and Cardiovascular Disease

Long before modern scientific studies of personality characteristics, emotions, and cardiovascular diseases, there was a general belief in many societies that "pressure" builds up within an individual who is emotionally upset until he "blows his stack" or has a heart attack. One of the earliest studies of essential hypertension, high blood pressure with no apparent organic cause, was reported by Saul (1939), involving seven patients who were being treated by psychoanalysis. Saul found that in spite of their generally gentle outward manner, his patients suffered from intense chronic anger that was strongly inhibited.

Twenty years later, Friedman and Rosenman (1959) identified a "coronary-prone behavior pattern" that ever since has been widely studied as a major risk factor for coronary heart disease. Known as Type A behavior, this pattern was initially characterized by a excessively competitive drive, impatience, hostility, and quick movements. More recently, epidemiological studies have found a significant relationship between Type A behavior and risk of subsequent coronary heart disease in both men and women. Psychologists have been extensively involved in studying Type A behavior. Some of this research has been aimed at learning more about the basic mechanisms underlying the physiological responses to psychological stressors among individuals with high Type A behavior characteristics. Other kinds of research have focused more on examining particular components of Type A behavior, studying their origins in children, and experimenting with ways of modifying Type A behavior patterns.

The most ambitious Type A experimental intervention study thus far is the Recurrent Coronary Prevention Project. This longitudinal study is designed to determine whether Type A behavior can be modified in cardiac patients by group psychotherapy using cognitive restructuring, relaxation training, and guided practice (Thoresen, 1990; Thoresen, Friedman, Gill, & Ulmer, 1982). The study began in 1978 when 1,012 volunteers who had already suffered heart attacks were given a physical examination, several questionnaires, and a special videotaped interview. On the basis of this information, each participant was rated on Type A behavior. One group of 270 volunteers was randomly chosen to receive lectures, reading material, and group discussions led by a cardiologist who emphasized the importance of diet, nutrition, exercise, and medication. A second group of 592 volunteers participated in small, experimental intervention groups in which they received group psychotherapy designed specifically to change any Type A behavior. A third group of 150 heart patients volunteered to serve as a control group, receiving free examinations and testing but no special treatment.

The treatment was continued for four and a half years, with the experimental groups meeting twice a month for sessions lasting one and a half hours. A second video interview was recorded for each patient at the end of the treatment. The long-term effects of the different treatments were examined at the end of four more years, when the health status of all but one of the original volunteers was determined. Results were obtained not only by comparing the three different groups, but also by analyzing the amount of change for each individual patient over the eight and a half years.

At the end of the four and a half years during which behavioral treatment occurred, it was found that those who had participated in the small group counseling aimed at reducing Type A behavior had 44% fewer heart attack recurrences than did those who were in the educational program led by the cardiologist. The long-term effects were similar, although the differences between the groups after eight and a half years were less dramatic. Patients who had substantially altered their Type A behavior, regardless of their treatment group, had an almost 50% lower mortality rate than did those who did not change substantially.

Singling out the higher risk patients who had initially suffered a very severe first attack revealed that Type A behavior was not as useful in predicting a recurrence as were physiological characteristics of the initial heart attack itself. Type A behavior proved to be an especially strong predictor of death by arrhythmic heart attack, which can occur without warning and can cause death within minutes.

The changes over four and a half years among the patients receiving behavioral treatment indicate that hostility was particularly important. These patients reported an improved ability to relax, to control anger, to listen to others, and to appreciate daily events and people in their lives.

Much of the contemporary research on Type A personality characteristics deals with the problems of measuring and defining hostility. Paper-and-pencil self-report inventories yield different results from behavioral observations in small group experimental settings, which can also vary from one social context to another. Part of this problem is due to the complexity of hostility, which includes cognitive, emotional, and behavioral characteristics, all three of which do not always occur together. The cognitive aspects consist of negative beliefs about other people, which make an individual think of them as threatening. Such emotions as anger, annoyance, disgust, contempt, and resentment underlie the emotional states characteristic of hostility, whereas the behavioral aspects involve overtly aggressive acts. In addition, many people tend to deny their hostile feelings and acts. Current studies are under way aimed at understanding better how these psychological components of hostility interact to increase the likelihood of severe heart attacks.

## Cessation of Smoking

One of the major risk factors in many illnesses is the smoking of tobacco. Public campaigns to encourage smokers to quit have spread to many countries, and millions of smokers would like to stop but have great difficulty doing so. Psychologists have been in the forefront of research on why people continue smoking even though they know it is bad for them. For many smokers who try to quit, the adverse side effects of cessation, such as weight gain due to overeating or feeling mildly depressed or anxious, encourage them to smoke once again.

Typical of the studies that have examined both smoking and overeating is an experiment by Spring, Wurtman, Gleason, & Wurtman (1991) testing the hypothesis that d-fenfluramine would be of value in suppressing the desire to overeat and the tendency to feel blue or dysphoric. This drug releases serotonin, a brain hormone that is also affected by nicotine, the chemical in tobacco that gives a smoker a "lift" and suppresses appetite. To test this hypothesis, a double-blind study was conducted in which neither the therapists nor the subjects knew whether a participant had been randomly assigned to the experimental group receiving the drugs or to the control group given an inert placebo.

Subjects for the study were 31 volunteer, overweight, female smokers who responded to a community announcement offering a free five-week treatment program to stop smoking. At the time of enrollment, everyone completed questionnaires about their personal habits and history as well as a standardized inventory to measure their feelings of anxiety and depression. The actual amount of food eaten during the five weeks that they quit smoking was also recorded. At the end of treatment, mood measures and weight were again obtained.

As predicted, the women receiving the placebo during abstinence from smoking had withdrawal symptoms of mild depression and an average weight gain of 3.5 pounds. Whereas the women who were given d-fenfluramine not only felt good but enjoyed an average weight loss of 1.8 pounds. The study proved that a serotonin-releasing drug can prevent withdrawal symptoms for smokers trying to quit. Other studies have shown that nicotine-containing chewing gum reduces withdrawal symptoms and helps smokers to quit.

# Conclusion

These seven research topics are only a small sample of the many interesting and socially significant research projects being undertaken by scientists working in the field of health psychology. The list could be expanded greatly by adding such topics as the promotion of health through mass media, treatment programs for the reduction of alcohol consumption, understanding the psychobiological factors underlying drug abuse and addiction, alternative interventions for changing the behavior of individuals at high risk of being stricken by AIDS, and understanding the nature of risk-taking behavior as it relates to accidents and to illicit drugs and other self-destructive acts.

Those who are interested in delving more deeply into the methods and findings of research in health psychology will find excellent reviews of contemporary research in the *Annual Review of Psychology* (Krantz, Grunberg, & Baum, 1985; Rodin & Salovey, 1989). Another review in this series is scheduled to appear in 1993 (Adler & Matthews, in press). The U.S. Institute of Medicine commissioned a major study on health and behavior (Hamburg, Elliott, & Parron, 1982). Another more recent review of topics in health psychology was edited by Maes, Spielberger, Defares, and Sarason (1988). A general review of the contributions of psychology to the improvement of health and health care throughout the world can be found in the *Bulletin of the World Health Organization* (Holtzman, Evan, Kennedy, & Iscoe, 1987). Because the great majority of scientific research activities take place in the highly developed industrial societies of the West, the topics on which the greatest amount of research has been done is limited to those areas of health and illness of particular concern to societies in North America and Europe.

Psychologists are major contributors to health throughout the world in many ways other than by conducting scientific research. Clinical and counseling psychologists provide extensive diagnostic and treatment services for individuals; school and industrial psychologists contribute significantly to health care in many countries by working in educational or industrial settlings; and social and community psychologists are concerned with community development, leadership training, and social organization for improving the delivery of health services. Some of the most rapid growth in the professional training of psychologists is taking place in the dynamically developing countries of Latin America and, to some extent, Asia. Therefore, it is highly likely that in the next several decades research in health psychology will expand vigorously in other parts of the world than the highly developed countries, where most such research is now done.

It is safe to conclude that, together with other social and behavioral scientists, psychologists will play a key role in devising and disseminating new behavioral technologies for the promotion of health, the changing of lifestyles, and the reduction of behavioral factors that produce disease, as well as of the deleterious aspects of the environment. Wider access to health care throughout the world will require expanded cooperation with other culturally indigenous health care providers, as well as with professionals in a variety of other fields. Health psychology and the larger concept of behavioral medicine will continue to be truly interdisciplinary. An important challenge for the future will be the dissemination of new knowledge and technology in sufficiently clear, relevant, and appealing forms so that important ideas growing out of research can be applied by others with less specialized training in psychology for the benefit of people throughout the world.

# References

Ader, R. (in press). Psychoneuroimmunology. *Annual Review of Psychology, 44.*

Ader, R., & Cohen, N. (1984). Behavior and the immune system. In W. D. Gentry (Ed.), *Handbook of behavioral medicine* (pp. 117–173). New York: Guilford Press.

Adler, N., & Matthews, K. (in press). Health psychology. *Annual Review of Psychology, 45.*

Badura, B., Kaufhold, G., Lehmann, H., Pfaff, H., Richter, R., Schott, T., & Waltz, M. (1988). Soziale Unterstützung und Krankheitsbewältigung: Neue Erkenntnisse aus der Oldenburger Longitudinal Studie 4½ Jahre nach Erstinfarkt [Social support and coping with chronic disease: New results of the Oldenburg longitudinal study 4½ years after infarction]. *Psychotherapie, Psychosomatik, Medizinische Psychologie, 38,* 48–58.

Bernal, G., & Marin, B. (Eds.). (1985). Community psychology in Cuba [Special issue]. *Journal of Community Psychology, 13,* 103–235.

Cohen, S., Tyrrell, D. A. J., & Smith, A. P. (1991). Psychological stress and susceptibility to the common cold. *New England Journal of Medicine, 325,* 606–612.

Cohen, S., & Williamson, G. (1988). Perceived stress in a probability sample of the United States. In S. Spacapan & S. Oscamp (Eds.), *The social psychology of health* (pp. 31–67). Newbury Park, CA: Sage.

Coyne, J. C., & Downey, G. (1991). Social factors and psychopathology: Stress, social support, and coping processes. *Annual Review of Psychology, 42,* 401–426.

Dasen, P. R., Berry, J. W., & Sartorius, N. (Eds.). (1987). *Health and cross-cultural psychology: Toward applications.* London: Sage.

Dawber, T. R., Meadors, G. F., & Moore, F. E., Jr. (1951). Epidemiological approaches to heart disease: The Framingham study. *American Journal of Public Health and the Nation's Health, 41,* 279–286.

Fernandez, E. L., & Guthrie, G. M. (1984). Belief systems and breast-feeding among Filipino urban poor. *Social Science and Medicine, 19,* 991–995.

Friedman, M., & Rosenman, R. H. (1959). Association of specific overt behavior pattern with blood and cardiovascular findings—blood cholesterol level, blood clotting time, incidence of arcus senilis, and clinical coronary artery disease. *Journal of the American Medical Association, 162,* 1286–1296.

Gardell, B. (1981). Strategies for reform programmes on work organization and work environment. In B. Gardell & G. Johansson (Eds.), *Working life: A social science contribution to work reform* (pp. 3–13). Chichester, England: Wiley.

Grossarth-Maticek, R., Eysenck, H. I., Vetter, H., & Schmidt, R. (1988). Psychosocial types and chronic disease: Results of the Heidelberg prospective psychosomatic intervention study. in S. Maes, C. D. Spielberger, P. B. Defares, & I. G. Sarason (Eds.), *Topics in health psychology* (pp. 57–75). New York: Wiley.

Guthrie, G. M., Fernandez, T. L., & Estrera, N. O. (1984). Small-scale studies and field experiments in family planning in the Philippines. *International Journal of Intercultural Relations, 8,* 391–412.

Hamburg, D. A., Elliott, G. R., & Parron, D. L. (Eds.). (1982). *Health and behavior: Frontiers of research in the biobehavioral sciences.* Washington, DC: National Academy Press.

Hanninen, H. (1971). Psychological picture of manifest and latent carbon disulphide poisoning. *British Journal of Industrial Medicine, 28,* 374–381.

Heidbreder, E. (1933). *Seven psychologies.* New York: Appleton-Century.

Henderson, S., Byrne, D. G., & Duncan-Jones, P. (1981). *Neurosis and the social environment.* Sydney, Australia: Academic Press.

Holtzman, W. H., Evan, R. I., Kennedy, S., & Iscoe, I. (1987). Psychology and health: Contributions of psychology to the improvement of health and health care. *Bulletin of the World Health Organisation, 65,* 913–935.

Jenkins, C. D. (1971). Psychologic and social precursors of coronary heart disease. *New England Journal of Medicine, 284,* 244–255.

Johnson, B. (Ed.). (1987). *Prevention of neurotoxic illness in working populations.* New York: Wiley.

Kittel, F. (1984). The interuniversity study on nutrition and health. In J. D. Matarazzo et al. (Eds.), *Behavioral health: A handbook of health enhancement and disease prevention* (pp. 1148–1153). New York: Wiley.

Krantz, D. S., Grunberg, N. E., & Baum, A. (1985). Health psychology. *Annual Review of Psychology, 36,* 349–384.

Lazarus, R. S., & Folkman, S. (1984). *Stress, appraisal, and coping.* New York: Springer.

Levy, S. M. (1985). *Behavior and cancer: Lifestyle and psychosocial factors in the initiation and progression of cancer.* San Francisco: Jossey-Bass.

Maes, S. (1990, July). *Health psychology in Europe.* Paper presented at the 22nd International Congress of Applied Psychology, Kyoto, Japan.

Maes, S., Spielberger, C. D., Defares, P. B., & Sarason, I. G. (Eds.). (1988). *Topics in health psychology.* New York: Wiley.

Matarazzo, J. D. (1980). Behavioral health and health psychology. *American Psychologist, 35,* 807–817.

Miller, N. E. (1969). Learning of visceral and glandular responses. *Science, 163,* 434–445.

Peltzer, K. (1990, July). *Health psychology in Africa.* Paper presented at the 22nd International Congress of Applied Psychology, Kyoto, Japan.

Puska, P. (1984). Community-based prevention of cardiovascular disease: The North Karelia project. In J. D. Matarazzo et al. (Eds.), *Behavioral health: A handbook of health enhancement and disease prevention* (pp. 1140–1147). New York: Wiley.

Rodin, J., & Salovey, P. (1989). Health psychology. *Annual Review of Psychology, 40,* 533–580.

Rodriguez, D., Hernandez-Pozo, R., & Ramos-Lopez, T. (1990, November). *Status of health psychology in Latin America.* Paper presented at the First International Congress of Health Psychology, Mexico City.

Russell, R. (1990). Introduction. In R. Russell, P. Flattau, & A. Pope (Eds.), *Behavioral measures of neurotoxicity.* Washington, DC: National Academy Press.

Saul, L. J. (1939). Hostility in cases of essential hypertension. *Psychosomatic Medicine, 1,* 153–161.

Shigehisa, T., Fukui, I., & Motoaki, H. (1989). Stress coping strategy and mode of coping, in relation to proneness to cancer and cardiovascular disease (I): Analyses in males, in relation to their parents. *Japanese Journal of Health Psychology, 2*(12), 1–11.

Spring, B., Wurtman, J., Gleason, R., & Wurtman, R. (1991). Weight gain and withdrawal symptoms after smoking cessation: A preventive intervention using d-fenfluramine. *Health Psychology, 10,* 216—233.

Thoresen, C. E. (1990, June). *Recurrent coronary prevention project: Results after 8½ years.* Symposium presented at the First International Congress of Behavioral Medicine, Uppsala, Sweden.

Thoresen, C. E., Friedman, M., Gill, J. K., & Ulmer, D. (1982). Recurrent coronary prevention project: Some preliminary findings. *Acta Medica Scandinavica Supplementum, 660,* 172–192.

U.S. Department of Health and Human Services. (1984). *Proceedings of the 4th Joint U.S.–U.S.S.R. Symposium on Hypertension* (NIH Publication No. 86-2704). Bethesda, MD: National Institutes of Health.

Visser, M. (Ed.). (1990). *Health psychology in South Africa: Proceedings of the seminar on health psychology presented by the Institute for Psychological and Edumetric Research on 1 November 1989.* Pretoria, South Africa: Human Sciences Research Council.

Wolf, S., & Wolff, H. G. (1942). Genesis of peptic ulcer in man. *Journal of the American Medical Association, 120,* 670–674.

World Health Organization. (1987). *Evaluation of the strategy for health for all by the year 2000: Seventh report on the world health situation* (Vol. 1). Geneva, Switzerland: Author.

Yach, D., Cameron, N., Padayachee, N., Wagstaff, L., Richter, L., & Fonn, S. (1991). Birth to ten: Child health in South Africa in the 1990's, rationale and methods of birth cohort study. *Paediatric and Perinatal Epidemiology, 5,* 211–233.

# CHAPTER 8

# Research on Psychotherapy

Larry E. Beutler and Paulo P. P. Machado

W ithin the last two decades, psychotherapy research has begun to emerge from being a cottage industry to become recognized as a viable and credible scientific endeavor. This emergence appears to be a common development in most industrialized countries of the western world, although it has progressed at different rates in each. Collectively, the growth of psychotherapy research has followed a pattern that is characterized by at least three distinct phases. For want of better terms, these phases may be described as the periods of *case analysis, descriptive assessment,* and *controlled experiments.* Indeed, research on psychotherapy may now be entering a fourth and still more mature stage of growth characterized by methods that are designed to address complex interactions among treatment, patient, outcome, and process variables.

## The Phase of Case Analysis

With the introduction of the "talking cure" by Freud and his followers, research during the first three decades of this century was confined largely to intensive descriptions and analyses of individual cases, accompanied by elaborate theoretical formulations to explain the observations. These case analytic methods in psychotherapy were initiated in Europe and paralleled the use of similar methods in the biological sciences during that

*Work on this chapter was partially supported by National Institute of Alcohol Abuse and Alcoholism Grant No. 1 RO1 AA08970 awarded to Larry E. Beutler.*

period. This latter trend was reflected most directly in medical writings where descriptions of exemplary cases clarified the nature and treatment of physical pathologies. Following the lead of medical disciplines, the theoretical formulations of mental pathologies that were espoused by the newly developed psychoanalytic theory of the mind during this phase were mysteries that were assumed to be beyond the reasoning of ordinary people. Paradoxically, the mystery and novelty of these concepts generated considerable interest among the upper class and educated members of the public, but they were so far removed from then-existent medical concepts that they achieved little standing in the larger scientific community for whom they were intended. This wider community of science was rapidly rejecting the uncontrolled observations of case analyses in favor of an empirical model of research that was borrowed from the physical sciences of the day.

The methods associated with the empirical model of science introduced a shift of scientific influence from its previous center in continental Europe to North America. This model of research contrasted with the older one by the value placed on objective observations and statistically based inferences and by its rejection of metaphysical, explanatory concepts. The survival of psychotherapy research required that it acclimate to these new research values.

### The Phase of Descriptive Assessment

Psychotherapy research during the postwar period of the late 1940s and 1950s found a compatible home in the conventional "empiricism" of middle America. In this environment, research programs began to adopt empirical methods from the physical sciences and entered a period of "descriptive" research. Descriptive research methods gradually permeated research in most of the industrialized nations of Western Europe and replaced uncontrolled single case analyses with investigations of several individuals at once (i.e., group designs), therapist observations with systematic and quantitative measurement, and complex or metaphysical explanations with more parsimonious formulations. With these methods, researchers began to discover empirical relationships among therapist, client, and outcome characteristics. During this time, for example, Carl Rogers (1957) excited great interest among psychotherapy researchers and practitioners because of his empirical demonstrations that outcome was correlated with certain "facilitative therapist" qualities. Better outcomes were experienced by clients who viewed their therapists as empathic, congruent in their communications, and having high regard for others. Although not a surprising finding to clinicians, the confirmation of these relationships by objective means (e.g., Truax & Carkhuff, 1965) demonstrated to the scientific community that the concepts of psychotherapy were subject to understanding through standard scientific methods.

Through the 1960s, the demands of descriptive research methods led to the development of theories that were less mystical to lay observers than were their predecessors, and, consequently, psychotherapy became understandable and accessible to the "ordinary person." In spite of its profound benefits to the field, this period of descriptive research still failed to earn a place for psychotherapy research within the mainstream of science. This failure can be attributed to at least two important reasons. The first of these is that physical science had since moved beyond the point at which rationally constructed theories were accepted solely on the basis of naturally occurring relationships among uncontrolled events. During the postwar years, the controversies that had been initiated decades earlier by Darwin's work intensified. These controversies eventually gave rise to a movement that sought ways to prove causal relationships. The resulting "experimental" methods emphasized the value of the direct manipulation of events and circumstances as a method of testing the presence of causal relationships. In biology, this movement led to the selective breeding of animals and insects as a means of studying the genetic transmission of characteristics. In the arena of psychotherapy, this movement was expressed, somewhat belatedly, in the use of college students, rats, and primates to develop principles of behavior change that were then extrapolated for use with clinical populations by behavior therapists. When these extrapolated procedures proved effective, advocates of this new "behavior therapy" touted the superiority of their methods over conventional psychotherapies (Eysenck, 1952).

A second reason for the failure of descriptive research to establish the scientific credibility of psychotherapy research may be because the research itself was largely restricted to demonstrating relationships that seemed intuitively obvious and relatively uninteresting to those who practiced the clinical arts. For example, only in the late 1970s were psychotherapy researchers finally able to conclude that scientific evidence supported the belief that psychotherapy was effective (Bergin & Lambert, 1978). By that time, however, the news seemed old and of little consequence to psychologists, psychiatrists, and social workers, who, after years of training and practice, had developed a profound faith in the effectiveness of their efforts. Research of this type followed rather than informed clinical practices and, unsurprisingly, was considered to be of little value to practitioners (Barlow, 1981; Strupp, 1981). Another change of research methods was required for research to begin to exert a direct effect on clinical practice.

## The Phase of Controlled Experiments

In North America, the 1960s and 1970s were characterized by an unheralded interest in psychotherapy among the public. New theories developed at an exponential rate that far exceeded the ability of psychotherapy researchers to assess their clinical efficacy (Parloff, 1980). By the mid 1970s, there were literally hundreds of different approaches, each touting its superiority over the others (e.g., Corsini, 1981), but most lacked even the most rudimentary empirical support (Beutler, 1979). This proliferation of untested theories presented a major problem for the health care industry in the United States, which was asked to pay for services provided within these theoretical frameworks. Investing unbridled credibility in a host of unvalidated theories proved to be a hard pill to swallow for the health insurance industry.

Most countries did not experience the explosion of psychotherapy theories and research that characterized North America during the 1960s and 1970s. However, they did experience the fallout when private and national health service providers in the United States began to question the efficacy of spending millions of dollars for psychotherapeutic services that were provided within numerous and often contradictory frameworks, few of which were supported by evidence of clinical efficacy. Initiated by these pressures, several well-intentioned efforts in the United States attempted to test various theories against one another. The most notable efforts of the time (Luborsky, Singer, & Luborsky, 1975; Sloane, Staples, Cristol, Yorkston, & Whipple, 1976) not only suggested that the average effects of several different theoretical approaches were similar, but also noted that there were frequently as many differences in how two practitioners who shared the same theoretical framework conducted psychotherapy as there were when practitioners who represented two different theoretical frameworks did so. This recognition led to a concerted effort in the late 1970s to develop experimental methods that would provide more control over the actual procedures used and more systematic measurement both of what comprised the applications of clinical theories and of the resulting therapeutic outcomes than had previously existed. These efforts initiated the use of "treatment manuals" and thereby resulted in the application of true experimental designs in psychotherapy research.

The construction of treatment manuals was the result of efforts to operationalize and standardize different models of psychotherapy. They embodied detailed procedural descriptions along with performance criteria for assessing compliance with the theoretical model and skill in the conduct of the therapy. Although initially seen as a necessary step for reducing the high degree of therapist variability that overshadowed the outcome

differences associated with different psychotherapies in research, the manuals have sub-
sequently been applied to efforts to increase the efficacy of training in psychotherapy
(Dobson & Shaw, 1988; Lambert & Ogles, 1988; Luborsky & DeRubeis, 1984).

The development of treatment manuals paved the way for direct, controlled comparisons of different treatments (i.e., controlled clinical trials). Together, the advent of
treatment manuals and the use of randomized trial designs initiated what has since become a revolution of research activity throughout much of the industrialized world. This
research is beginning to result in the acceptance of psychotherapy research within
the scientific community and, at long last, has allowed research to begin to set the directions that will be taken in clinical practice, rather than being relegated to proving the
obvious.

Principal among the procedures that characterize the period of controlled research
in psychotherapy have been the following: the introduction of standard measures of psychotherapy outcomes (Lambert, Christensen, & DeJulio, 1983; Waskow & Parloff, 1975);
the extension of descriptive manuals to the training of therapists in many different theoretical systems and formats (Beutler & Clarkin, 1990; Luborsky, Crits-Christoph, Mintz, &
Auerbach, 1988); the development of measurement instruments for assessing the internal
processes of psychotherapy (Greenberg & Pinsoff, 1986); and the development of sophisticated statistical procedures for assessing effect sizes and clinical significance levels.
Some of these last procedures allow comparisons of findings across widely different studies (Berman, Miller, & Massman, 1985; Shapiro & Shapiro, 1982; Smith, Glass, & Miller,
1980); some offer sophisticated means for intensively studying individual treatment responses (Barlow & Hersen, 1984; Kazdin, 1984), others allow the translation of statistical
data into estimates of clinical worth (Jacobson & Truax, 1991), and still others provide
means for assessing complex interactions among many different variables at once (Bentler, 1985).

## Contemporary Trends

Psychotherapy research appears to be entering a fourth methodological phase characterized by (a) programmatic and collaborative studies rather than by individual, single-
setting efforts; (b) explorations of sophisticated combinations of procedures representing
different theoretical models, rather than investigations of single-theory approaches; and
(c) assessment of the differential efficacy of different approaches for different problems

and client types (i.e., client $\times$ therapy interactions) rather than assessment of treatment main effects only (Beutler & Crago, 1991).

## Research Methods

Traditionally, the objectives of psychotherapy research were loosely grouped into two categories: those that aimed to understand the internal workings of therapy (*process research*) and those that aimed to evaluate the efficacy of psychotherapy (*outcome research*). However, contemporary researchers find it difficult to categorize their objectives neatly into these two groups. Much of contemporary psychotherapy research comprises systematic efforts to understand the linkages among several classes of variables. Elements in these linkages may include two or more of the following: (a) those things that place one at risk for emotional disturbance; (b) interventions that may prevent these disturbances; (c) characteristics that typify patients and therapists at the beginning of treatment; (d) interpersonal processes occurring between the participants; (e) naturally occurring sequences in process events that characterize the stages of treatment; (f) intermediate outcomes that are assumed to precipitate long-term gains (e.g., the development of working relationships over time); (g) end-of-treatment outcomes; and (h) long-term maintenance of gains, and relapse.

To address these interrelationships, three research methodologies or strategies are typically used (Kazdin, 1991). *Naturalistic* research designs represent the correlational methods developed during the period of descriptive assessment. These methods are marked by their focus on evaluating treatments as they usually or typically occur. This focus contrasts with that of the *true experiment*, which adopts the methods of the period of controlled experimentation. The focus of these latter methods is upon "ideal" or "pure" treatments—how they would be performed by maximally competent and skilled practitioners in circumstances that are uncluttered by adjunctive treatments and extraneous influences.

Combinations of naturalistic and controlled research designs represent the third methodology: *quasi-experimental* research. This type of research method typically compares naturally occurring treatments that frequently cannot be manipulated directly (e.g., male vs. female patients and therapist pairs). These designs represent a compromise between the advantages of studying an ideal and a usual treatment.

All three of these research strategies incorporate the following ideals to one degree or another: (a) carefully screened subjects from actual clinical settings; (b) confirmatory monitoring of the therapeutic procedures used; (c) assessment of therapist skill, compliance, or proficiency in using the treatment; (d) periodic reevaluation of patient response; (e) systematic and standard measurement of both subjective and objective responses to treatment; and (f) long-term follow-up.


## Implementation

The "true experiment" is the most difficult of the three methodologies to implement (Kazdin, 1991). True experiments require a high level of control over the assignment of patient-subjects to treatments and over the treatments themselves. The usual true experiment uses manual-directed therapies, provides direct assurance of equivalence among the skill levels of therapists in the various conditions, validates therapist compliance with the manuals, and uses random assignment of equivalent and usually diagnostically homogeneous patient groups. Demands for this level of control arose from the factors that precipitated the phase of controlled studies described earlier. The strength of this type of investigation is its ability to detect causal relationships among treatments, processes, and outcomes while ruling out, within the limits of reasonable probability, the effects of extraneous factors related to settings, patients, and therapists.

"Comparative Treatments" research program at the University of Bern (Grawe, 1991) and the "Psychotherapy of Depression" research program at the University of Arizona (Beutler et al., 1991b) represent variations of this type of methodology and, at the same time, illustrate differences that are frequently observed between North American and European research designs. In the University of Arizona controlled assignment research program, a diagnostically homogeneous group of 61 moderately depressed outpatients were carefully screened and then randomly assigned to three treatment conditions: cognitive therapy, focused expressive psychotherapy, and supportive, self-directed therapy. The therapies were manualized, therapists were experienced practitioners who were pretrained to defined levels of compliance and skill, therapy was closely monitored and supervised over a constant period of time (20 sessions), and outcomes were assessed after sessions, at the end of treatment, and several months after treatment's end (Beutler et al., 1991a).[1]

---

[1] In 1990, L. E. Beutler, the principal investigator for the Arizona project, moved to the University of California at Santa Barbara (UCSB). Since that time, this program has been a collaborative one between T. Jacob and V. Shoham-Salomon at the University of Arizona and L. E. Beutler at UCSB. The program has now expanded to the study of alcoholism, serious mental disorder, and family therapies.

The University of Bern research project (Grawe, 1991) is one of relatively few European programs that have used controlled experimental assignment and manualized therapies. Like the Arizona program, the Bern project maintained careful control over therapeutic procedures. The therapists were carefully trained, and the therapies were monitored throughout to ensure their distinctiveness and internal consistency. Outcomes as well as treatment process variables were monitored throughout the treatment.

The distinctions between the Arizona and the Bern programs are, for example, in the specificity of the manuals by which the treatments were run, the heterogeneity of the samples selected, and the types of therapies studied. Characteristic of programs in Western Europe, the Bern program used somewhat less control over the selection of subjects and the nature of the treatments, particularly in terms of standardizing treatment lengths and internal structure. In the Bern program, the four manualized treatment conditions were: (a) interactional behavior therapy in group, (b) interactional individual therapy, (c) broad spectrum behavior therapy, and (d) client-centered therapy. Each of these treatments varied in length, depending on the assessed needs of the patients. Likewise, the patient sample was not diagnostically homogeneous, comprising 63 patients presenting with varied symptoms associated with interpersonal problems, anxiety, and depression.

These departures from the usual controls established in North American programs like the Arizona project reflect relatively less interest in time-limited therapies among European investigators, as well as their investment in studying populations and treatment conditions that are more similar to those encountered in actual practice. Hence, they represent a step more toward a focus on the *usual* than the *ideal*, when compared with North American investigators.

Among the disadvantages of research that controls both the nature of the samples and the nature of the treatment are the time and expense required to carry out such studies. Moreover, the procedures frequently require such highly selected samples of patients, therapists, and treatments that they may be unlike the usual conditions under which treatment occurs in the real world. In this sense, European programs like the one at the University of Bern have greater "external validity" (i.e., are more easily generalized to the populations with which psychotherapy is usually conducted), whereas North American programs such as the one at Arizona have greater internal validity (i.e., one can be sure that the influence of extraneous variables is controlled). In either case, "true experiments," because they operate according to preestablished and standardized manuals, are best used to demonstrate and test new treatments, to determine what types of patients are best suited to different treatments, and to define the efficacy limits of defined treatment packages or specific, isolated procedures.

The "true experiment" contrasts with "naturalistic" research methods, which draw from the methods developed during the phase of descriptive research. These naturalistic procedures rely less often on establishing control over either the assignment of patients to treatments or the treatments themselves than does the true experiment. Patient and treatment characteristics are carefully monitored, however, and sophisticated statistical procedures are typically used to assess relationships among variables and to estimate the likelihood of causal linkages. Although this type of research does not allow a direct determination of causal relationships, solid grounding in theory and prior empirical research, coupled with sophisticated statistical procedures that are able to test the closeness of fit between observations and predicted sequential patterns of variables, help identify those causal relationships that are most likely to be present.

An example of a program that uses naturalistic methods is the "Long-Term Psychotherapy: Patients, Process and Outcomes" project of Northwestern University (Howard et al., 1991). In this research project, every patient that is accepted for long-term psychotherapy is asked to participate in the study, and answers a set of process and outcome questionnaires throughout the course of therapy. Responses, characteristics, and observations are then correlated with subsequent outcomes. No effort is made to control the use of various psychotherapy procedures, the assignment of the patients, or the length of treatments. All of these variables are allowed to vary in their normal fashion to maximize their external validity (i.e., their similarity to usual treatment conditions and settings).

This program also incorporates a variety of planned comparisons of naturally occurring groups through post hoc analyses and statistical methods of correcting for the lack of precise control. Such comparisons characterize the third, or "quasi-experimental," strategy (Kazdin, 1991). These methods blend procedures that dominated research during the phase of descriptive research with those that dominated the phase of controlled research. This set of methodologies is used when the investigator cannot control entirely either the nature of subjects/patients to be studied or the nature of the treatment offered. Typically, this method involves the systematic comparison of groups that are selected from naturally occurring assignments of patients to therapies. These groups are selected to approximate the type of control that would be imposed if a true experiment were possible. For example, if the setting or nature of the investigation does not allow the controlled assignment of patients to one or another treatment, samples of patients who are receiving two different treatments might be selected and matched in an effort to approximate equivalent groups by which the treatments could be compared. Likewise, if the setting does not allow the investigator systematically to train therapists in different treatment procedures, one may select from a large sample of ongoing therapies certain therapy–patient pairs that approximate the treatment differences that are of concern. The two naturally occurring treatments may then be compared to see if the treatments are related to different effects.

In the case of the Long-Term Psychotherapy Project at Northwestern University, therapies of different lengths are compared for immediate and long-term efficacy. In this way, the study maintains a close correspondence with treatments as they are ordinarily practiced. The patient and therapy samples are similar to those usually seen in clinical practice, and the procedures themselves can be carried out at a lower cost of time and money than those of true experiments. Unfortunately, the relative lack of precise control in these types of studies precludes a precise determination of cause and effect relationships, and they are not designed to contribute knowledge of the nature of "optimal" or "ideal" treatment, as true experiments might.

Finally, the advent of more sophisticated statistical procedures and the introduction of compact, speedy, and powerful computers has reintroduced, at a new level of status, an interest in individual case analyses. Although such an individual level does not represent a distinct methodology or strategy for conducting research on the order of the true experiment, the quasi-experiment, or the naturalistic design, all three of the foregoing methodologies can be applied to individual patient–therapist relationships as well as to groups of treated patients. This application to individual cases is a far departure from the uncontrolled investigations that typified early case analysis. Experiments on individual cases can now incorporate experimental manipulations and assessment of interactions among variables that allow fairly precise determinations of causal sequences. Although results based on single cases always suffer when one seeks to generalize their conclusions to other patients, therapists, and situations, these procedures are fruitfully used to explore prototypical cases from larger samples, to develop hypotheses for future study with groups, and to refine and pretest treatment procedures.

The "Ulm Textbank Research Program" at the University of Ulm in Germany is a good example of new technologies applied to individual case studies in psychotherapy. In this project, transcripts of individual therapy sessions are stored in a large computer database that integrates techniques of linguistic data and text processing. These data are then available for several longitudinal studies of the process of change in long-term psychotherapy. Data are analyzed using correlational methods and mathematical models.

# A Review of International Research Programs

Beutler and Crago (1991) recently reviewed 40 different psychotherapy research programs from many different countries. This review disclosed a considerable amount of diversity among the objectives and methods used. It concluded that psychotherapy research is a vital and growing field of scientific inquiry that is characterized by considerable creativity. The vitality of this field of research is marked by the growth and multinational membership of the Society for Psychotherapy Research (SPR), the major research organization in the field. This group now includes over 1,000 members in nearly 30 countries and is divided into three regional divisions (North America, the United Kingdom, and continental Europe). The advent of electronic mail, the introduction of multinational market economies, the accessibility of Eastern European countries, and a growing interest in the public sector have encouraged international communication and collaboration. For example, the SPR and other organizations with similar or related interests have begun journals and electronic mail services whose specific aims are to speed communication and to facilitate collaborative efforts among investigators in different countries. In the following sections, the programs previously mentioned will be reviewed in greater depth to illustrate some international trends in this area of research. These are only representative examples that have been selected for illustrative purposes. A more complete picture of international research in this area can be obtained from Beutler and Crago (1991).

## Illustrative Programs

### The Arizona/University of California at Santa Barbara Project

The Arizona and University of California (Santa Barbara) psychotherapy research project was initiated at the Arizona Health Sciences Center in 1979 (see Beutler et al., 1991a) with the establishment of two parallel programs emphasizing naturalistic studies, on the one hand, and controlled studies, on the other. Until its move to the University of California at Santa Barbara (UCSB) in 1990 and its implementation of controlled studies on family therapies, alcoholism, and serious/chronic mental disorders, the Psychotherapy for Depression project was the most developed controlled study within this program. The objectives of this latter study were to (a) develop and test the relative efficacy of several models of group and individual psychotherapy; (b) assess how the level of emotional arousal in psychotherapy contributed to both treatment maintenance and outcome in depression; and (c) determine if there were effects when different therapies were conducted with patients who also varied along two independent dimensions: coping style (externalization vs. internalization) and resistance potential (reactance level). The major objective of this depression project was to investigate, prospectively, the proposition that even when average outcomes among psychotherapies are equivalent, different therapies exert their best effects among different types of patients. The specifics of this project were published in 1991 (Beutler et al., 1991a).

Three manualized psychotherapeutic approaches for depression, varying in two theoretically derived dimensions, were developed and compared in this project: (a) focused expressive psychotherapy (FEP), a group Gestalt-based therapy that encourages affective arousal by identifying awareness and facilitating expression of unwanted emotions (Daldrup, Beutler, Engle, & Greenberg, 1988); (b) cognitive therapy (CT), a treatment that improves emotional control through identifying, challenging, and then reframing automatic thought patterns that are presumed to be the root of emotional conflict (Yost, Beutler, Corbishley, & Allender, 1986); and (c) a nondirective supportive, self-directed therapy (S/SD) that uses brief telephone sessions along with suggested readings (Scogin, Hamblin, & Beutler, 1987). Two of the treatments (CT and FEP) were selected both to reflect high levels of therapist directiveness and to contrast with the third treatment (S/SD), which used low levels of therapist directiveness. Directiveness was expected to correlate negatively with improvement among highly resistant patients but to correlate positively with improvement among nonresistant patients.

Likewise, two of the treatments (FEP and S/SD) were selected and developed to focus on internal experience, in contrast with the other (CT), which focused on external change. The degree of external focus was expected to correlate positively with improvement among patients who maintained externalizing coping styles and to correlate negatively with improvement among patients who maintained internalizing coping styles.

A diagnostically homogeneous sample of moderately depressed outpatients composed the sample of this study. Eligibility criteria for subjects entering the Psychotherapy for Depression study were a reliable *DSM–III–R* (American Psychiatric Association, 1987) diagnosis of major depression, a score of 16 or above on the 17-item form of the Hamilton Rating Scale for Depression (Hamilton, 1967), and an absence of psychotic features, of suicidal ideation, and of evidence of substance abuse.

Patients were selected from 376 individuals who were referred to the depression research program through newspaper advertisements, word of mouth, and health professionals. Of this initial sample, 81 were found to meet the criteria, and 5 declined further participation. Seventy-six subject/patients were randomly assigned to one of the treatment protocols. After those who dropped out prior to the scheduled evaluation after the fourth session were excluded, the final analysis was based on 63 subjects.

Screening instruments and interviews were given prior to treatment. Treatment process variables and depression were measured weekly using the Beck Depression Inventory (Beck, 1978) and session report forms. More intensive evaluations, including self-report measures and structured interviews, were administered every five weeks, at termination, and at 3-, 5-, and 12-month follow-up periods.

As expected, this study failed to find differences in overall effectiveness among the three psychotherapeutic approaches. The differences observed among treatments were specific to patients of different types. Both the dimensions of coping style and resistance potential predicted the relative efficacy of the different therapies. Depressed patients who coped with unwanted emotions by acting out and externalizing did best in CT. On the other hand, both S/SD and FET favored the nonexternalizing depressed patient.

Data on the role of resistance potential (reactance) also confirmed the hypothesis that directive treatments (CT and FEP) would be of greatest benefit to patients who have less propensity for resistance. S/SD therapy was remarkably effective for patients who were initially judged to have high levels of defensiveness and to be resistant to therapeutic procedures.

### The University of Bern Project

The "Differential Psychotherapy Research Program" (Grawe, 1991) at the University of Bern, Switzerland, started in 1979. Like the Arizona/UCSB project, the focus of this study was on the match between treatment and patient types rather than on main effect differences among different psychotherapies. The treatments studied were (a) interactional behavior therapy; (b) interactional individual therapy; (3) broad-spectrum behavior therapy; and (4) client-centered therapy. However, unlike the Arizona/UCSB project, no specific, a priori patient characteristics were predicted to be differentially affected by these therapies. The assessment of differential effects with different patient characteristics was explored in a naturalistic, ex post facto fashion (correlations of 54 different measures with outcomes among four treatments).

Four different but related studies have been the focus of investigation in this research center. The first study was a comparative investigation in which a form of psychotherapy developed at the University of Bern was compared with other approaches; the second dealt with the development and refinement of this form of therapy, which came to be designated "Schema-Theory and Heuristic Psychotherapy." The third study consisted of an evaluation of all controlled studies with clinical populations, and the fourth was an analysis of efficacy within individual cases.

In the comparative treatment study, 63 patients with interpersonal problems, but otherwise varied symptoms, were randomly assigned to the four treatments. The evaluation of these types of psychotherapy was centered on two general issues: (a) Do the outcomes of interactional behavior therapy in individual and group formats differ from those of broad-spectrum behavior therapy and client-centered therapy? and (b) Which measurement procedures and methods are most suitable for assessing differential effects of the different therapies?

Comparisons of the four treatment conditions on more than 60 outcome measures showed only minimal differences. However, when differential effects were assessed, data showed that both client-centered therapy and broad-spectrum behavior therapy were less successful with the more socially disturbed patients than was interactional therapy. Client-centered therapy was more successful than others with patients who had good interpersonal skills and the ability to make autonomous decisions. Behavior therapy, on the other hand, exerted its greatest success among patients who tended toward dependency in interpersonal relationships.

### Northwestern University

The "Long-Term Psychotherapy Project" at Northwestern University (see Howard et al., 1991) is currently in process and has two major goals. The first goal is to intensively investigate the psychotherapeutic process itself and to determine what happens in therapy or in the therapeutic context both within and between sessions. This goal is being addressed in a naturalistic fashion by observing the patterns of relationships that occur over time. The second goal of this project is to gather information on the psychotherapy delivery system in order to determine who uses psychotherapy, under what circumstances they do so, for how long, and for what reasons. This goal is being pursued by means of a quasi-experimental design that is comparing the distinguishing characteristics of various naturally occurring groups. Most notably, the following variables are being considered as representing potentially important distinctions among patients in successful and unsuccessful short- and long-term psychotherapy: clinical and demographic qualities; early therapy experiences; and relevant psychotherapeutic processes over the course of time.

All patients seeking treatment through the Department of Psychiatry's Psychotherapy Clinic are asked to participate in this research project. Those who agree to participate are asked to complete a set of self-report questionnaires. They are then evaluated through a comprehensive battery of interview and self-report measures throughout therapy and throughout a follow-up period without direct effort to modify the course or duration of treatment.

The questionnaires are designed to evaluate the extent and type of psychopathology, environmental stress, and readiness for treatment. A general survey of the patients' experiences in individual psychotherapy is also completed after the first, third, fifth, and sixth sessions and every tenth session thereafter. Although unusual in a study of this type, therapist conformity with the initial treatment plan is also assessed as a means of exploring therapist skill level as a contributor to treatment gain. All of these variables are correlated with clinical outcomes on the basis of pre–post self-reports and interviews.

The research developed in this program is based on two interdependent models of psychotherapy: the dosage model, based on varying numbers of sessions (Howard, Kopta, Krause, & Orlinsky, 1986), and the generic model, which stresses components of the therapeutic process (Orlinsky & Howard, 1987). The preliminary results of the dosage model that are now becoming available suggest that a positive relationship exists between the dose (number of sessions) of psychotherapy and improvement. Eight sessions is the mean dose of psychotherapy required to demonstrate positive therapeutic effects among 50% of the subjects. By the time 26 sessions have been completed, 75% of those obtaining treatment experience benefits. Overall, the relationship between dosage and outcome is represented by a gradually decreasing but positive function.

The generic model of psychotherapy (Orlinsky & Howard, 1987) postulates that certain input variables, process events, and outcome realizations are common to all therapies. This model identifies five components of the therapeutic process. Variations within each of these five dimensions are hypothesized to be related to variations of treatment outcome regardless of the type of psychotherapy being used. These dimensions are (a) the therapeutic contract, which specifies the terms and limits of the treatment; (b) the therapeutic interventions; (c) the therapeutic bond; (d) the way in which the patient directs and controls his or her own behavior throughout the therapeutic encounter; and (e) the therapeutic realizations or interactive processes that occur in therapy. Although still preliminary, research findings are beginning to accumulate in support of some of the dimensions of this model. The results are strongest in regard to the power of the therapeutic bond: The rated quality of the therapeutic bond in very early sessions appears to be a good predictor of subsequent therapeutic outcome.

## The Ulm Textbank Project

Since 1968, a major research effort at the University of Ulm (Germany) has been the intensive study of the processes of individual psychoanalytic work. The group involved with this work pioneered the use of computer technology to study psychoanalytic narratives. Tape recordings of long-term psychoanalytic psychotherapy and analysis have generated a large number of verbatim transcripts; these transcripts have been stored as narrative files in a computerized data bank. This archival data is used to explore dialectic and thematic aspects of the therapy process, facilitated by the computer's ability to search and sort words and topics. The goals of the "Ulm Textbank Research Program" (Mergenthaler & Kächele, 1991) makes the verbatim transcripts of psychotherapy sessions available to researchers. The Textbank Management System integrates techniques of linguistic analysis and text processing to make texts in the field of psychotherapy accessible to a wide range of users.

The two major areas of work at the Textbank include longitudinal and cross-sectional studies. Longitudinal studies concentrate on texts from a relatively small number of long-term psychoanalytic cases, with the goal of studying the process of change in psychoanalysis. Cross-sectional studies concentrate on a larger number of intake interviews and explore the influence of client demographic (e.g., gender, age, and socioeconomic status) and clinical (e.g., diagnostic) variables, as well as therapist variables, on interview processes and treatment outcome measures.

The database of psychoanalytic psychotherapy texts includes extensive excerpts of four cases and individual sessions of another nine cases. The database of initial interviews, on the other hand, includes several hundred cases and is referenced and cross-listed by clients' and therapists' gender and clients' diagnostic status. The latter database is being expanded to included patient variables like socioeconomic status and age, as well as therapist variables like level of experience and theoretical orientation. Two thirds of the material in the Ulm Textbank comes from the Psychotherapy Department at the University of Ulm. The other third has been supplied by other research institutions both in Germany and in other countries such as Austria, Sweden, Switzerland, and the United States.

Current research projects using the Textbank include studies on vocabulary change in the course of short-term psychotherapy, as well as the construction of an emotion-word dictionary that allows therapy processes to be referenced to changes in verbalized emotions, dialectic aspects of speech, and patterns of speaker interactional sequences.

Computer-aided text analysis has proven to be an efficient tool in psychotherapy process research. Further developments in this program will include the use of artificial intelligence technology, as well as cognitive science. The first steps in this direction include the development of computer-knowledge based procedures that are able to identify early childhood experiences in the therapeutic transcripts.

## Summary of International Trends

As a result of such efforts as those described in the previous sections, psychotherapy research is catching the interest of scientists internationally. A host of research reports are now accumulating from countries that have not traditionally been known to support psychotherapy research. These reports attest to increasing interest among scientists in Italy (e.g., Guidano, 1987, 1991), Portugal (Goncalves, 1990), and Spain (Feixas i Viaplana & Villegas i Besora, 1990).

Although worldwide collaboration has resulted in the development of some common methods and conclusions about psychotherapy process and outcomes, there continues to be considerable variability among programs and countries in the goals of research, in the nature of the problems addressed, and in the ways that even standard procedures are applied. These differences led Beutler, Crago, and Machado (1991) to conclude that the differences among programs and regions may be a stronger index of the vitality of the field than are the similarities.

Beutler et al. (1991) concluded that regional as well as programmatic differences are apparent in at least four domains: (a) the relative focus on process and outcomes; (b) the theoretical models of psychotherapy targeted for investigation; (c) the modality of service delivery studied; and (d) the methodologies preferred. These differences will be briefly summarized below.

### Process Versus Outcome Focus

Research programs tend to separate themselves into those that are principally interested in psychotherapy processes and those that are interested in psychotherapy outcomes. However, this distinction is now far less clear than it has been in the past. There is a consistent movement by many programs (e.g., Henry & Strupp, 1991; Piper, Azim, McCallum & Joyce, 1991; ) toward combining the two domains of focus to emphasize specifically the relationships among process and outcome variables. The conclusion that there is an escalating interest in merging process and outcome interests may be supported by the observation that the programs claiming increasing interest in the combination of process and outcome emphases represent all regions of Europe and North America in similar proportions. This movement has resulted in an increasing similarity among programs around a common interest in process and outcome relationships.

In spite of this increasing similarity, both interprogram and interregional variations are sufficient to suggest that there are regional and geographical differences in the degree to which process and outcome research is valued. Beutler, Crago, & Machado (1991) concluded that most research programs that intensively study psychotherapy processes, to the relative exclusion of efficacy assessment, are clustered in northern Europe, especially Germany (e.g., Mergenthaler & Kächele, 1991), and the coastal regions of North America (e.g., Horwitz et al., 1991). On the other hand, programs that place relative value on efficacy studies are less easily assigned a geographic concentration in North America because they represent all of the regions of the United States and Canada. This is not the case in Europe, however, where programs that emphasize outcome studies tend to be proportionately distributed more in the United Kingdom and Scandinavia than in Germany, France, and adjoining countries.

## Theoretical Models of Psychotherapy Studied

In the last two decades, a large number of distinctively different theoretical models of psychotherapy have evolved. These various models or types range in complexity, focus, and history. Research programs have demonstrated various degrees of commitment to studying one or more of these psychotherapy types. Some programs are uncommitted to a given theoretical posture and are drawn to study whatever type is of interest in the changing zeitgeist. Others, however, have distinct allegiances to one or another type of psychotherapy and are devoted to testing the theoretical principles on which that therapy is based.

The review by Beutler and Crago (1991) suggests that the type or model of psychotherapy explored is closely related to whether a program values processes or outcomes. Those programs that emphasize the study of the internal processes of psychotherapy over the study of treatment outcomes have almost uniformly targeted for study variations of psychodynamic and psychoanalytic treatments (e.g., Henry & Strupp, 1991). Outcome researchers, on the other hand, favor the study of interpersonal, behavioral, and cognitive therapies (e.g., Emmelkamp & Albersnagel, 1991), perhaps because the outcomes that these treatments target are more easily observed and measured than those that are addressed by psychodynamic therapies.

Those programs that are systematically committed to assessing the linkages between internal workings and external outcomes are the most diverse of all. They include studies of naturally occurring psychotherapies, unsystematic combinations of psychotherapeutic procedures, cognitive therapies, behavioral interventions, experiential or humanistic models, psychodynamic therapies, interpersonal therapies, and therapies that systematically integrate different approaches.

The geographical distributions of studies with varying commitments to psychodynamic and alternative methods reveal again the psychodynamic leanings of Germany and the coastal regions of North America. However, there are also some clear indications of continuing interest in client-centered therapy among Western European scientists (e.g., Stuhr & Meyer, 1991). This latter interest contrasts with the strong disposition in North America toward the more recently developed cognitive therapies (e.g., Jarrett, 1991). Finally, interest also appears to be present for both experiential therapies and integrative therapies, although the geographical distributions of these interests are not obvious.

## The Modality of Delivery

Although much of psychotherapy research has focused on individually administered treatment, there are some notable exceptions. Several programs have systematically investigated group therapies as well as marital and family therapies (e.g., Klass & Barlow, 1991). A small group of programs have also focused on the relationship between psychotherapy and various drug therapies (e.g., Luborsky, Crits-Christoph, & Barber, 1991), and some have concentrated on research on the prevention of emotional problems (e.g., Markman, Stanley, Floyd, Hahlweg, & Blumberg, 1991).

At the same time, the preponderance of investigations of short-term and time-limited treatments are located in North America. This distribution contrasts with the proportional attention given to research on long-term psychotherapies and psychoanalysis in continental Europe. Interestingly, the health care delivery system and research funding priorities of Germany appear to encourage the use and investigation of these long-term treatments, especially psychoanalysis. In contrast, there appears to be little federal support for studying long-term therapies like psychoanalysis in North America.

## Preferred Methodologies

A review of the programs reported by Beutler and Crago (1991) suggest that there are also variations in the degree to which different geographic regions use the methods of true experiments, quasi-experiments, and naturalistic observations. There is also variation in the degree to which they rely on intensive analyses of single cases versus groups or aggregates of similar individuals, and on mathematical procedures models of psychotherapy processes.

As suggested by the extent and variety of their use, Beutler, Crago, & Machado (1991) concluded that the methodologies preferred among programs based in North America embody three central qualities: the random assignment of subjects to treatments, the use of manual driven therapies, and the selection of diagnostically homogeneous samples. These are the defining characteristics of "true experiments." There are a few programs outside of North America that incorporate all three of these elements, but European programs prefer and more frequently use quasi-experimental and naturalistic methods. When true experiments are conducted in Europe, they are often modified to exclude the use of diagnostically similar samples of patients in favor of diverse and unselected samples (e.g., Grawe, 1991).

In both Europe and North America, by far the largest number of studies that do not routinely restrict entry to a specific set of diagnostic groups have used naturalistic rather than either true experimental or quasi-experimental research methods. In this type of study, descriptive relationships are explored between therapy or therapist characteristics and the outcomes of treatment. Sometimes, this procedure is varied to incorporate the group comparison procedures of quasi-experiments (e.g., Howard et al., 1991).

Intensive case-study methodologies have been used most often as the primary method for assessing psychoanalytic treatments, but they are also increasingly used as secondary analyses for a variety of psychotherapies (e.g., Jacobson & Truax, 1991; Luborsky et al., 1991). In these case-study methodologies, it is more difficult than in controlled comparison and clinical trials studies to tease out the type of patient to which the results can be applied.

Finally, a number of research programs have used statistical procedures as a primary method in psychotherapy research. These approaches have included meta-analysis (e.g., Berman et al., 1991), mathematical modeling of therapeutic interactions and outcomes (e.g., Langs & Badalamenti, 1991), and textual analysis of process data (e.g., Mergenthaler & Kächele, 1991). These innovations may mark the evolution of new means of compiling psychotherapy data, with the development of computer technologies. The applications are varied, but at this point they are too infrequent to detect regional differences in their use.

The pattern of regional differences suggests that North American research programs tend to value randomized clinical trials methods, as applied in diagnostically homogeneous samples, process and process-to-outcome patterns, the use of manualized therapies, and the exploration of diverse therapies. In contrast, researchers in continental Europe appear to value naturalistic studies of psychoanalytic processes occurring in non-manualized treatments among heterogeneous samples. Some movement toward randomized clinical trials and manualized treatments has been noted in Europe, but largely without the restriction of samples to diagnostic groupings.

It should be emphasized that Europe is more diverse in its interests and values than this summary indicates, with considerable variation seen among countries. Variations run from the biological focus of France (e.g., Gerin & Dazord, 1991) to the strongly behavioral focus of the Netherlands (e.g., Emmelkamp & Albersnagel, 1991).

It is difficult to determine the preferences of either Scandinavian investigators or those from the United Kingdom because of their infrequent representation among research programs. However, on the basis of the limited data available, it might be concluded that in the United Kingdom there is a preference for randomized clinical trial designs, and a focus on process-to-outcome relationships and structured, short-term therapies, more similar to North America than to the other countries of northern Europe.

Notably lacking in the foregoing discussion is research from Asian countries. Difficulties of translation and the relatively undeveloped nature of psychotherapy research programs in countries of this region account for this absence of information. The need for international linkages and collaboration is apparent.

## Conclusions

Lambert (1991) has outlined six conclusions about psychotherapy from contemporary research: (a) Psychotherapy is effective, (b) it is more effective than "placebo" interventions, (c) clients who improve in therapy maintain that improvement for extended periods, (d) some treatments have a negative effect on some clients, (e) common factors and specific therapy interventions affect client posttreatment status, and (f) the client is a principal determiner of the effectiveness of a given treatment.

Although these conclusions seem safe from significant contradiction, it should be pointed out that methodologies are continuing to evolve and are being directed toward discovering differences among the efficacy rates of specific psychotherapy models. Some of these methodologies are arising from a continuing controversy about whether psychotherapy effects are the result of principles and procedures that are common to all models of change or if mean outcomes mask differential efficacy rates. This new push for comparisons differs from early horse race comparisons of psychotherapy in that it seeks to unmask the therapy and patient interaction effects and thereby to reveal the conditions under which different models are effective for different client groups (Beutler et al., 1991a).

Additionally, controversy still exists around the importance of understanding psychotherapy processes in the absence of specific outcome data. Many programs still emphasize the importance of discovering principles of change from individual samples, even in the absence of a clear demonstration of efficacy. Generally, however, the field seems to be moving toward an integration of these process-focused studies and research on outcome efficacy.

Investigators also differ in the relative value placed on studying diagnostically homogeneous groups. Although some investigators and programs have found value in developing treatments for specific diagnostic conditions, others have emphasized the cross-cutting nature of psychotherapy and have suggested that variables yet undisclosed in diagnosis may be more important to understanding psychotherapy efficacy.

Finally, there continues to be disagreement about the relative value of different methods of delivering psychotherapy. Group, family, and individual delivery systems are being developed and compared. It is likely that, once again, all will win and all will have prizes until we discover the limitations and indicators for each of these delivery mechanisms.

# References

American Psychiatric Association. (1987). *Diagnostic and statistical manual of mental disorders* (3rd ed., rev.). Washington, DC: Author.

Barlow, D. H. (1981). On the relation of clinical research to clinical practice: Current issues, new directions. *Journal of Consulting and Clinical Psychology, 49,* 147–155.

Barlow, D. H., & Hersen, M. (Eds.). (1984). *Single-case experimental designs: Strategies for studying behavior change* (2nd ed.). New York: Pergamon Press.

Beck, A. T. (1978). *Depression inventory.* Philadelphia: Center for Cognitive Therapy.

Bentler, P. M. (1985). *Theory and implementation of EQS, a structural equation program.* Los Angeles: BMDP Statistical Software.

Bergin, A. E., & Lambert, M. J. (1978). The evaluation of psychotherapeutic outcomes. In S. L. Garfield & A. E. Bergin (Eds.), *Handbook of psychotherapy and behavior change: An empirical analysis* (pp. 139–190). New York: Wiley.

Berman, J. S., Miller, R. C., & Massman, P. J. (1985). Cognitive therapy versus systematic desensitization: Is one treatment superior? *Psychological Bulletin, 97,* 451–461.

Berman, J. S., Neimeyer, R. A., Houts, A. C., Shadish, W. R., Meyers, A. W., & Whelam, J. P. (1991). The psychotherapy research program at Memphis State University. In L. E. Beutler & M. Crago (Eds.), *Psychotherapy research: An international review of programmatic studies* (pp. 285–289). Washington, DC: American Psychological Association.

Beutler, L. E. (1979). Toward specific psychological therapies for specific conditions. *Journal of Consulting and Clinical Psychology, 47,* 882–897.

Beutler, L. E., & Clarkin, J. (1990). *Systematic treatment selection: Toward targeted therapeutic interventions.* New York: Brunner/Mazel.

Beutler, L. E., & Crago, M. (Eds.). (1991). *Psychotherapy research: An international review of programmatic studies.* Washington, DC: American Psychological Association.

Beutler, L. E., Crago, M., & Machado, P. P. (1991). The status of programmatic research. In L. E. Beutler & M. Crago (Eds.), *Psychotherapy research: An international review of programmatic studies* (pp. 325–328).Washington, DC: American Psychological Association.

Beutler, L. E., Engle, D., Mohr, D., Daldrup, R. J., Bergan, J., Meredith, K., & Merry, W. (1991a). Predictors of differential and self directed psychotherapeutic procedures. *Journal of Consulting and Clinical Psychology, 59,* 333–340.

Beutler, L. E., Engle, D., Shoham-Solomon, V., Mohr, D., Dean, J. C., & Bernat, E. M. (1991b). University of Arizona: Searching for differential treatments. In L. E. Beutler & M. Crago (Eds.), *Psychotherapy research: An international review of programmatic studies* (pp. 90–97). Washington, DC: American Psychological Association.

Corsini, R. J. (1981). *Handbook of innovative psychotherapies.* New York: Wiley.

Daldrup, R. J., Beutler, L. E., Engle, D., & Greenberg, L. S. (1988). *Focused expressive psychotherapy: Freeing the overcontrolled patient.* New York: Guilford Press.

Dobson, K. S., & Shaw, B. F. (1988). The use of treatment manuals in cognitive therapy: Experience and issues. *Journal of Consulting and Clinical Psychology, 56,* 673–680.

Emmelkamp, P. M. G., & Albersnagel, F. A. (1991). University of Groningen: Experimental psychotherapy and psychopathology. In L. E. Beutler & M. Crago (Eds.), *Psychotherapy research: An international review of programmatic studies* (pp. 251–260). Washington, DC: American Psychological Association.

Eysenck, H. J. (1952). The effects of psychotherapy: An evaluation. *Journal of Consulting Psychology, 16,* 319–324.

Feixas i Viaplana, G., & Villegas i Besora, M. (1990). *Constructivismo y psicoterapia* [Constructivism and psychotherapy]. Barcelona, Spain: PPU.

Gerin, P., & Dazord, A. (1991). Psychotherapy research at the Institut National de la Santé et de la Recherche Medicale. In L. E. Beutler & M. Crago (Eds.), *Psychotherapy research: An international review of programmatic studies* (pp. 274–278). Washington, DC: American Psychological Association.

Goncalves, O. F. (1990). Psicologia clinica: Estado actual e perspectivas de futuro [Clinical psychology: Current state and future trends]. *Jornal de Psicologia, 9*(1), 8–13.

Grawe, K. (1991). University of Bern: Differential psychotherapy research. In L. E. Beutler & M. Crago (Eds.), *Psychotherapy research: An international review of programmatic studies* (pp. 202–211). Washington, DC: American Psychological Association.

Greenberg, L. S., & Pinsoff, W. M. (1986). *The psychotherapeutic process: A research handbook.* New York: Guilford Press.

Guidano, V. F. (1987). *Complexity of the self: A developmental approach to psychopathology and therapy.* New York: Guilford Press.

Guidano, V. F. (1991). *The self in process: Toward a post-rationalist cognitive therapy.* New York: Guilford Press.

Hamilton, M. (1967). Development of a rating scale for primary depressive illness. *British Journal of Social and Clinical Psychology, 6,* 278–296.

Henry, W. P., & Strupp, H. H. (1991). Vanderbilt University: The Vanderbilt Center for Psychotherapy Research. In L. E. Beutler & M. Crago (Eds.), *Psychotherapy research: An international review of programmatic studies* (pp. 166–174). Washington, DC: American Psychological Association.

Horwitz, L., Allen, J. G., Colson, D. B., Frieswyk, S. H., Gabbard, G. O., Coyne, L., & Newsom, G. E. (1991). Psychotherapy of borderline patients at the Menninger Foundation: Expressive compared with supportive interventions and the therapeutic alliance. In L. E. Beutler & M. Crago (Eds.), *Psychotherapy research: An international review of programmatic studies* (pp. 48–55). Washington, DC: American Psychological Association.

Howard, K. I., Kopta, S., Krause, M., & Orlinsky, D. (1986). The dose–effect relationship in psychotherapy. *American Psychologist, 41,* 159–164.

Howard, K. I., Orlinsky, D. E., Saunders, S. M., Bankoff, E., Davidson, C., & O'Mahoney, M. (1991). Northwestern University–University of Chicago psychotherapy research program. In L. E. Beutler & M. Crago (Eds.), *Psychotherapy research: An international review of programmatic studies* (pp. 65–73). Washington, DC: American Psychological Association.

Jacobson, N. S., & Truax, P. (1991). Clinical significance: A statistical approach to defining meaningful change in psychotherapy research. *Journal of Consulting and Clinical Psychology, 59,* 12–19.

Jarrett, R. B. (1991). University of Texas Southwestern Medical Center at Dallas: Psychosocial program in mood disorders. In L. E. Beutler & M. Crago (Eds.), *Psychotherapy research: An international review of programmatic studies* (pp. 142–148). Washington, DC: American Psychological Association.

Kazdin, A. E. (1984). Statistical analyses for single-case experimental designs. In D. H. Barlow & M. Hersen (Eds.), *Single-case experimental designs: Strategies for studying behavior change* (2nd ed., pp. 285–394). New York: Pergamon Press.

Kazdin, A. E. (1991). *Research design in clinical psychology* (2nd ed.). New York: Pergamon Press.

Klass, E. T., & Barlow, D. H. (1991). The University at Albany, State University of New York Center for Stress and Anxiety Disorders: Psychotherapy research at the Phobia and Anxiety Disorders Clinic. In L. E. Beutler & M. Crago (Eds.), *Psychotherapy research: An international review of programmatic studies* (pp. 74–81). Washington, DC: American Psychological Association.

Lambert, M. J. (1991). An introduction to psychotherapy research. In L. E. Beutler & M. Crago (Eds.), *Psychotherapy research: An international review of programmatic studies* (pp. 1–11). Washington, DC: American Psychological Association.

Lambert, M. J., Christensen, E. R., & DeJulio, S. S. (Eds.). (1983). *The assessment of psychotherapy outcome.* New York: Wiley.

Lambert, M. J., & Ogles, B. M. (1988). Treatment manuals: Problems and promise. *Journal of Integrative and Eclectic Psychotherapy, 7,* 187–204.

Langs, R., & Badalamenti, A. (1991). Nathan S. Kleine Institute for Psychotherapy Research: Quantitative studies of the therapeutic interaction guided by consideration of unconscious communication. In L. E. Beutler & M. Crago (Eds.), *Psychotherapy research: An international review of programmatic studies* (pp. 294–298). Washington, DC: American Psychological Association.

Luborsky, L., Crits-Christoph, P., & Barber, J. (1991). University of Pennsylvania: The Penn psychotherapy research projects. In L. E. Beutler & M. Crago (Eds.), *Psychotherapy research: An international review of programmatic studies* (pp. 133–141). Washington, DC: American Psychological Association.

Luborsky, L., Crits-Christoph, P., Mintz, J., & Auerbach, A. (1988). *Who will benefit from psychotherapy? Predicting therapeutic outcomes.* New York: Basic Books.

Luborsky, L., & DeRubeis, R. J. (1984). The use of psychotherapy treatment manuals: A small revolution in psychotherapy research style. *Clinical Psychology Review, 4,* 5–14.

Luborsky, L., Singer, B., & Luborsky, L. (1975). Comparative studies of psychotherapies. *Archives of General Psychiatry, 32,* 995–1008.

Markman, H. J., Stanley, S. M., Floyd, F. J., Hahlweg, K., & Blumberg, S. (1991). Prevention of divorce and marital distress. In L. E. Beutler & M. Crago (Eds.), *Psychotherapy research: An international review of programmatic studies* (pp. 115–122). Washington, DC: American Psychological Association.

Mergenthaler, E., & Kächele, H. (1991). University of Ulm: The Ulm Textbank Research Program. In L. E. Beutler & M. Crago (Eds.), *Psychotherapy research: An international review of programmatic studies* (pp. 219–225). Washington, DC: American Psychological Association.

Orlinsky, D. E., & Howard, K. I. (1987). A generic model of psychotherapy. *Journal of Integrative and Eclectic Psychotherapy, 6,* 6–28.

Parloff, M. B. (1980, April). *Psychotherapy and research: An anclitic depression.* Frieda Fromm-Reichman Memorial Lecture, Washington School of Psychiatry, Washington, DC.

Piper, W. E., Azim, H. F. A., McCallum, M., & Joyce, A. S. (1991). The University of Alberta Psychotherapy Research Center. In L. E. Beutler & M. Crago (Eds.), *Psychotherapy research: An international review of programmatic studies* (pp. 82–89). Washington, DC: American Psychological Association.

Rogers, C. R. (1957). The necessary and sufficient condition of therapeutic personality changes. *Journal of Consulting Psychology, 21,* 95–103.

Scogin, F., Hamblin, D., & Beutler, L. E. (1987). Bibliotherapy for depressed older adults: A self-help alternative. *Gerontologist, 27,* 383–387.

Shapiro, D. A., & Shapiro, D. (1982). Meta-analysis of comparative therapy outcome studies: A replication and refinement. *Psychological Bulletin, 92,* 581–604.

Sloane, R. B., Staples, F. R., Cristol, A. H., Yorkston, N. J., & Whipple, K. (1976). *Psychotherapy versus behavior therapy.* Cambridge, MA: Harvard University Press.

Smith, M. L., Glass, G. V., & Miller, T. I. (1980). *The benefits of psychotherapy.* Baltimore: Johns Hopkins University Press.

Strupp, H. H. (1981). Clinical research, practice and the crisis of confidence. *Journal of Consulting and Clinical Psychology, 49,* 216–219.

Stuhr, U., & Meyer, A. E. (1991). University of Hamburg: Hamburg short-term psychotherapy comparison study. In L. E. Beutler & M. Crago (Eds.), *Psychotherapy research: An international review of programmatic studies* (pp. 212–218). Washington, DC: American Psychological Association.

Truax, C. B., & Carkhuff, R. R. (1965). The experimental manipulation of therapeutic conditions. *Journal of Consulting Psychology, 29,* 119–124.

Waskow, I. E., & Parloff, M. B. (Eds.). (1975). *Psychotherapy change measures* (Publication No. 74–120). Rockville, MD: National Institute of Mental Health.

Yost, E., Beutler, L. E., Corbishley, M. A., & Allender, J. R. (1986). *Group cognitive therapy: A treatment approach for depressed older adults.* New York: Pergamon Press.

# CHAPTER 9

# Psychological Assessment

Kurt Pawlik

I ndividual differences are an essential feature of behavior. People may differ widely in how they react in similiar or identical situations: when meeting a stranger, when facing an examination, or just in celebrating one's birthday. Individual differences in overt behavior, in psychophysiological responses, in mood states, and in conscious experience have long been recognized as essential to understanding human behavior and human social action. Methods of psychological assessment have been developed to describe, analyze, and interpret (for example, through statistical comparisons) such differences. In this chapter, different types of psychological assessment and important psychometric and ethical standards of test construction, test use, and test interpretation will be explained. Major assessment techniques will be presented according to a taxonomy of psychodiagnostic data sources.

The first attempts to develop methods of psychological assessment go back to 1884 and to the work of Sir Francis Galton in Great Britain and of J. McKeen Cattell (1890) in the United States (Anastasi, 1976). Toward the end of the last century, the first prototypes of "mental tests" were developed: selected tasks designed to study individual differences in memory performance, reasoning, speed of perception, and other mental functions. Research using these first tests later became instrumental in the development of a new branch of psychological science: differential psychology, the study of systematic interindividual differences in behavior. As early as 1900, William Stern published his founding text *Ueber Psychologie der individuellen Differenzen: Ideen zu einer Differentiellen Psychologie* ("On the Psychology of Individual Differences: Ideas Toward a Differential Psychology"). The methodological framework of psychological assessment developed in this book was to become influential for several decades thereafter. Today, more than 90 years later, methods of psychological assessment are available for all major aspects and dimensions of human behavior, meeting high standards of test construction and interpretation. And the scope of psychological assessment has shifted well beyond the initial emphasis on aspects of differential psychology. Methods of assessment have been developed to meet more specific psychodiagnostic needs in clinical and medical psychology (including psychotherapy), educational psychology, industrial and organizational psychology, forensic psychology, and environmental psychology, to mention only a few very prominent areas of application. Although much progress has been made, the field of psychological assessment continues to evolve.

The following two examples illustrate the range of problems for which methods of assessment are currently used by psychologists:

*Case 1: Neuropsychological diagnostics.* Jimmy K., age eight and a half, experienced serious brain injury in a traffic accident. Riding his bike home from school, Jimmy was hit by a car when he was about to cross a busy road at an intersection. According to the police report, he had misjudged his speed and that of an approaching car when the crosswalk lights were already flashing. In the accident, Jimmy sustained serious open-head injury and severe brain trauma, with unconsciousness continuing in the hospital until the next morning. He showed complete retrograde amnesia (i.e., he was unable to recall any event up to 20 minutes prior to the accident).

Following his release from the hospital, Jimmy's parents noticed significant changes in his behavior: His ability to concentrate was reduced, back in school he had difficulties paying attention for a full class period, his memory seemed impaired, and his parents were concerned that his drive and level of motivation were reduced. After consulting with a neurologist, they saw a clinical neuropsychologist for advice on how serious Jimmy's mental deficits were and if they would improve with time or require special remedial treatment (rehabilitation).

In a case like this, the psychologist will conduct a detailed assessment of Jimmy's performance on various mental tests (of perceptual and memory capacities, attention, concentration, etc.) and personality tests (of anxiety, level of motivation, emotional responsiveness to mental tasks, interpersonal attitudes, etc.). The test results will be analyzed by comparing them with Jimmy's (estimated) premorbid level of personality and performance and with statistical "test norms" available from large samples of same-age, noninjured children with a similiar background (cf. Filskov & Boll, 1981). In this way, reliable information is obtained to describe and explain Jimmy's behavior problems and to decide on suitable methods of intervention. Similiar methods of assessment will be used later to evaluate the effectiveness of such interventions.

*Case 2: Lead poisoning: An ecobehavioral assay of toxicology.* In some countries, lead is still an acceptable additive to gasoline (to improve engine lubrication); it is emitted into the environment around traffic following combustion. Because lead has been shown to be toxic to a number of metabolic processes, the question arose as to what extent lead may also be detrimental to nervous system functioning and, as a result, to behavior. To answer this question, matched samples of subjects experiencing different levels (concentrations) and durations of lead exposure in their habitual environment were tested on measures of speed of reaction and performance, of speed–accuracy trade-off in perception and vigilance over longer operating periods, and of memory and higher mental functions. On the basis of these test results, psychologists were able to quantify the ecotoxicological effects of lead on different dimensions of human behavior and experience (cf. Winneke, 1985). These results are used, for example, in defining maximum tolerance thresholds of lead concentration in the environment.

# The Types and Heuristics of Psychological Assessment

Methods of psychological assessment are used to provide reliable information about variations in overt human behavior, subjective experience (through verbal self-report data), and their psychophysiological bases. Psychologists apply these methods for different purposes, under different heuristics, and in different contexts of psychological intervention. In this first section, some principal distinctions and different prototypes of psychological assessment will be examined.

### The Heuristics of Assessment: Description, Modeling, and Intervention

*Heuristic* refers to the kind of scientific question in the pursuit of which psychodiagnostic information is sought. In principle, three variants of assessment heuristics can be distinguished: description, modeling, and intervention.

## Description

Assessing the immediate memory span of a person exposed to a certain concentration of lead for a certain period of time, and measuring Jimmy K.'s speed of reaction in a choice-reaction test are examples of psychodiagnostics in the narrow sense of "describing a given behavioral reality." The term *diagnostics* (from the Greek "diágnosis": differentiation, ability to differentiate) refers to this descriptive heuristic of assessment. In many applications, psychologists move beyond this first level, however, and also make use of this information in the context of a more advanced heuristic called *diagnostic inference* and in modeling (interpretation) and intervention.

## Type A Modeling, or Prognosis

Will Jimmy's behavior problems improve with time or remain unchanged? To answer this question, the psychologist needs to resort to a model (theory) of behavior development at Jimmy's age, at his level of performance, and following his kind of brain injury (the so-called "antecedents"). By applying this model to the diagnostic information at hand, the psychologist will arrive at a *prognosis* (prediction) of Jimmy's most likely test performance in, say, a year's time. In many applications of psychological assessment, heuristics of prognosis or prediction play an important role.

## Type B Modeling, or Explanation

Explanation is diagnostic inference in a direction opposite to that of prediction. By applying a model to a given state of affairs (e.g., Jimmy's current deficits in tests of concentration) in a "backward direction," the psychologist seeks to identify conditions (such as the kind and extent of Jimmy's brain injury or his anxiety response to the accident as such) that are likely antecedents (or causes) for his current state and thus serve to explain it. In this way, explanation is "postdiction" of the most likely antecedents for a given behavioral state. Prediction and explanation are the most frequently used heuristics of diagnostic inference.

## Intervention

Which remedial psychological treatment, if any, is indicated in a case like Jimmy's? Under this third type of heuristic, psychodiagnostic information is sought to optimize decisions among alternative treatments. (These decisions require a prediction of behavioral outcomes of a treatment from knowledge about the effectiveness of different kinds of treatments in subjects differing in assessment status.) Psychological assessment under the intervention heuristic is most common in clinical and educational settings. As a rule, it is combined with a subsequent second descriptive assessment (the so-called "evaluation") conducted after the intervention has taken place, to test its effectiveness.

## Alternative Dimensions of Assessment

As explained in detail elsewhere (e.g., Pawlik, 1976), psychological assessments may be designed to meet different aims of psychodiagnostics, which in turn imply different rationales of test construction and interpretation.

### Assessment of Status Versus Assessment of Process

In *status assessment*, diagnostic information is sought as representative of a testee's concurrent overall status in a certain variable of behavior, irrespective of the specifics of the testing situation or of fluctuations of a testee's behavior over time. Conversely, *process assessment* is designed to diagnose changes in a testee's behavior between different occasions of testing (situations, or stages of development or therapeutic intervention, for example). Process assessment poses special problems of psychometrics because difference scores are, in general, less reliable than status scores (Harris, 1963).

### Norm-Referenced Versus Criterion-Referenced Assessment

Here, "norm" is used in a purely statistical (rather than prescriptive) sense. For example, the mean and standard deviation of an assessment variable like "speed of perception" in a reference group of people may serve as a statistical norm to interpret a patient's performance on this test. In *norm-referenced assessment*, a person's test results are evaluated with respect to such statistical norms (e.g., as equal to, below, or above the group average). Most interindividual difference testing is norm-referenced, as is most clinical status diagnostics.

In *criterion-referenced* assessment, the assessment results of a person are evaluated by reference to a behavioral standard (the *criterion*) rather than to a group-statistical norm. Criterion-referenced assessment techniques have been developed for a wide range of behavioral criteria: with reference to the behavioral aims of psychotherapeutic interventions (such as reducing a client's anxiety in social situations or prior to exams), to scholastic achievement criteria (mastery tests for scholastic and other training programs), and to behavioral criteria of neuropsychological rehabilitation. Criterion-referenced assessment poses special problems of psychometric test construction and evaluation. As a rule, assessment techniques developed for norm-referenced assessment cannot be applied directly to criterion-referenced assessment, and vice versa (Hambleton, Swaminathan, Algina, & Coulson, 1978).

### Representative Testing (Sampling) Versus Inventory-Taking of Behavior

What does it mean to refer to a person's immediate-memory capacity? There are numerous ways to assess immediate-memory performance, depending on the type of material (figural, verbal, numerical), on the sensory modality (visual, auditory, somesthetic) and content (the specific figures, words, numbers) of information to be kept in memory, on the delay between the presentation of information and its recall, and on the type of recall requested (free recall, cued recall, recognition). Clearly, any given assessment procedure of immediate memory performance can cover only a selection, or sample, of all of these possibilities. Psychological assessment techniques following this sampling principle are called *tests* (in the restricted sense of the term). A test is made up of a limited number of tasks (e.g., memory), questions, or other occasions providing for the observation of behavior. An important aspect of the psychometric quality of a psychological test is the degree to which these elements, or items, of a test constitute a representative (unbiased) sample of the universe of items (e.g., of all possible memory tasks) for which the test is to stand.

In most tests, the assessment result is expressed in numerical form, typically the number of test items passed (answered in the scored direction). The scoring instructions for a test define rules to map differences in test behavior into different numerical test results (test scores). In this sense, psychological tests are instruments of behavioral measurement. Most personality and ability tests follow this measurement rationale. When interpreting numerical test results, one has to take into account the level of measurement or type of scale inherent in a scoring procedure, which specifies the highest level of operation that is admissible in comparing test results (simple nominal comparisons; ordinal comparisons; linear operations of addition/subtraction; nonlinear operations of multiplication/division).

Take as an example the assessment of ambient temperature. Common temperature adjectives can be used to form a simple ordinal scale: frigid–cold–tepid–warm–hot–burning hot. The familiar Fahrenheit scale is an interval scale (as is the Celsius scale): The difference between degrees is equal everywhere along the same scale. It would not be correct, however, to say that 70° Fahrenheit is twice as warm as 35° Fahrenheit: Expressed in degrees centigrade, the two temperatures correspond to (approximately) 21° and 0.2° Celsius, yielding a ratio of more than 100 (as compared with a ratio of 2 in the Fahrenheit scale). The reason for this discrepancy is obvious: The two temperature scales, although both perfectly linear, differ in scale unit and in zero point. Ratio comparisons (e.g., value A is twice or one third the amount of value B) are admissible only in scales with an absolute zero point (so-called ratio scales, like the Kelvin scale of temperature).

Similarly, IQ tests, as well as most other psychological tests, yield numerical results only at an interval scale level. Results of these tests can be interpreted with respect to test score differences, but not with respect to test score ratios. Interpretations involving percentages ("person A yielded a test result 15% higher than person B") are thus not admissible for IQ (and almost all other psychological) tests, which establish measurement only up to interval scale level. (See Lord & Novick, 1968, for a detailed account of different measurement principles in behavioral research.)

A totally different kind of psychological assessment, not following this sampling principle of tests, is *inventory taking* (Pawlik, 1982). Consider a patient seeking psychotherapy to overcome anxiety problems. Assessing that person's overall level of anxiety, tested across a representative sample of anxiety-inducing situations, will not prove sufficient for devising an effective intervention program. In addition, detailed one-by-one information will be needed as to which conditions do and which do not elicit which kind of anxiety response in that patient. Taking only a sample of these conditions or responses would be unsatisfactory; what is needed is an item-by-item inventory of (possibly all) stimuli eliciting anxiety responses, and a detailed stock-taking of the nature of these responses. Assessment instruments of this second type follow principles of *exhaustion* rather than of sampling. Fear schedules and other clinical tests designed in recent years for application under the heuristics of intervention programs follow this inventory-taking rationale of psychological assessment (cf. McReynolds, 1989).

### The Object of Assessment: Schedules of Behavior, Traits, and States

For more than half a century, psychological assessment has been predominantly trait oriented. *Traits* are hypothetical (latent, i.e., not directly observable) variables introduced to account for variations in observable test results. Intelligence, speed of perception, eye–hand coordination, extraversion–introversion, and emotional stability–lability are examples of psychological traits that have been the object of frequent test construction. In differential psychology, methods of analysis have been developed that enable the researcher to investigate the number and (inferred) nature of latent variables underlying observable test score variation in a group of subjects. The best-known and most widely used are methods using principles of multivariate statistical analysis of test score intercorrelations (factor analysis, principal components analysis, multivariate discriminant function analysis, and canonical correlation analysis; Guilford, 1959; Harman, 1960; Pawlik, 1972; Thurstone, 1947). Given the test results of $N$ subjects on $n$ psychological tests (with $N < n$), these methods enable the researcher to express the observed test scores as linear functions of a smaller number ($k$) of factors or traits ($k < n$).

Many psychological tests have been designed to measure traits identified by these or related methods of analysis. A psychological trait is called *general* if it has been demonstrated to determine individual differences in a wide range of behavioral variables. Most psychological traits are of the medium-range level of generality, termed *common factors* in Thurstone's (1947) method of factor analysis, such as many cross-replicated factors of intelligence (verbal comprehension, spatial orientation, visualization, speed of perception, word fluency, speed of closure, etc.). A trait is called *specific* if it determines interindividual differences only within a narrow field of test content. Dimensions of knowledge competence tend to belong to this second category.

Traits of behavior that have been shown to determine test score variations in different subject populations are called *universal*. In this sense, the general traits referred to above are also of high universality. A trait that applies only to a subset of the general population is called *group specific*. Many traits of interest in clinical psychological assessment, for example, are specific to groups of patients with particular kinds of behavior problems.

By contrast, systematic sources of test score variations within a person across different occasions (situations, times) of testing are called *states*. Psychological state measurement is closely related to process assessment in clinical and educational applications. State tests follow a principle of test construction different from that of trait tests; they have to demonstrate high sensitivity to within-subject variations in behavior. Their design owes a lot to the work of Cattell (1957) and his group.

Both trait and state assessments are targeted toward measuring latent dimensions of behavior. By contrast, *schedules of behavior* are designed to assess surface attributes of behavior such as those focused on in the experimental study of behavioral learning (and behavior modification) and defined in terms of directly observable characteristics of behavior. Example are conditions eliciting a certain kind of behavior (*stimulus* variables), overt characteristics of a behavior (*response* variables), and factors associated with the maintenance of this behavior in a given person (*organismic* variables and variables of *reinforcement* and of reinforcement *contingency*). Schedules of behavior have been used for assessment in clinical psychology and in research on the therapy of problem behaviors (fears, anxiety responses and phobias, smoking and drinking problems, drug problems, etc.; e.g., McReynolds, 1989, and the chapter by Holtzman in this volume). Such assessment schedules typically follow an inventory-taking rather than a testing design.

# Psychometric and Ethical/Legal Standards of Assessment and Psychodiagnostic Inference

In psychodiagnostic assessment, information that can be part of people's personal sphere of privacy is obtained about their behavior and their personal experience. Therefore, the acquisition of such information (test construction and administration) and the use of such data (test interpretation, report writing, data handling) has to meet the highest psychometric/scientific and ethical/legal standards. In many countries, these standards have been incorporated into formal regulations that are obligatory for any kind of psychological testing (see, for example, American Psychological Association, 1985). They include both ethical/legal standards of psychological testing (protecting the client/testee against the misuse of psychological tests and test results) and psychometric standards (to guarantee established scientific criteria of test construction and interpretation). Every technique of psychological assessment has to be evaluated in terms of these psychometric standards, and the result of this evaluation has to be presented in detail in the published test manual. In this section, I will discuss first the most important psychometric/scientific standards of psychological assessment, and then major ethical/legal standards.

## Psychometric/Scientific Standards
### The Objectivity of Administration

The results of an assessment procedure remain ambiguous unless a clear definition is provided as to which aspects of behavior are to be studied (observed, tested) in which way and under which conditions. The extent to which a diagnostic instrument fulfills this requirement is called the *objectivity of administration*. This refers to the degree to which relevant details of test administration are standardized. Important aspects are the testing situation as such, the social and physical conditions under which the assessment is to be conducted, the instruction to be given to the testee, and the behavior of the psychological examiner (for example, if and in which way he or she is allowed or requested to lend help to the testee in the case of queries). All of this has to be spelled out in sufficient detail in the manual of an assessment procedure. As a rule, group tests show better objectivity of administration than do individual tests, and computer-assisted tests better objectivity than manipulative (performance) or situation tests. One way to test an assessment procedure for the degree of administration objectivity is to have matched samples of testees assessed independently by different examiners; proper administration objectivity is shown when there are no systematic (significant) differences in assessment results between different samples (and assessment conditions).

## Scoring Objectivity

Test results must be free of scoring errors and unaffected by scoring idiosyncracies on the part of the examiner. The degree to which independent scorers of the same behavior protocol arrive at identical results is called *scoring objectivity*. Scoring rules also have to be laid out in full detail in the manual of an assessment procedure. As a rule, tests providing open-ended items (*inventive response–format*) are less objective to score than tests providing multiple-choice items (*selective response–format*). Scoring objectivity tends to become a problem in broad-band assessment procedures like interviews, projective techniques, and expression analysis.

## Statistical Norms

How good (or poor) is the performance of a testee who has solved 22 out of 30 mental arithmetic problems or 14 out of 20 essay-type items on a 7th-grade biology test? The most common way of evaluating a test result is to compare it with statistical norms obtained in a appropriate reference group (norm population) of testees examined on that test before. The manual for a psychodiagnostic method explains the type of norms offered by the author. A simple test norm is the *standard score*,

$$z = \frac{X - \overline{X}}{s_X},$$

which expresses the deviation of a test score $x$ from the test score mean $\overline{x}$ in the reference population in units of the test score standard deviation ($s_x$) in that population. Standard scores have a mean ($m$) of 0 and a standard deviation ($s$) of 1. Other test norms used are *normalized standard scores* ($T$; $m = 50$, $s = 10$), *standardized IQ scores* ($m = 100$, $s = 15$), and *stens* ($m = 5$, $s = 2$). *Percentile norms* ($P$) give the percentage of testees in the reference population yielding the same or a lower test score as the individual being considered. As a rule, an assessment instrument like a test needs to be restandardized (after the translation of test items) before it can be applied in another country or culture. Furthermore, cohort differences between different age groups make it necessary to restandardize many tests from time to time even within the same country or culture. Similarly, special norms are worked out for subsets of a population that differ systematically in their test results. For example, many tests of intelligence are standardized separately for different age groups and for groups differing in educational level (years of schooling).

## Discriminative Power

This term relates to the degree to which an assessment procedure will in fact detect genuine differences in behavior. For example, many tests show better discrimination in the middle of the range of scores than in the extreme sections of this range. Other things being equal, the discriminative power of a psychological test is a (negatively accelerated) function of the number of items: The more items in a test (the longer the test), the higher its discriminative power.

## Internal Consistency

If the different items of a test happen to measure totally different aspects of behavior, different traits, or different states, scores from that test are ambiguous to interpret. *Internal consistency* is the degree to which the items of a test measure the same aspect of behavior or the same trait or state. The internal consistency of a psychological test shows in the intercorrelations between the test items. For a test to be consistent, each item has to correlate highly with the total score computed from all remaining test items (item index of discrimination).

## Reliability

Reliability refers to a key concept of psychometric test theory: the degree to which test results are unaffected by unsystematic errors of observation, assessment, and measurement. It is interesting to note that the psychometric concept of error in test reliability theory is equivalent to the concept of error of measurement used in the norms for physical and technical measurement as established by the International Standards Organisation (International Standards Organisation, 1981). (Curiously enough, this instructive equivalence of physical/technical and psychological concepts of the precision of measurement has not been recognized by psychologists in the past.)

In both contexts, "error" is defined as unintended unsystematic variation affecting the results from repeated testing of the same person (the same physical object) with the same or an equivalent test procedure. If the variance of these unsystematic error variations is labeled $s_e^2$, and if $s_x^2$ denotes the variance of the raw test scores (including error variation), the quantity

$$1 - \frac{s_e^2}{s_x^2}$$

is called the *reliability* of that test. Assuming the errors to be uncorrelated (over people and over repeated tests) with the error-free or *true* component $x_t$ in each raw test score $x$, this can be rewritten as *reliability coefficient*

$$R = \frac{s_t^2}{s_x^2},$$

with $s_t^2$ denoting the variance of the true score components. In this sense, the reliability of a psychological test is the percentage of true score variance in raw test score variance. The reliability coefficient $R$ can vary only between 0 (0% true score variance) and 1 (100% true score variance). The complement $(1 - R)$ gives the percentage of error variance in the raw test score variance:

$$1 - R = \frac{s_e^2}{s_x^2}.$$

The positive square root of the error variance $s_e^2$, $s_e$, is identical to the average deviation (in raw score units) of the raw test scores from the respective true scores. The quantity $s_e$ is called the *standard error of measurement* (SEM) of that test.

For psychological assessment, standards have been established and generally accepted according to which the reliability of an assessment procedure must not fall short of .80, if this procedure is to be admissible for individual assessment. (In statistical large-group comparisons, slightly lower reliabilities may be acceptable.) A necessary condition for the SEM not to exceed half of the raw score standard deviation is that $R$ reach or exceed .75 because

$$s_e = s_x \sqrt{1 - R}.$$

A systematic theory of psychological measurement, *classical test theory* (CTT), has been developed on the basis of this concept of psychological test reliability. (See Lord & Novick, 1968, for a systematic treatment of this theory and of a somewhat different concept of error of measurement as used in modern *probabilistic* or *item-response theory* of psychological measurement, which builds on the work of Rasch, Birnbaum, and others.)

In CTT measurement, "error" comprises all sources of nonsystematic variation affecting raw test scores that are unrelated to the true scores components of the test scores. Typical sources of error variance in psychological assessment include unintended effects of the test situation (social conditions; physical conditions such as insufficient illumination, noise disturbances, etc.) and variations in examiner behavior (both due to insufficient standardization of test administration); errors in scoring (i.e., insufficient scoring objectivity), inadequate test make-up (poor printing, labeling, or figure work; unclear instructions; ambiguous answer sheets, etc.), and irrelevant specifics of item content. It is important to note that trait and state measurements presuppose slightly different reliability concepts. For example, unintended variations on the part of the testee (such as fluctuations of attention, test-taking attitude, mood state, and level of activation or fatigue) may be additional sources of error variance in trait assessment, whereas these same variations may be part of intended true score variance in state measurement.

Several methods have been developed for estimating psychometric test reliability from interindividual raw score correlations. Those applied most widely are the method of repeated testing (reliability estimated from stability); the correlation of parallel test forms (reliability estimated from equivalence); and the estimation of reliability from the correlation of test half-scores or of test items (internal consistency estimates of reliability: the SPEARMAN–BROWN split-half reliability, and the KUDER–RICHARDSON reliability coefficient; for details, see again Lord & Novick, 1968). Coefficients of reliability are not strictly comparable across different methods of estimation, which tend to capitalize on slightly different portions of total error variance. The classical parallel-form reliability theory of psychological tests can be extended to a (limited or unlimited) universe of parallel tests or items measuring the same true score component to different degrees; this important extension by Cronbach has been called the *theory of generalizability* (Cronbach, Gleser, Nanda, & Rajaratnam, 1972).

## Validity

Test validity is the degree to which a psychological test measures that and only that psychological variable or attribute it is designed to measure. For example, a test constructed to measure the level of anxiety, although highly reliable, may still fall short of validity if true score components on the test depend more on the testees' level of activation than on their level of fearfulness and anxiety.

Several types of psychological test validity have been distinguished: *External* or *criterion validity* is estimated by correlating test scores (for example, scores on a test of psychomotor coordination) with an external measure (the *criterion*) of the psychological attribute in question (for example, success in civil air pilot training). (This notion of "criterion" is not to be confused with the concept of "criterion" in "criterion-referenced testing" referred to earlier.) To estimate *internal validity*, test scores are correlated with scores of the same subjects on other tests whose validity has been previously established. In both cases, test validity is expressed in a *coefficient of correlation r* (between testees' test scores and their criterion values or scores on other psychological tests); *r* can again vary between 0 and 1, with 0 indicating no validity and 1 indicating perfect validity of the test for the attribute in question. By computing $r^2$, the square of the validity coefficient, one obtains the percentage of test raw score variance accounted for by the attribute the test is to measure. It can be shown that this squared test validity cannot exceed test reliability: $r^2 \leq R$.

Yet another approach to investigating psychological test validity is *construct validation*. This is the method of choice for determining the validity of an assessment procedure designed to measure an attribute, for which neither a suitable criterion nor other previously validated tests exist. First, hypotheses are derived for the construct in question (for example, anxiety) from a theory in which this construct is defined (for example, the theory of anxiety as a secondary or learned drive). In the next step, these hypotheses are tested in suitably designed studies, using the test raw scores to measure the construct in question. Then construct validity shows in the degree to which the hypotheses can be verified on the basis of the test scores.

Methods of construct validation have gained increasing importance in test validation research in recent years. In this way, psychology has moved far beyond the old (and rightly criticized) commonplace that "intelligence is what intelligence tests measure." Rather than taking assessment results at their face value, psychologists have succeeded in unraveling the theoretical nature of a wide range of test variables.

### Test Fairness

What would have happened if Jimmy K., an English boy, had had his accident in a foreign country and, upon release from the hospital, had to be examined by a non-Anglophone neuropsychologist using psychological tests written in a language other than English? Clearly, it would have been difficult if not impossible to ascertain to what extent a poor test performance was due to the aftereffects of the brain trauma or to difficulties, on the part of Jimmy K., in taking the test in a foreign language and in a foreign environment. *Test fairness* refers to the extent to which the results of a psychological assessment are not affected or "biased" by differential degrees of familiarity with the nature of the assessment procedure, its language, or its cultural background. In this sense, lack of test fairness obviously works against test validity.

Specific aspects of the fairness of psychological assessment have been studied in detail in the United States in relation to such dimensions of culture as ethnicity and native language, also, more recently, with respect to gender and age discrimination. A variant of test fairness, *culture fairness*, has been given wide attention in cross-cultural testing and comparisons (Segall, Dasen, Berry, & Poortinga, 1990; see also Chapter 5, this volume) since R. B. Cattell's original use of the term for a new kind of intelligence test (Cattell, 1957). Special troubleshooting techniques of research have been developed to guard against effects of overt or covert sources of cultural bias. These include the testing of a control group of bilinguals experienced in both cultures under comparison, and retranslation of test or questionnaire instruments into the original language, with a subsequent bilingual expert rating of equivalence. With growing mobility and cross-national exchange of people, aspects of test fairness gain additional weight in test construction and test interpretation in general. For example, labor market regulations among the European Community countries will speed up multicultural developments in Europe, particularly within multinational enterprises. One consequence will be a growing demand for psychological assessment procedures fulfilling high standards of multicultural test fairness. The psychological testing of applicants for astronauts to be trained for future European Space Administration spaceflights may serve as a recent example (Goeters & Fassbender, 1991).

A psychological assessment procedure may fulfill overt linguistic and cultural criteria of test fairness and yet lack in test fairness at a more advanced level of analysis. (Detailed examples are given by Reynolds & Brown, 1984). Systematic checks on multicultural fairness at different levels of analysis are an important part of psychological test construction today.

## *Response Objectivity*

Personality questionnaires and other verbal self-report inventories are open to distortion by (voluntary and involuntary) response tendencies (see "Data Sources for Psychological Assessment," below). The standard of *response objectivity* (not to be confused with "objectivity of administration" and "scoring objectivity," explained earlier) refers to the degree to which the results of a psychological assessment will not be affected by a testee's voluntary or involuntary response sets or faking tendencies. Setting aside voluntary dissimulation, many performance tests and certain methods of behavior observation are highly objective in this sense of "response objectivity," whereas many tests of personality, of motivation, and of interests inevitably fall somewhat short of this criterion.

In addition to these nine key psychometric standards of psychological assessment, a number of minor criteria have been introduced. Examples are the *economy* of an assessment procedure (in terms of costs incurred in administering and scoring the procedure as compared with its validity and interpretative benefits), the *acceptability* of an assessment procedure (in the judgment of the testee), and the *band-width* of an assessment procedure (the number and breadth of psychological attributes covered). Special techniques of test construction and psychodiagnostic inference have been developed for *multistage procedures of assessment* (test batteries and multistage logistics of diagnostic inference).

### Ethical/Legal Standards

In many countries, norms of professional–psychological ethics and legal regulations have been formulated to protect a testee's rights in the design and conduct of a psychological assessment and in the use to be made of the results of this assessment. These rules and regulations may be part of a national code of ethics of professional conduct of psychologists, of the penal code, of the code of criminal procedure, of the civil code, or of special laws against the misuse of personal data (in data processing), or they may be derived directly from the national constitution. They can be summarized in the following four ethical/legal standards of psychological assessment.

#### The Protection of Personality

Like medical examinations, psychological assessment also must not violate the testee's personal rights and integrity and must respect the testee's right of privacy and protection of personal interests. In the case of doubt, a professional ethics committee should be consulted to ensure that every assessment procedure will comply with this overriding ethical norm.

#### The Principle of Informed Consent

With the possible exception of assessment under formal court procedure (forensic assessment), conducting a psychological assessment is contingent on the testee's prior and informed consent. Behavior observation of identified (or identifiable) persons in nonpublic situations without their knowing and without their prior and informed consent is against the law in many countries.

### The Principle of Confidentiality

Excluding again special circumstances in formal court procedure, the psychologist is bound to observe the principle of professional confidentiality regarding anything that comes to the psychologist's knowledge in the course of a psychological assessment (or any other professional psychological activity, for that matter). In Article 52 of the German Penal Code, for example, which regulates the protection of "personal secrets," psychologists are one of the professional groups explicitly referred to as being bound by law to keep secret any information about other persons they get access to in the course of their professional activity. Before entering into a psychological assessment, the testee has to be informed explicitly (and prior to his or her consent to participate) as to the use to be made of the results of the assessment. Although this is of special relevance, for example, in employment testing, it also holds for assessments that are part of research studies.

### The Protection of Personal Data

Upon the completion of a psychological assessment, all assessment results should be kept in a way that will ensure full protection against the misuse of personal data, including the misuse of the computerized storage of test and other personal data. In Germany, for example, the Data Protection Act requires a psychologist to obtain, in writing and prior to the assessment, the testee's consent to have his or her assessment data stored electronically, even if the purpose of this assessment and data storage is purely scientific and the data will be analyzed only with respect to group statistics.

## Data Sources for Psychological Assessment

Although tests *sensu strictiore* (i.e., tests of ability and aptitudes) and questionnaires still constitute the bulk of assessment techniques in use, data instrumental to psychodiagnostics come from a much wider range of source. From a systematic point of view, at least 10 different data sources of psychological assessment can be distinguished (see Pawlik, in press). These sources are described in this section, with illustrative references to some procedures that have gained relatively wide use and acceptance in research or applied work.

### Actuarial and Biographical Data

This most elementary type of assessment information comprises data on a person's life history (age, years and kind of schooling and professional education, marital status, current employment position, etc.) or professional or medical record. As a rule, actuarial and biographical data can be obtained at high levels of objectivity and reliability, with viable validities, for example, of educational-record data for the prediction of future educational or professional performance criteria (Cascio, 1976). Special questionnaire-type instruments have been developed to collect biographical data on a self-report basis (e.g., for employment testing), and special interview schedules have been designed for collecting patients' medical-record data (e.g., in clinical in-take examinations; Goldstein & Hersen, 1984). Actuarial and biographical data also seem to deserve more attention in other applied psychodiagnostic contexts.

## Behavior Traces

Studying behavior by analyzing its products or "traces" also has some tradition outside of psychology. Students of fine arts have tried to interpret the personality of a painter like van Gogh through analysis of his paintings, and musicologists have attempted to unravel Bach's musical talent through analysis of his fugues or his famous passion music. Behavior traces studied in psychological assessment are less spectacular, of course. They comprise various material results of a person's behavior, ranging from attributes of a person's appearance (style of hair and dress, bitten fingernails) to accidental traces (for example, literal footprints on a sandy beach or signs of use in a children's playground or on tools and other equipment at work) and intentional products of behavior (handwriting, children's drawings, personal collections, etc.).

In the past, behavior traces have been studied most systematically in clinical contexts and in ecopsychological field research (for example, to analyze different patterns of visitors' behavior in a state park or a museum). One kind of behavior trace has attracted psychodiagnostic interest in a wider context, at least among researchers in the German-speaking and French-speaking countries: personal style of handwriting. Contrary to expectations (and promises!), careful scientific evaluation of the external validity of both measured and rated characteristics of a person's style of handwriting did not support graphology as a valid source of psychodiagnostic information (Guilford, 1959; Rohracher, 1969).

## Behavior Observation

In the broad sense of the term, any psychological assessment will involve behavior observation. In a more restricted sense, behavior observation refers to the study (recording, describing, classifying) of all kinds of behavior other than those that are scored as part of a test, questionnaire, interview schedule, or the like. Studying a child's behavior in an informal play group or while solving a mechanical puzzle, observing a psychotic patient's behavior in the initial phase of a panic attack, recording the behavior of a neurological patient suffering from Parkinson's disease attempting to control his or her tremor, or studying human operator behavior in a flight control center—these examples illustrate the wide range of assessment tasks and of research settings for which techniques of behavior observation may be, and have been, implemented. Irrespective of the specifics, some general points pertaining to direct behavior observation in assessment can be summarized.

There are no such things as "natural units" in the stream of human behavior; to the contrary, the proper breadth and definition of such units have to depend on and match the question under study. "Naive" behavior observation tends to vary in the breadth of units of observation used (Newtson, Hairfield, Bloomingdale, & Cutino, 1987), rendering it unsuitable for scientific purposes. In schedules for behavior observation, units of observation should be clearly defined without recourse to interpretative (intuitive) judgment, sticking closely to directly observable features of behavior. (In this sense, "X smiles" is a proper unit, whereas "X is happy" is not.) Observations by trained observers work well in stationary or quasi-stationary environments such as hospitals, schools, places of work, and playgrounds. Elsewhere, techniques for the self-monitoring of behavior are to be preferred over having records taken by direct observers. Self-monitoring is preferable for technical and cost-effective reasons and in the interest of the protection of privacy, given appropriate instruments for the recording of observations and adequate pretraining of subjects in the use of protocol instruments. Recent research has demonstrated the feasibility and satisfactory psychometric reliability (including low proneness to artifacts of reactivity) of self-monitoring data obtained by trained adult lay subjects under unrestrained everyday life conditions, using a computerized recording and a time-sampling design of data collection (*ambulatory psychodiagnostics or in-field testing*, Pawlik, 1988; Pawlik & Buse, in press).

## Behavior Rating

Unlike behavior observation, ratings of behavior do involve elements of judgment, of comparison, and even of interpretation on the part of the examiner. In behavior ratings, the rater is to judge the frequency, intensity, or some other attribute of a testee's behavior, trait, or state. In the interest of satisfactory scoring objectivity, the attribute to be rated needs to be defined very carefully, preferably both in general terms and by giving illustrative, representative examples. Rating scales differ in the response format provided for the recording of ratings (graphic rating scales, numerical rating scales, verbal rating scales, percentage scales). One way to improve interrater objectivity is to use representative sample records of behavior (photographs, audiotaped or videotaped records of behavior) to define major subdivisions of a behavior rating scale (a *standard scale* or *master scale*).

Rating scales continue to be widely used in personality research and in many areas of psychological assessment. Assessment techniques using behavior observation and behavior rating have been the object of intensive psychodiagnostic and psychometric research for decades. In addition to obvious sources of psychometric error in behavior observation (poor definition of behavioral units or of time periods of observation; errors of observation/perception or of recording or coding), a number of basic judgmental errors of behavior ratings have been identified. Once identified, these can be duly taken into account in the construction of rating scale instruments. The six most common sources of judgmental error in behavior ratings are generalized tendencies of judgment (the severity vs. mildness of the rating); the central tendency error (avoiding the extreme categories of a rating scale); a positive or negative halo effect (overgeneralizing a single positive or negative rating so that it affects other ratings given for that same person, a common effect of stereotyped judgment); errors of semantics (because of poor definition or misunderstanding of rating categories); a rater–attribute interaction error (rating a testee relative to the examiner's implicit self-rating on that same scale); and a logical error (because of an examiner's implicit "theory" about how different scales or attributes may interrelate when, in reality, these scales or attributes are related differently or not at all). Modern textbooks of psychological assessment provide detailed accounts of how to guard against such errors of judgment in the construction of behavior rating schedules.

## Expressive Behavior

In everyday life, we are used to two sources of information about other people's states of feeling: their explicit verbal reports ("I am hungry"; "I do not like this noise"), and common-sense interpretations of how other people behave, look, move, or talk. *Expression* refers to these latter attributes of a person's behavior that impress an observer to draw inferences about that person's inner states of feeling or mood or other psychological processes. Facial expression, paralinguistic attributes of speech (pitch, intonation, speed, loudness, pauses, etc.), tics, gestures, poise, and gait are among the fields of expressive behavior that have been studied as further sources of data in psychological assessment. Early attempts toward the psychodiagnostic use of expressive behavior have been largely intuitive, and failed to reach satisfactory objectivity, reliability, or validity. Different social stereotypes in interpreting expressive motions, the highly multivariate nature of expressive behavior, and the fact that expressive motions may change extremely fast with time explain why intuitive interpretations of expressive behavior tend to be of unsatisfactory reliability and validity. In recent years, therefore, analytical instruments for recording and describing expressive behavior have been introduced; these have improved the situation drastically. For example, the FACS technique by Ekman (1982) for recording and describing a person's facial expression yields results of satisfactory scoring objectivity and reliability as well as promising evidence of validity. Similar systems are being developed for gross bodily movements of expression and for interpersonal expressive behavior. Because of the fast time course of these behaviors and their highly multivariate nature, these methods require high-quality videotaped records for repeated analysis at reduced viewing speed.

## Interview

Asking another person about his or her personal situation, past history, future expectations, motives, interests, or personal problems may well be the oldest "method" to get to know that person. Modern psychological interview techniques are much more refined than such simple question asking. Different types of interviews are distinguished depending on the degree of structuring (standardization) and the diagnostic purpose.

In an *exploratory interview* (also called *exploration*), the examiner enters into a free dialogue with the testee to learn about his or her general situation or simply to find out why this person comes to consult a psychologist. Most psychological assessment and psychological experiments start with a brief exploration of this kind. *Anamnestic interviews* are conducted to collect information about a testee's past, his or her educational and medical record, and so forth. Anamnestic interviews are a standard component of clinical in-take examinations and are conducted routinely following admission of a patient to the hospital as well as in vocational guidance and employment testing.

In an *unstructured interview*, it is up to the examiner which questions to ask and in what order. It presupposes considerable assessment experience on the part of the examiner. Unstructured interviews have some use in exploratory interviews, as a means to introduce a psychological assessment as a social encounter, or simply to "warm up" the testee for subsequent assessment procedures. Beyond such general purposes, the psychometric quality of unstructured interviews is low because, given the low degree of standardization, an interview protocol may tell more about the examiner (or the testee's reaction to the examiner as a person) than about the testee per se. In the hands of experienced examiners, unstructured interviews may prove useful for developing hypotheses about a testee, although of little to no validity for testing such hypotheses (Guilford, 1959).

*Structured interviews* are interview techniques designed according to principles at the opposite end of the standardization scale: In a structured interview, the content (often even the wording) of questions and their sequence is worked out in advance and laid down, in detail, in an *interview schedule* (*interviewer guide*). The task of the examiner is reduced to that of reading these questions to the testee and of taking notes of the testee's answers. The interview schedule may provide for a multiple-choice or a free-response answer format; in the latter case, the testee's answers should be audiotaped (for subsequent scoring by content or descriptive rating scales). Structured interview schedules also provide instructions as to which question to ask next depending on the testee's response to the previous question. In a sense, a standardized structured interview can be visualized as a tree-like algorithmic design organizing the course of the interview as a function of the testee's responses.

Fully structured interviews require a high degree of familiarity with the interview schedule on the part of the examiner. Therefore, computerized versions of interview schedules have been developed in recent years, especially for application in clinical research and practice. The interviewer types the examinee's answers on the computer keyboard, and the program selects the most salient next question, which the interviewer is to read to the examinee from the computer monitor. An example of a highly developed interview schedule of this type is the Structured Clinical Interview (Spitzer, Williams, & Gibbon, 1987) developed to implement clinical assessments following the revised third edition of the *Diagnostic and Statistical Manual* (American Psychiatric Association, 1987). Results obtained with these structured diagnostic interviews fulfill psychometric standards of objectivity and reliability at the level of objective tests (Widiger & Trull, 1991).

*Semistructured interviews* range somewhere between the extremes of a fully structured and a fully unstructured interview, the idea being to combine the strengths of both while avoiding the rigidity of a fully structured schedule. Semistructured interview schedules have been developed for use in educational, employment, and clinical applications. An early and psychometrically very successful example, taken again from clinical psychology, is the Inpatient Multidimensional Psychiatric Scale (IMPS) by Lorr, Klett, and McNair (1965). In this system, the patient's behavior in a semistandardized clinical intake examination is observed with respect to a 75-item behavior observation schedule giving rise to 10 factors (syndromes) of psychopathology. These can be measured with an average scoring objectivity of .88 and an average internal scale consistency of .85. The IMPS has since become a model for the development of several similar scales for semistructured clinical assessment, including some in languages other than English (see Baumann & Stieglitz, 1983; Pawlik, 1982, pp. 302–343).

## Questionnaires

Personality inventories, interest surveys, attitude and opinion schedules, and other questionnaire-type methods constitute one of the two major sources of information for psychological assessment (the other one being objective tests, discussed later). A *questionnaire* is essentially a list of printed questions. For each question, two or more alternatives for response are provided; the testee is instructed to check off the alternative closest to his or her perception, attitude, recollection, opinion, or interest. The first questionnaires were introduced as shortcut alternatives to interviews, suitable for mass administration in selection assessments, at the same time avoiding problems of insufficient objectivity in scoring open-ended questions (e.g., Woodworth Personal Data Sheet, Franz, 1920). In questionnaires developed later, items were usually presented in statement format rather than in question format. A typical personality or interest questionnaire contains statements phrased in the first person, such as "Sometimes I feel nervous without being able to give a reason" or "I prefer to play football to playing chess," usually with three response alternatives per item (e.g., YES–?–NO; or AGREE–DON'T KNOW, CAN'T DECIDE–DISAGREE).

In this way, personality questionnaires have been developed for assessing selected personality traits like extraversion–introversion and emotional stability–neuroticism and — since the early 1930s, in the form of *multidimensional inventories*—also for clinical use. A class questionnaire of this type, still in use today, is the Minnesota Multiphasic Personality Inventory (Hathaway & McKinley, 1943; recently revised and restandardized by Butcher, Dahlstrom, Graham, Tellegen, & Kaemmer, 1989). Its clinical scales correspond to a priori dimensions of psychopathology. A different principle of construction was followed in another widely used personality questionnaire, the Sixteen Personality Factor Questionnaire (16 PF) by Cattell, Eber, & Tatsuoka (1970; revised in 1986). The items of the 16 PF were selected so as to represent salient aspects of 16 basic personality dimensions identified in factor analyses of questionnaire item response covariations in nonclinical samples (the general population). The questionnaire methodology has also been adapted to assess variations in state, for example, in situational variations of anger or anxiety (Spielberger, 1983).

The questionnaires referred to above have all been translated into many other languages. In addition, personality questionnaires following similar principles of construction have been developed independently in many non-anglophone countries. Today, the literature abounds in data on criterion validity and internal validity (questionnaire scale intercorrelations) and, to a lesser extent, in cross-cultural comparisons on the basis of personality questionnaire results. (Detailed references are beyond the scope of this introductory presentation.) Other areas of assessment for which questionnaire-type instruments have been developed include the measurement of interests and motives (Edwards, 1959), of attitudes and personal orientations (such as honesty and dependability; Goldberg, Grenier, Guion, Sechrest, & Wing, 1991), and of preclinical or clinical symptomatology. Furthermore, questionnaire-type instruments are being used widely as research instruments.

The psychometric construction of questionnaires has to safeguard against well-established *response sets* on the part of the testee, which have been shown to affect the validity of questionnaire scale values. Response sets that have been given broad attention in personality research include *acquiescence* (the systematic tendency to prefer response categories of agreement over those expressing disagreement), *social desirability* (the systematic tendency to prefer the response alternative of higher social value), and various kinds of semantic and voluntary distortion errors. Although questionnaires have perfect scoring objectivity, as a rule they lack in response objectivity, which has led some authors to classify them as "subjective methods" of assessment.

Another restriction of the questionnaire methodology relates to the fact that a testee's response to the behavioral content of a questionnaire item need not be *behaviorally veridical* at the item level. For example, a testee expressing agreement with the questionnaire item "I frequently suffer from serious headaches" may do so for several reasons, including inter alia the following:

- the testee experiences intense headaches at high objective frequency (e.g., several times a day);
- in the testee's perception, even once every two weeks means "frequently";
- the testee classifies even minor (and thus more frequent) forms of headache as "serious"; or
- the testee, upon reading the item, is reminded vividly of a period during which he or she had particularly frequent spells of headaches.

Questionnaires are no shortcut substitutes for much more laborious and methodologically demanding direct methods of behavior observation. As a rule, questionnaires cannot tell what people actually do or how they behave or react; rather, they tell us how people think, believe, or conceptualize their behavior, or their likely behavior in a situation as described in an item. Questionnaires are methods of psychological assessment of testee's mental representation of his or her actual or likely behavior, subjective experience, fears and anxieties, and so forth. In this way, questionnaires are response-objective only at the level of recorded reactions to the verbal stimuli of the items as such. Because of this restriction, psychologists have come to interpret questionnaire results diagnostically only in terms of validated scale scores. At this level, personality and other questionnaires show satisfactory to high levels of psychodiagnostic validity. For example, questionnaires designed for clinical use reach external clinical scale validities as high as .50 to .60 (Goldstein & Hersen, 1984; Guilford, 1959). Reliabilities of questionnaire scale scores depend on the nature of the personality variable measured. Well-designed personality questionnaire scale scores have been shown to reach reliabilities of .80 and higher.

## Projective Techniques

Consider an incomplete text like the following: "Yesterday we met again in the village square. We were both surprised. I was the first to calm down and . . . ." (after Wartegg, 1939). The testee is asked to complete this text into a full story. Different people will interpret the two and a half sentences in different ways, from different backgrounds of culture and personal experience, and as a stimulus for different kinds of emotional response.

This is a simple example of a *projective technique* in psychological assessment. The term *projective* is borrowed from classical psychoanalytic theory and refers to the (hypothetically unconscious) tendency of a person to perceive ambiguous stimuli according to his or her own personal experience, motives, hopes, or fears—as if that person "projects" (in the literal sense of the word) his or her personality into the apperception of the ambiguous stimulus when preparing a response to it.

In the early days of psychological assessment, some authors put great faith (and hope!) into projective techniques as a means to "unravel the deeper layers of personality" (such as processes of nonadmitted, "repressed" fears) and thus "transcend" the surface level of directly observable behavior. Subsequent research (e.g., by Murstein, 1963) soon showed that this far-reaching expectation could not be verified empirically. As in many other situations, testees tend to control (select, reinforce, inhibit, or activate) their responses to projective tests, depending on how they interpret the testing situation, the test material, the examiner's behavior, or conclusions likely to be drawn from the evaluation of their test responses.

Still, the term *projective techniques* has been kept as a generic label for a class of assessment instruments that follow the same principle of design: presenting the testee with ambiguous, more or less unstructured stimulus material to which he or she is to respond as spontaneously as possible. One of the oldest projective techniques is the Rorschach (1921) inkblot interpretation test. This test consists of 10 symmetrical inkblots (some in black and white, some in color, some following simple patterns, some more complex in design) that Hermann Rorschach, a Swiss psychiatrist, selected out of several hundred inkblots pretested for differentiating between psychiatric patients and controls in their responses. Rorschach had in fact intended to establish his procedure as an "objective" test of psychopathology; today's classification of the test as a projective technique is due to later researchers and their use of the test design. Roschach devised a complex scoring system to describe, in a formal way, characteristics of a testee's responses to the inkblots. As one would expect, the original test turned out to be of medium (to low) psychometric quality because of insufficient scoring objectivity and score reliability (Guilford, 1959). Some of these weaknesses have been improved in more recent test designs following the inkblot principle, such as the Holtzman Ink-Blot Test (Holtzman, Thorpe, Swartz, & Herron, 1961), which has also been applied successfully in cross-cultural research.

A second type of projective technique follows the *thematic apperception* principle: The testee is presented with ambiguous drawings or photographs, each showing one or several persons, with the task to describe each scene and invent a story around it. The oldest and most widely used test of this type is the Thematic Apperception Test (TAT; Murray, 1943), which has undergone many revisions of stimulus material and scoring instructions, differing considerably in scoring objectivity and in reliability. Research by McClelland and others inaugurated a tradition of using the TAT to assess individual and group differences (including cross-cultural differences) in the need for achievement (McClelland, 1971).

Other projective techniques use formats such as construction play with puppets, story completion, or the completion of abstract drawing designs. In clinical research and practice, once their chief domain of application, projective techniques have lost much of their appeal in the course of the last two decades as a result of improved nosological and therapeutic theory development favoring more objective techniques of assessment rooted in learning theory and neuroscience approaches to psychopathology.

## Objective Tests
In terms of the number of assessment methods published, objective tests represent by far the largest and most important data source of psychodiagnostics. The term *objective*

refers to administration, scoring, and response objectivity in test design. Objective psychological tests have been developed for practically all aspects and facets of human behavior, far too many to be listed or even classified here in any complete sense. The following is a brief overview of existing tests of established psychometric quality and broad application in research and practical assessment work.

## Behavior Tests of Performance

Literally thousands of performance tests of behavior have been constructed (see Conoley & Kramer, 1989; Keyser & Sweetland, 1984; Sweetland & Keyser, 1983) to measure trait or state variations in the speed and accuracy of human sensation (mostly visual and acoustic), perception (the identification, classification, and recognition of figural, symbolic, and semantic stimulus material), psychomotor coordination, past memory, immediate and long-term anterograde memory, cognition (thinking and problem solving), originality (creativity), and linguistic capacities, to mention only the most prominent classes of test development. (See Guilford's, 1985, structure-of-intellect model for an instructive and comprehensive taxonomy of objective test designs.)

Depending on its aim and form, an objective test calls for a testee's verbal, numerical, or manipulative responses. In recent years, performance tests of behavior have been adapted or newly constructed for computer-assisted testing (CAT); a higher degree of standardization and of economy of test administration are one motive behind this. Still more important, computerized psychological tests provide for important additional possibilities for behavioral analysis (for example, detailed chronometric analysis of a testee's behavior at the item level). Furthermore, CAT allows for more flexible ways of test administration, called *tailored* or *adaptive testing* (Lord, 1980). Tests constructed according to item-response theory standards of test design (mentioned earlier) can be administered under conditions of optimum trade-off between individual score reliability and the time needed for testing—an advantage particularly relevant in testing of handicapped patients in clinical neuropsychology, for example.

A group of performance tests of behavior that have attracted wide attention, also among educationists and outside of psychology, are tests of intelligence. Intelligence testing has undergone major changes since the first prototype tests 90 to 100 years ago (see Anastasi, 1976). An early test design that was to become influential for decades of test construction goes back to the French lawyer and psychologist Alfred Binet. In 1905, he and Théophile Simon, a French physician, published their first "échelle métrique" for the assessment of the "intelligence" of school children. The "metric scale" comprised some 30 tasks (items) selected to differentiate between children getting along well in grade school and children in need of special remedial education. The Binet–Simon scales went through several revisions. As a simple statistical norm, they proposed to express a child's test performance as a score called "mental age", the average age of children of normal development showing a level of test performance exactly like the given child. As early as 1912, Stern proposed the term "intelligence quotient" (IQ) to be used for the ratio "mental age divided by chronological age, multiplied by 100."

The original Binet–Simon scale, as well as the IQ formula proposed by Stern, suffered from a number of psychological, psychodiagnostic, and psychometric weaknesses which were demonstrated clearly in later research. Subsequent developments in the field of intelligence testing have come a long way in several different areas of assessment. First, Stern's ratio-formula of IQ was replaced by an IQ to be computed as a normalized standard score (with a mean of 100 and a standard deviation of 15). In addition, numerous new test designs were introduced to sample human cognitive performance through items representative of all kinds of mental tasks a person may face. Tests of overall or "general" intelligence were improved to include both verbal–numerical and manipulative subtests, yielding separate "verbal IQs" and "performance IQs" (Wechsler, 1958). Tests of this type, like the WAIS (Wechsler Adult Intelligence Scale) and the WISC (Wechsler Intelligence Scale for Children), are now available translated and restandardized in many different countries.

Yet another line of research in test development was directed toward the identification and separate measurement of major components (latent dimensions or factors) of human cognitive abilities and aptitudes. The work of the Thurstones, Guilford, and many others succeeded in providing a reference system of well-replicated factors of intelligence (French, 1951; Guilford, 1959; Pawlik, 1972). Multifactor and differential tests of intelligence and aptitude, widely in use today, have been constructed that allow psychologists to describe a testee's intelligence in terms of a profile of scores across major components of cognition and aptitude. Tests of this type play a key role in modern vocational guidance, for example, and in modern aptitude research. In addition, a variety of multidimensional tests of vocational aptitudes (e.g., the Differential Aptitudes Tests Battery; Bennett, Seashore, & Wesman, 1981) have been developed, which are widely in use today.

A third line of development was to devise performance tests of behavior for special groups: for mentally handicapped children or adults, for gifted children, or, more recently, for patients suffering from brain injuries or other kinds of neurological trauma or disease. In the neuropsychological assessment of memory functions, for example, special test designs, in addition to those developed for assessment in healthy normals, are needed to assess the nature and degree of a patient's amnesia (Poon, 1986).

## Behavior Tests of Personality

This second kind of behavior test was developed to assess individual differences in habitual style of behavior: in emotionality, dimensions of temperament, motivation, or interest. The idea behind these tests was to replace traditional questionnaires (of personality, interest, etc.) by tests intended to assess the same traits and states at a higher standard of response objectivity. For some traits and states—such as anxiety, emotional stability/lability, or level of activation/arousal—this ambitious program of psychodiagnostic development has been more successful than for others (e.g., extraversion–introversion). Systematic cross-studies analysis of available correlational evidence (Hundleby, Pawlik, & Cattell, 1963) clearly showed that some traits and states of personality, by their very psychological nature, are more amenable to measurement by objective tests than are others. A first compendium of objective personality tests was made available from the research of Cattell (the Objective–Analytic Battery of Tests; see Cattell & Warburton, 1965). In recent years, research on objective tests of personality has been concentrating on more specific, miniature-type laboratory tasks, notably on potential behavioral "markers" of psychopathology (See Buchsbaum & Haier, 1983; Widiger & Trull, 1991).

## Psychophysiological Assessment

During the last 40 to 60 years, a wealth of research evidence has accumulated (See Chapter 4, this volume) relating variations in human behavior and experience to measurable variations in biosignal indicators of central or peripheral nervous system functioning. Important examples of psychophysiological variable domains studied are the following: variations in the electrical activity of the brain (recorded from scalp electrodes; electroencephalogram; EEG), cardiovascular system activity (electrocardiogram; ECG) electrodermal activity (electrical skin resistance and conductance; EDA), gaze and pupillary response (electrooculogram; EOG; electropupillogram; EPG), muscle tonus (electromyogram; EMG), and variations in breathing (pneumogram). Standardized procedures have been developed for recording and analyzing these major types of biosignals and for cross-relating their measurements to variations in human experience and behavior. Online recording and parametrization of such biocorrelates of human behavior, including recording under field conditions outside of the laboratory, has been greatly facilitated by the availability of modern laboratory computing facilities.

Restrictions of space prohibit a detailed account of this rich research approach. Research on the psychometric quality of psychophysiological methods of assessment has yielded promising behavioral validity for purposes of state measurement (especially, of level of arousal and activation) and somewhat lower behavioral validity for purposes of trait measurement (See Fahrenberg, 1983; Martin & Venables, 1980). By using on-line methods of recording, state variations in the level of activation/arousal, in the level of excitement or relaxation, in anxiety, and in mental fatigue can be monitored and assessed in a nonreactive way (i.e., without impeding the testee or requesting him or her to respond to tests, items, or questions). For example, an increase in the level of emotional arousal is revealed by higher average (tonic) electrical skin conductance (and higher skin conductance variability), larger heart-rate variability, and higher average muscle tonus.

In addition, measures of phasic EDA, ECG and EMG response can be used to monitor a person's arousal response to a stimulus or environmental change. The frequency spectrum of the EEG is correlated with changes and individual differences in the level of mental activation, with 8-to-13-Hz EEG waves (alpha waves) indicative of relaxed wakeful states, 15-to-30-Hz EEG waves (beta waves) of mentally activated states, and different slow-wave patterns of different sleeping stages. Event-related potentials obtained by averaging EEG recordings taken shortly before or after presentation of a stimulus can be scored for component measures related to different stages of neuropsychological encoding of that stimulus (brain stem transduction; primary cortical or sensory response; secondary cortical or cognitive response). Different kinds of stimuli and different levels and qualities of arousal and emotion can be compared on the basis of these and other biosignal indicators (differential psychophysiology). In this way, psychophysiological methods of assessment may soon become the methods of first choice, at least for psychological state assessment.

More recent research has been devoted to the study of inter- and intraindividual variations in biochemical assays of hormonal levels in the blood, and of neurotransmitter release and uptake in the brain, as related to state and trait differences in behavior, activation, or mood state. Studies by Deakin (in press) and Netter and Rammsayer (1989), for example, provided strong experimental evidence that serotonin (5-HT) release and uptake in the brain is related to concurrent variations in the levels of depression and anxiety, so that a patient's behavioral response to a drug influencing this neurotransmitter balance may be taken as an objective psychophysiological marker. In the context of aptitude testing, Eysenck and Barrett (1985) reported high correlations between subjects' IQ test scores and parameters of event-related evoked EEG potentials. Some of these findings will probably also give a rise to improved psychophysiological contributions in the field of ability and personality assessment.

# Method Variance and Multivariate Assessment: A Concluding Comment

Each method of psychological assessment, each source of psychodiagnostic information, carries its specific psychometric strengths and weaknesses and has its specific indications and contraindications as well as its method-specific sources of variance. There is ample empirical evidence (for example, from the systematic construct validation of questionnaires, objective tests, and psychophysiological assessments; Campbell & Fiske, 1959) that some portion of the variance sampled by each method is specific to the respective assessment approach. Questionnaires, psychological tests, psychophysiological assessments, behavior ratings, and interview data—all show some inter- and intraindividual variance that does not correlate across methods because it is unique to one approach. Hundleby et al. (1963), for example, presented an early summary of inherent instrument-specific limitations of personality testing. Other researchers have since presented similar findings for other areas of assessment (Wiggins, 1973).

This leads to an important scientific and practical consequence: Psychological assessment must, whenever and wherever possible, be planned according to a multivariate design that combines techniques of assessment from different types of methods (different sources of data). By this comparative approach, an assessment can be safeguarded against fallacies of instrument-specific sources of variance. This has become widely accepted, for example, in employment testing, following the methodology of assessment centers. In this case, objective test information, questionnaire results, "simulated-situation" tests, and observations of behavior (alone and in social interaction) are combined with interview data, biographical data, and testing data. Similarly, in modern clinical psychodiagnostics, results from objective tests, questionnaires, behavior observations, and ratings of patients in the daily hospital routine (by psychologists, physicians, nurses, and other hospital staff) are combined with interview data, observations of expressional behavior, psychophysiological recording, and, often, therapy-outcome data. In this way, results from one method of assessment can be cross-checked against psychodiagnostic information obtained through procedures of assessment that follow totally different principles of design. The development of algorithms of *psychodiagnostic inference* that enable the psychologist to combine and cross-validate assessment results from such diverse sources constitutes a key area of psychodiagnostic research.

# References

American Psychiatric Association. (1987). *Diagnostic and statistical manual of mental disorders* (3rd ed., rev.). Washington, DC: Author.

American Psychological Association. (1985). *Standards for educational and psychological tests.* Washington, DC: Author.

Anastasi, A. (1976). *Psychological testing* (4th ed.). New York: Macmillan.

Baumann, U., & Stieglitz, R. D. (1983). *Testmanual zum AMDP-System* [Test manual for the AMDP system]. Berlin: Springer.

Bennett, G. K., Seashore, H. G., & Wesman, A. G. (1981). *Differential Aptitude Tests (DAT)* (5th ed.). New York: Psychological Corporation.

Buchsbaum, M. S., & Haier, R. J. (1983). Psychopathology: biological approaches. *Annual Review of Psychology, 34,* 401–430.

Butcher, J. N., Dahlstrom, W. G., Graham, J. R., Tellegen, A., & Kaemmer, B. (1989). *Manual for administration and scoring, MMPI-2, Minnesota Multiphasic Personality Inventory-2.* Minneapolis: University of Minnesota Press.

Campbell, D., & Fiske, D. (1959). Convergent and discriminant validation by the Multitrait–Multimethod Matrix. *Psychological Bulletin, 56,* 81–105.

Cascio, W. F. (1976). Turnover, biographical data, and fair employment practice. *Journal of Applied Psychology, 61,* 576–580.

Cattell, J. M. (1890). Mental tests and measurement. *Mind, 15,* 373–380.

Cattell, R. B. (1957). *Personality and motivation structure and measurement.* Yonkers, NY: World Book.

Cattell, R. B., Eber, H. W., & Tatsuoka, M. M. (1970). *Handbook for the Sixteen Personality Factor Questionnaire (16PF).* Champaign, IL: Institute for Personality and Ability Testing.

Cattell, R. B., & Warburton, F. W. (1965). *Principles of personality measurement and a compendium of objective tests.* Champaign, IL: University of Illinois Press.

Conoley, J. C., & Kramer, J. J. (Eds.). (1989). *The tenth mental measurement yearbook.* Lincoln, NE: Buros Institute of Mental Measurement.

Cronbach, L. J., Gleser, G. C., Nanda, H., & Rajaratnam, N. (1972). *The dependability of behavioral measurements: Theory of generalizability of scores and profiles.* New York: Wiley.

Deakin, J. F. W. (in press). 5-HT receptor subtypes in depression. In T. Archer, P. Bevan, & A. Cools (Eds.), *Behavioral pharmacology of 5-HT.* New York: Erlbaum.

Edwards, A. L. (1959). *Edwards Personal Perference Profile.* New York: Psychological Corporation.

Ekman, P. (1982). *Emotion in the human face.* New York: Cambridge University Press.

Eysenck, H. J., & Barrett, P. (1985). Psychophysiology and the measurement of intelligence. In C. R. Reynolds & V. L. Willson (Eds.), *Methodological and statistical advances in the study of individual differences* (pp. 1–49) New York: Plenum Press.

Fahrenberg, J. (1983). Psychophysiologische Methodik [Psychophysiological methodology]. In K.-J. Groffmann & L. Michel (Eds.), *Enzyklopädie der Psychologie:* Vol. B/II/4. *Verhaltensdiagnostik* [Behavior diagnostics]. Göttingen, Germany: Hogrefe.

Filskov, S. B., & Boll, T. J. (Eds.). (1981). *Handbook of clinical neuropsychology.* New York: Wiley.

Franz, S. I. (1920). *Handbook of mental examinations.* New York: Macmillan.

French, J. W. (1951). The description of aptitude and achievement tests in terms of rotated factors. *Psychometric Monographs, 5.*

Goeters, K. M., & Fassbender, C. (1991). *Definition of psychological testing of astronaut candidates for Columbus missions.* [Research report]. Hamburg: German Aerospace Research Establishment.

Goldberg, L. R., Grenier, J. R., Guion, R. M., Sechrest, L. B., & Wing, H. (1991). *Questionnaires used in the prediction of trustworthiness in pre-employment selection decisions: An APA task force report.* Washington, DC: American Psychological Association Science Directorate.

Goldstein, G., & Hersen, M. (Eds.). (1984). *Handbook of psychological assessment.* New York: Pergamon Press.

Guilford, J. P. (1959). *Personality.* New York: McGraw-Hill.

Guilford, J. P. (1985). The structure-of-intellect model. In B. Wolman (Ed.), *Handbook of intelligence* (pp. 225–266). New York: Wiley.

Hambleton, R. K., Swaminathan, H., Algina, J., & Coulson, D. B. (1978). Criterion-referenced testing and measurement: A review of technical issues and developments. *Review of Educational Research, 48,* 1–47.

Harman, H. H. (1960). *Modern factor analysis.* Chicago: University of Chicago Press.

Harris, C. W. (1963). *Problems in measuring change.* Madison: University of Wisconsin Press.

Hathaway, S. R., & McKinley, J. C. (1943). *Manual for the Minnesota Multiphasic Personality Inventory.* New York: Psychological Corporation.

Holtzman, W. H., Thorpe, J. S., Swartz, J. D., & Herron, E. W. (1961). *Ink-blot perception and personality.* New York: Wiley.

Hundleby, J. D., Pawlik, K., & Cattell, R. B. (1963). *Personality factors in objective test devices.* San Diego, CA: Knapp.

International Standards Organisation. (1981). *ISO Norm 5725: Precision of test methods.* Geneva: International Standards Organisation.

Keyser, D. D., & Sweetland, R. C. (Eds.). (1984). *Test critiques.* Kansas, MO: Test Corporation of America.

Lord, F. M. (1980). *Applications of item response theory to practical testing problems.* Hillsdale, NJ: Erlbaum.

Lord, F. M., & Novick, M. R. (1968). *Statistical theories of mental test scores.* Reading, MA: Addison-Wesley.

Lorr, M., Klett, C. J., & McNair, D. M. (1965). *Syndromes of psychosis.* Elmsford, NY: Pergamon Press.

Martin, J., & Venables, P. H. (Eds.). (1980). *Techniques in psychophysiology.* New York: Wiley.

McClelland, D. C. (1971). *Assessing human motivation.* New York: General Learning Press.

McReynolds, P. (1989). Diagnosis and clinical assessment. *Annual Review of Psychology, 40*, 83–108.

Murray, H. A. (1943). *Thematic Apperception Test.* Cambridge, MA: Havard University Press.

Murstein, B. (1963). *Theory and research in projective techniques (emphasising the TAT).* New York: Wiley.

Netter, P., & Rammsayer, T. (1989). Serotonergic effects on sensory and motor responses in extraverts and introverts. *International Clinical Psychopharmacology, 4*, 21–26.

Newtson, D., Hairfield, J., Bloomingdale, J., & Cutino, S. (1987). The structure of action and interaction. *Social Cognition, 5*, 191–237.

Pawlik, K. (1972). *Dimensionen des Verhaltens* [Dimensions of behavior] (3rd ed.). Bern, Switzerland: Huber.

Pawlik, K. (1976). Modell-und Praxisdimensionen psychologischer Diagnostik [Dimensions of psychological assessment with respect to modeling and practice]. In K. Pawlik (Ed.), *Diagnose der Diagnostik* [Diagnosis of diagnostics] (pp. 13–43). Stuttgart, Germany: Klett.

Pawlik, K. (Ed.). (1982). *Multivariate Persönlichkeitsforschung* [Multivariate personality research]. Bern, Switzerland: Huber.

Pawlik, K. (1988). "Naturalistische" Daten für Psychodiagnostik: Zur Methodik psychodiagnostischer Felderhebungen. ["Naturalistic" data for psychological assessment: The methodology of psychodiagnostic in-field studies]. *Zeitschrift für Differentielle und Diagnostische Psychologie, 9*, 169–181.

Pawlik. K. (in press). *Lehrbuch der Psychologischen Diagnostik* [Textbook of psychological assessment]. Bern, Switzerland: Huber.

Pawlik, K., & Buse L. (in press). Felduntersuchungen zur transsituativen Konsistenz individueller Unterschiede im Verhalten und Erleben [In-field studies of transsituational consistency of individual differences in behavior and mood-state]. In K. Pawlik & K. Stapf (Eds.), *Umwelt und Verhalten. Perspektiven und Ergebnisse ökopsychologischer Forschung* [Environment and behavior: Perspectives and results of ecopsychological research]. Bern, Switzerland: Huber.

Poon, L. W. (Ed.). (1986). *Handbook for clinical memory assessment of older adults.* Washington, DC: American Psychological Association.

Reynolds, C. R., & Brown, R. T. (Eds.). (1984). *Perspectives on bias in mental testing.* New York: Plenum Press.

Rohracher, H. (1969). *Kleine Charakterkunde* [Brief characterology] (12th ed.). Vienna: Urban & Schwarzenberg.

Rorschach, H. (1921). *Psychodiagnostik* [Psychodiagnostics]. Bern, Switzerland: Huber.

Segall, M. H., Dasen, P. R., Berry, J. W., & Poortinga, Y. H. (1990). *Human behavior in global perspective.* Elmsford, NY: Pergamon Press.

Spielberger, C. D. (1983). *State–Trait Anxiety Inventory manual.* Palo Alto, CA: Consulting Psychologists Press.

Spitzer, R. L., Williams, J. B. W., & Gibbon, M. (1987). *Instruction manual for the structured clinical interview for DSM–III–R.* New York: State Psychiatric Institute.

Stern, W. (1900). *Ueber Psychologie der individuellen Differenzen* [On the psychology of individual differences]. Leipzig, Germany: Barth.

Sweetland, R. C., & Keyser, D. J. (Eds.). (1983). *Tests.* Kansas City, MO: Test Corporation of America.

Thurstone, L. L. (1947). *Multiple factor analysis.* Chicago: University of Chicago Press.

Wartegg, E. (1939). Gestaltung und Charakter [Design and character]. *Zeitschrift fuer angewandte Psychologie,* Beiheft *84,* 1–261.

Wechsler, D. (1958). *The measurement and appraisal of adult intelligence.* Baltimore: Williams & Wilkins.

Widiger, T. A., & Trull, T. J. (1991). Diagnosis and clinical assessment. *Annual Review of Psychology, 42,* 109–133.

Wiggins, J. (1973). *Personality and prediction: Principles of personality assessment.* Reading, MA: Addison-Wesley.

Winneke, G. (1985). Blei in der Umwelt [Lead in the environment]. *Lehr- und Forschungstexte Psychologie* (Vol. 16). Berlin: Springer.

# Questionnaire Used in the 1991 Survey by the International Union of Psychological Science (IUPsyS)

After most questions, a number in brackets shows the page(s) in the text where information from that question appears.

# IUPsyS International Survey on Research in Psychology

[January 1991]

Respondent: Please check the
accuracy of your name and
address; correct any errors.

[Respondent name and
address here.]

Please reply using this questionnaire. Print all answers clearly. Additional attachments and documents are welcome.

First we would like to find what fields of psychological research are especially important in different countries and regions of the world.

1.a. Considering the main fields of psychology, please check below which ones show
   (a) a high level of research activity in your country,
   (b) a moderate level of research activity in your country,
   (c) a low level of research activity in your country:

| Fields | (a) High | (b) Moderate | (c) Low |
|---|---|---|---|
| Clinical | _____ | _____ | _____ |
| Cognitive | _____ | _____ | _____ |
| Comparative | _____ | _____ | _____ |
| Counseling & Guidance | _____ | _____ | _____ |
| Developmental & Gerontological | _____ | _____ | _____ |
| Educational | _____ | _____ | _____ |
| Experimental | _____ | _____ | _____ |
| Industrial/Organizational | _____ | _____ | _____ |
| Personality | _____ | _____ | _____ |
| Physiological | _____ | _____ | _____ |
| Psychometrics | _____ | _____ | _____ |
| Quantitative | _____ | _____ | _____ |
| School | _____ | _____ | _____ |
| Social | _____ | _____ | _____ |
| Other (_____) | _____ | _____ | _____ |

[Material based on this question appears on text pages 4, 28–29; Table 3, p. 28.]

1.b. Are there fields of psychological research (see the list above and feel free to add others) that are characteristic of your country and that tend to differentiate it from other countries?
   Yes _____ No _____.
   If yes, please name and describe these fields.
   [pp. 29–30]

2. Is there a national plan or set of priorities for research in psychology in your country?
   Yes _____ No _____.
   [pp. 30, 59]

If yes, in what year was the plan established? _____. Also, please tell how the plan was established:

Also, please send a copy of the plan or give sources for information about it; if the sources are published, please give full citations.

---

Here we want to obtain information about the total number of psychologists in your country and the number who are engaged in research. For this survey, "psychologist" means anyone who has earned a degree equivalent to Bachelor of Arts in psychology with at least 3 years of post-secondary studies.

---

3.   Human resources for research in psychology in your country.
     a. Total psychologists in your country's labor force, whether employed or not _____
     [p. 23; Table 2, p. 24]
     (Please state the most recent year for this information: 19____)
     How many are men? _____ How many are women? _____
     [p. 25]
     b. If possible, give the number of psychologists in your country by each level of
     university degree (e.g., B.A. or B.S.; M.A. or M.S.; Ph.D.; or equivalent degrees within
     your national system).

| Degree | Number |
|---|---|
| B.A., B.S. (or equivalent) ........................................... | _____ |
| M.A., M.S. (or equivalent) ........................................... | _____ |
| Ph.D. (or equivalent) ............................................ | _____ |
| Other degree (state name:                    ) ............... | _____ |
| [p. 21] | |

     c. Please state the number of psychologists in your country who do research as their
     primary or secondary activity: _____
     [pp. 21, 23; Table 2, p. 24]

---

Information about trends in numbers of psychologists in your country is also important for planning.

---

4.a. Over the past 10 years, has the number of students getting degrees in psychology
increased ____, remained the same ____, or decreased ____?
[p. 35]
b. Over the last 10 years, did the number of psychologists engaged in research increase ____,
remain the same ____, or decrease ____?
[p. 35]
c. Over the past 10 years, were there important shifts in the numbers active in different
fields of psychology? Yes ____ No ____.
[p. 30; Table 4, p. 31]

If yes, please indicate below which fields have gained in numbers of psychologists over the last 10 years and which fields have lost:

| Fields | Gained | Lost |
|---|---|---|
| Clinical | _____ | _____ |
| Cognitive | _____ | _____ |
| Comparative | _____ | _____ |
| Counseling & Guidance | _____ | _____ |
| Developmental & Gerontological | _____ | _____ |
| Educational | _____ | _____ |
| Experimental | _____ | _____ |
| Industrial/Organizational | _____ | _____ |
| Personality | _____ | _____ |
| Physiological | _____ | _____ |
| Psychometrics | _____ | _____ |
| Quantitative | _____ | _____ |
| School | _____ | _____ |
| Social | _____ | _____ |
| Other (_____) | _____ | _____ |

[p. 30]

---

Next, we want to obtain information about the amount of financial support available annually for research and development in psychology in comparison with the entire research and development effort in your country, and also to look at trends over the last 10 years.

---

5. Financial resources for research and development in psychology.
   a. What is the total amount of financial support available annually from all sources in your country for psychological research and development? Please state the amount in your currency _____.
   [p. 38]

   b. What is the amount available in your country annually for research and development in *all* fields of science? Please state the amount in your currency _____.

   c. Trends and projections for research support.
   Over the last 10 years, has financial support for psychological research in your country increased ____, remained the same ____, or decreased ____?
   [p. 48]

   d. Is support for psychological research in your country shifting from one field to another? Yes ____ No ____.
   If Yes, please indicate below which fields of psychology have gained in financial support for research over the last 10 years and which fields have lost in support over the last 10 years:

| Fields | Gained in support over last 10 yrs | Lost in support over last 10 yrs |
|---|---|---|
| Clinical | ———— | ———— |
| Cognitive | ———— | ———— |
| Comparative | ———— | ———— |
| Counseling & Guidance | ———— | ———— |
| Developmental & Gerontological | ———— | ———— |
| Educational | ———— | ———— |
| Experimental | ———— | ———— |
| Industrial/Organizational | ———— | ———— |
| Personality | ———— | ———— |
| Physiological | ———— | ———— |
| Psychometrics | ———— | ———— |
| Quantitative | ———— | ———— |
| School | ———— | ———— |
| Social | ———— | ———— |
| Other (————) | ———— | ———— |

[p. 48]

    e. Compared to financial support for research and development in other fields of science and engineering, is psychology faring better ———, about the same ———, or worse ———?
[p. 45]
Please comment on financial support for research and development in psychology:

---

The ability of psychologists to obtain support for research and development may be related to the kinds and amount of recognition that psychological research receives in the country. In order to explore this, the next questions ask for information about recognition for psychological research in your country.

---

6. What kinds of recognition does psychological research receive in your country?
    a. Are psychologists in your country elected to the National Academy of Sciences or similar organization? Yes ——— No ———.
    [p. 61; Table 10, p. 62]
        If Yes, please give the following information:
        The name of the academy or similar organization:
        The proportion of psychologists in its membership:
        The year or period when psychologists were first elected:

    b. Do psychologists receive other kinds of official recognition or prizes? If so, please give some main examples.
    [p. 65]

c. How often is psychological research reported in the news media in your country? Check the frequency below for a major newspaper in your country:

\_\_\_\_ Daily
\_\_\_\_ At least once a week
\_\_\_\_ At least once a month
\_\_\_\_ A few times a year
\_\_\_\_ Almost never
\_\_\_\_ Never
[p. 66]
Please comment:

d. What are trends in recognition of psychological research in your country? Is recognition increasing \_\_\_\_, remaining the same \_\_\_\_, or decreasing \_\_\_\_?
[p. 61]
Please comment:

7.  How is psychology classed at universities in your country?
    As a natural science \_\_\_\_.   As a biological or life science \_\_\_\_.
    As a social science \_\_\_\_.   As a humanity \_\_\_\_.
    In a category of its own \_\_\_\_.
[p. 7]
Does the classification of psychology differ at different universities?
Please comment on the classification of psychology:

8. What is your organization doing to help and to encourage research in psychology?
[p. 54; Table 8, p. 55]
If possible, please give documentation and list source(s) for information about helping and encouraging psychological research.

9. Major obstacles or barriers exist in every country to achieving a satisfactory amount of high-quality psychological research. These may include too few highly trained research psychologists, insufficient financial support, lack of recognition for psychological research, and so on. What do you consider to be the main obstacles in your country?
[pp. 35, 45, 60]

10. The International Union of Psychological Science fosters research in several ways including the following: assuring the continuity of the International Congresses of Psychology (the XXV Congress will take place in Brussels, July 19–24, 1992); representing psychological science in such international organizations as the International Council of Scientific Unions, the International Social Science Council, and UNESCO; publishing the *International Journal of Psychology*; sponsoring and giving partial support to international scientific networks, workshops, and research projects. What other activities would you like to see IUPsyS undertake to foster psychological research?
[p. 47]

11. Please add any further information and/or comments that you think may be helpful to this international survey on research in psychology.


_____

(Please print name of person
completing questionnaire. If
this is different from the name
on page 1, then also print address.)

Thank you for your help with this project. Please return the questionnaire promptly by airmail. A return envelope is enclosed.

                                        Sincerely yours,


                                        Mark R. Rosenzweig
                                        President, IUPsyS
                                        Department of Psychology
                                        3210 Tolman Hall
                                        University of California
                                        Berkeley, CA   94720   U.S.A.

# Index

Acquiescence, questionnaire, 276
Adaptive testing, 279
Additive color mixture, 174, 175
Advisory Board for the Research Councils
    (United Kingdom), 39
Ambient light, 189–190
Ambulatory psychodiagnostics, 271
*American Journal of Psychology*, 1
American Psychological Association (APA), 2, 22,
    35, 36, 46, 53, 57, 64, 65, 66
American Psychological Society, 60, 66
Amnesia
  brain sites and, 115–117
  hippocampal, 107–111
Amygdala, 115
Anamnestic interviews, 273
Anger, cardiovascular disease and, 220–222
Anisomycin, 120
*Annual Review of Psychology*, 53, 57–58, 64, 223
Anoxia and brain damage, 130
Anxiety, 282
Association of Science–Technology Centers, 65
Atkinson–Shiffrin model, 79, 84
Attention, 78, 79

Behavior
  expressive, 272–273
  observation of, 270–271
  performance tests of, 279–281
  personality tests of, 281
  rating of, 271–272

toxic effects of environmental chemicals on,
    213–215
traces of, 270
Type A, 220–222
*Behavioral and Social Sciences: Achievements
    and Opportunities*, 46
Belgian Federation of Psychologists, 33
Binet–Simon scales, 280–281
Binocular disparity, 185–189
Binocular vision, 181–182
  binocular disparity, 185–189
  convergence, 183–185, 186
  Cyclopean eye, 182–183, 187
Birth-to-Ten study, 206
Bottom-up processing, 89
Brain damage
  amnesia and, 80, 105, 106–117, 126–129
Brain grafts
  effects modulated by experience and training,
    131
  recovery from amnesia and, 131
Brightness contrast, 172
*British Journal of Mathematical and Statistical
    Psychology*, 64
British Psychological Society, 66
Broad-spectrum behavior therapy, 239, 240
Brown–Peterson method, 81

Cancer, 203, 204, 216–218
Capacity, 79
Cardiovascular disease, 203, 204, 205, 209, 210
  anger, hostility, and, 220–222

# About the Editor

M ark R. Rosenzweig teaches and conducts research as professor emeritus at the University of California at Berkeley, and he is president (1988–1992) of the International Union of Psychological Science. His main area of research is on neural mechanisms of memory, and he has also written extensively on organizational aspects of modern psychology. He has written or edited 10 books, some of which have been translated into French, Italian, and Spanish, and he has written or coauthored about 200 scientific papers. Since 1968 he has been an editor of the *Annual Review of Psychology*, and he has served on the editorial boards of other publications in psychology and neuroscience. Active in many ways in international psychology, Professor Rosenzweig has presented scientific papers and has lectured in over 20 countries in North and South America, Europe, Asia, Africa, and Oceania.

On the basis of his experience, Professor Rosenzweig is convinced that the scientific study of behavior and of its biological mechanisms, conducted on an international basis, is leading to increased knowledge and understanding of human and animal behavior; it is also leading to applications of psychological science, often in collaboration with other disciplines, that benefit human development and the achievement of human rights.

Professor Rosenzweig is a member of the National Academy of Sciences, U.S.A.; he was awarded an honorary doctorate by the University of Paris; he was given the Distinguished Scientific Contribution Award of the American Psychological Association; and he was named a William James Fellow by the American Psychological Society.